Clerical Employment and Technological Change

H. Allan Hunt
Timothy L. Hunt

1986

W. E. Upjohn Institute for Employment Research

Library of Congress Cataloging in Publication Data

Hunt, H. Allan.

   Clerical employment and technological change.

   Bibliography: p.
   1. Clerks—United States—Supply and demand.
2. Clerks—United States—effect of technological
innovations on.   3. Office practice—Automation.
I. Hunt, Timothy L.   II. Title.
HD5718.M392U65   1986   331.12'5165137'0973   86-26556
ISBN 0-88099-043-0
ISBN 0-88099-042-2 (pbk.)

iii

Preface

This monograph originated in a request from Heidi Hartmann of the National Academy of Sciences, Panel on Technology and Women's Employment. She asked the authors to review the trends in clerical employment since 1950, and to critique the existing forecasts of the future outlook for clerical jobs. The goal was to reduce the range of uncertainty about clerical employment trends. We thank Heidi for her personal encouragement and for providing us the opportunity to work with the panel.

Partial funding for this research effort was provided by the National Commission for Emploment Policy. We are indebted to Carol Romero and Steve Baldwin of the Commission staff for their support and their helpful comments. The Commission also published an abridged version of the monograph in their Research Report series.

Individuals who were gracious enough to share their unpublished work or their ideas with us included the following: George Treyz of Regional Economic Models, Inc. and the University of Massachusetts, David Roessner of Georgia Tech University, Faye Duchin of New York University, Ron Kutscher and his staff at the Bureau of Labor Statistics, and John Priebe of the Census Bureau. Robert Spiegelman, executive director of the Upjohn Institute, read the entire text and improved both the analysis and the presentation.

The staff of the W. E. Upjohn Institute for Employment Research as always did a splendid job in supporting our efforts. Specific mention should be made of Jim Stansell, Carol Riffenburg, Mike Burns, Doug Palmer, Hernando Torrealba, Susan Clements, Judy Gentry and Natalie Lagoni. With such staff support, there can be no doubt that any remaining errors are the sole responsibility of the authors.

Last, but by no means least, we thank our families for putting up with the usual lost weekends and late hours. Our only defense is that we had fun and we got paid for doing it.

Facts and observations presented in this document are the sole responsibility of the authors. The viewpoints do not necessarily represent positions of the W. E. Upjohn Institute for Employment Research.

H. Allan Hunt
Timothy L. Hunt

November 1986

CONTENTS

LIST OF FIGURES

LIST OF TABLES

LIST OF TABLES (cont.)

1

Overview

There is widespread concern about clerical employment trends today, largely because of the fears of office automation. Some are concerned about the employment impacts of office automation because they are impressed by the potential labor displacing capabilities of the new technologies. Others are worried about any threat that the new office technologies may pose for women's employment opportunities. If office automation eliminates these traditionally female jobs, there may be even greater problems ahead for women in the labor market.

Actual trends in clerical employment in the first half of the 1980s fueled these concerns. At roughly the same time that microprocessor technology was capturing the public imagination, clerical employment began to decline. Was this a coincidence? Do the new word processors, enhanced telephone capabilities, electronic mail and dictation systems represent revolutionary technological change for the office? What do these new technologies portend for clerical employment in the future?

The decline in clerical employment and the growing interest in office automation occurred at the same time that the economy suffered through the deepest recession since the 1930s. Unemployment levels rose to unprecedented postdepression levels. Are these events causally related?

1

Which is cause and which is effect? Are clerical workers going the way of farm workers, becoming so productive that they worked themselves out of their jobs?

Clerical jobs are important because they are the most numerous occupational group in the economy. They are also important because they present entry opportunities for young workers, disadvantaged workers, or those reentering the labor force after an absence of some kind. Over the years, one of the most productive training outlets for employment and training programs for disadvantaged Americans has been clerical work. Are these entry channels to be choked off now by machines that replace clerical workers?

This monograph reviews trends in clerical employment over the last 30 years in a search for indirect evidence of the impact of changes in process technology on clerical employment levels. The indirect approach to studying technological change is necessary because the information required to conduct a more rigorous investigation is unavailable. In the absence of data on capital inputs or clerical output, existing employment data are carefully analyzed to provide a picture of clerical employment changes through time.

Specifically, clerical employment trends from 1950 to 1980, and from 1972 to 1982 will be examined. The intent is to secure some understanding of the clerical employment impacts of technological change during the first computer revolution of the 1960s and 1970s. This should aid in assessing the likelihood of significant technological displacement among current clerical workers accompanying the new microprocessor-based office technologies of the 1980s.

The monograph also investigates the broad economic determinants of recent clerical employment changes. The influence of industry occupational structure and industry employment trends on clerical employment totals is examined. Changes in occupational employment patterns within particular industries are examined for possible association with technological changes. Evidence of the direct impact of technological change on office employment levels is sought for the finance and insurance industry, reputedly the most advanced user of office automation systems and the heaviest employer of clerical workers in the economy.

A review of prominent forecasts of clerical employment is also offered. The obvious purpose is to provide information about other researchers' expectations about clerical employment trends. It also provides an opportunity to examine the way in which assumptions about technological change and its employment impacts for the future have shaped those employment forecasts.

The monograph does not try to assess the influence of other important factors that will determine future labor market outcomes for clerical workers. In particular, there is no consideration of future supply issues. If female labor force participation rates continue to rise as they have in the past, the issue of job creation for women will be of even greater significance. On the other hand, if women increase their penetration of nontraditional female occupations, the number of females seeking clerical positions in the future may decline. Whether men are more likely to begin to look to clerical positions for career opportunities in the future presumably depends on labor market developments for clericals, as well as the job outlook in more traditional male occupations.

Clearly these considerations are crucial to understanding whether the supply and demand of clerical workers will be in approximate balance in the labor market of the future, but this question is beyond the scope of the present volume. We seek only to (1) illuminate past trends in clerical employment, (2) investigate the causes behind those trends, with particular attention to technological change, and (3) critically evaluate existing clerical employment forecasts. It is hoped that this review will help to narrow the range of uncertainty about the probable future impact of technological change on the demand for clerical employment.

This first chapter will provide an overview of the issues. Questions will be raised about the causes of recent trends in clerical employment. A discussion of the meaning of clerical automation will also be offered. Possible employment impacts of technological change will be outlined and offsetting tendencies considered. The chapter will conclude with some cautions about the comparisons that must be made between dissimilar data sources.

Chapter 2 presents the best available data on the historical employment patterns of clerical workers. It begins with a discussion of some of the difficulties in measuring occupational employment. Then the chapter presents the data base on occupational employment for clerical workers. The number and types of clerical jobs are discussed, as is the demographic makeup of the clerical workforce. The long-term trend in employment from 1950 to 1980 is presented first. It is followed by a brief discussion of more recent trends using annual data from 1972 to 1982. Finally, the trends in demographic characteristics of clerical workers are described.

Chapter 3 describes the employment trends for individual clerical occupations in some detail. The clerical occupations are divided into relatively homogeneous subgroups and both long-term and recent trends are reviewed, together with the demographic composition of the occupation and speculation on the past impacts of technological change. Chapters 2 and 3 are complementary in the sense that they both examine the same basic data. Chapter 2 concentrates on overall trends while chapter 3 takes individual clerical occupations as the focus of attention.

Chapter 4 investigates the determinants of clerical employment. It concentrates on clerical employment by industry and the role that industry growth trends play in explaining the expansion of clerical employment. The industry staffing ratio is developed as a tool to aid in this analysis. Then the specific question of technological change in the office and its impact on clerical employment is explored. Chapter 4 concludes with an analysis of the contributions that general economic growth, differential rates of industry growth and changes in occupational staffing ratios have made to overall clerical employment trends.

Chapter 5 reviews the major recent forecasts of clerical employment levels in the future. The national occupational projections program at the Bureau of Labor Statistics is examined, and other noteworthy forecasting efforts are also considered. The focus is on the way in which assumptions about technological change impact the employment projections for clerical workers over the next decade. In the concluding chapter, the findings are reviewed and more global interpretations are offered of the determinants of clerical employment levels, both past and future.

Overview of Clerical Employment Trends

Clerical jobs are the largest single occupational group in the economy; they are also one of the most diverse. Generally, people use the term "clerical workers" to refer to the traditional office occupations. Secretaries, typists, stenographers, file clerks, office machine operators and receptionists do make up a large proportion of all clerical workers. But bookkeepers and bank tellers are also clerical workers, according to the U.S. Bureau of the Census, as are bill collectors, insurance adjusters, postal clerks, expediters, dispatchers, and teachers' aides. While this listing is not exhaustive, it is indicative of the great variety among clerical jobs throughout the economy.

The tremendous growth in the number of clerical workers in the U.S. is well known, but the true magnitude of this expansion cannot be appreciated without comparing it to the growth in total employment. Figure 1.1 shows that the proportion of clerical workers to total employment has *doubled* in the last 40 years. In 1940, just under one employee in ten was a clerical worker. By 1980, this proportion had risen to one in five.[1] One of the most stimulating questions about future employment is whether this trend will continue. Such questions derive naturally from early disappointment with labor market results of the 1970s and early 1980s, but they are driven primarily by the developments in office technology of the last few years.

The first "computer revolution" in the 1960s was expected to impact clerical work adversely as well. Despite the fact that the dire consequences predicted by some for clerical worker employment in the 1960s did not materialize, these fears have been aroused again in the 1980s.[2] Those who are convinced that this time the fears are well founded base their case primarily on the introduction to the office of microprocessor-based technologies. The incredible reductions in the cost of computing power, combined with the reductions in bulk made possible by microprocessor technology, may possibly constitute a new revolutionary development.

Those who expect that automation will stop the long-term growth in clerical employment cite the apparent reduction in the rate of increase in the proportion of clerical workers. This can be seen in figure 1.1 as well. While the clerical proportion of all employment rose almost linearly from 1940 to

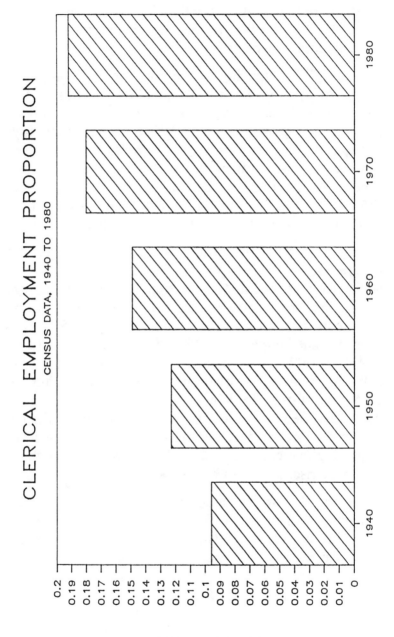

Figure 1.1

CLERICAL EMPLOYMENT PROPORTION
CENSUS DATA, 1940 TO 1980

1970, there is a slight reduction in the rate of increase between 1970 and 1980. Is this the beginning of the end of clerical employment growth?

Figure 1.2 helps illuminate the cyclical component in employment movements and shows how this can confuse the issue of the secular trend in clerical employment. Figure 1.2 indicates the growth in both clerical and total employment annually from 1958 to 1984.[3] Employment figures are reported in the form of index numbers to facilitate comparison between the two series. Using 1958 employment as the base, the index numbers indicate the growth in clerical and total employment over the levels in the base year.

The more rapid rise in clerical employment over most of this period is readily apparent in figure 1.2. However, the similarity in the employment trends since the last cyclical employment peak in 1979 is also indicated. Still, the absolute decline in clerical employment from 1981 to 1982 is the only time this has happened in the last quarter century (discounting the 1971 data anomaly). Generally, in recessionary periods production worker employment declines but clerical employment only slows in growth. Total employment movement then depends primarily on the severity of the change for production workers. In the 1975 recession, for instance, total employment declined while clerical employment continued to rise, although at a slower rate.

Figure 1.3 shows the proportion of clerical employment to total employment on an annual basis from 1958 to 1984, thus reflecting both the trends shown in figure 1.2. When total employment declines and clerical employment rises, the clerical proportion rises very rapidly as indicated in figure 1.3 for 1975. It is obvious in figure 1.3 that the rate of increase of clerical workers relative to all employment was much slower in the 1970s than it was in the 1950s.[4]

Figure 1.2

CLERICAL AND TOTAL EMPLOYMENT TREND

CPS DATA, 1958 TO 1984

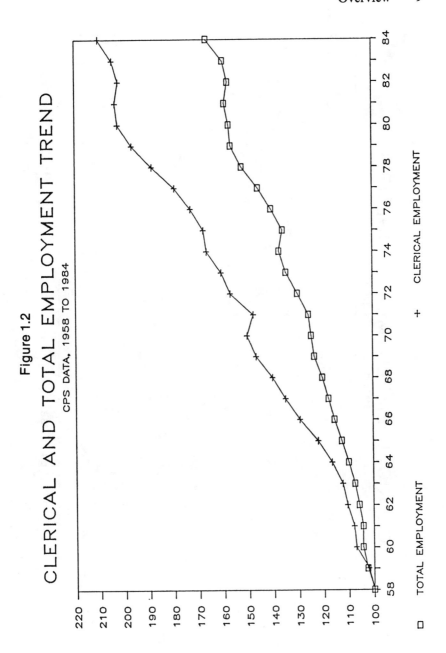

EMPLOYMENT INDEX (1958 = 100)

□   TOTAL EMPLOYMENT   +   CLERICAL EMPLOYMENT

Figure 1.3

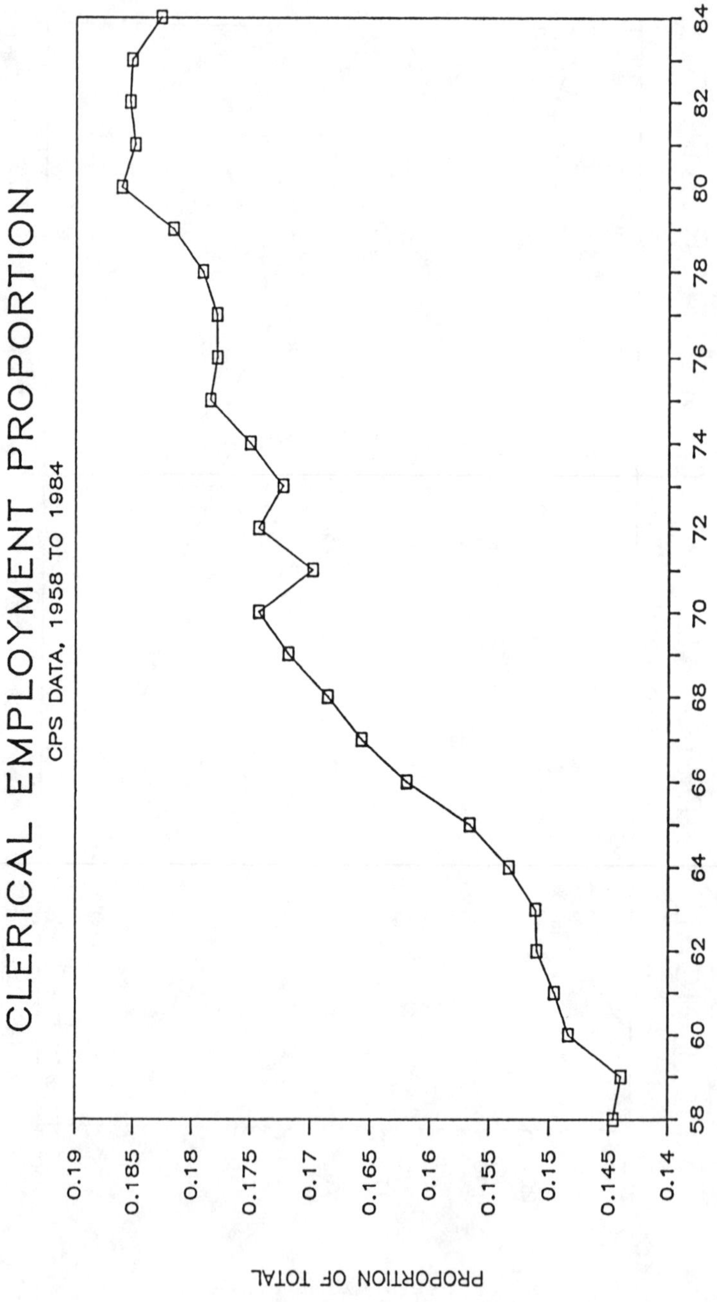

CLERICAL EMPLOYMENT PROPORTION

CPS DATA, 1958 TO 1984

PROPORTION OF TOTAL

What is even more apparent is the stagnation in the proportion of clerical workers since 1980. Clearly, clerical workers did not fare as well in the last recessionary period as they did earlier. It is less clear what the downturn in the clerical proportion in 1984 means. Such a decline has been typical of recovery periods in the past (as in 1976-77) when the number of production workers rises rapidly to restore the prerecession balance between production and nonproduction workers (including clericals). Whether the trend of the early 1980s is something different remains to be seen.

Figure 1.4 shows the employment ratio of clerical workers to managers and administrators reported in the Current Population Survey (CPS) from 1958 through 1982. Since these are aggregate figures, it would be risky to attach any particular importance to the actual numerical value of the ratio, but the trends are very suggestive. Figure 1.4 shows that the ratio of clericals to managers in the entire economy rose dramatically through the 1960s, reaching a plateau by the end of the decade. This ratio held very nearly constant through the 1970s (ignoring the 1971-72 distortion caused by conversion to Census benchmarks). However, the ratio has fallen slightly since the beginning of the recessionary period in 1979-80. This evidence is certainly not inconsistent with the hypothesis of a significant change in the employment trends of clerical workers in the last few years.

The last issue to be discussed in this overview is the extent to which clerical jobs are also female jobs. Is it a coincidence that the expansion of clerical employment occurred simultaneously with the expansion of female labor force participation rates? To what extent have female job opportunities been linked to the expansion of the clerical workforce?[5]

Figure 1.5 shows that the overwhelming majority of clerical workers are in fact female, and that this is even more

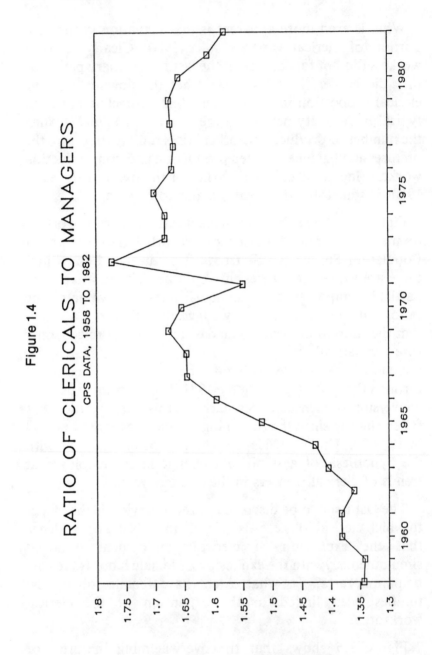

Figure 1.4

Figure 1.5

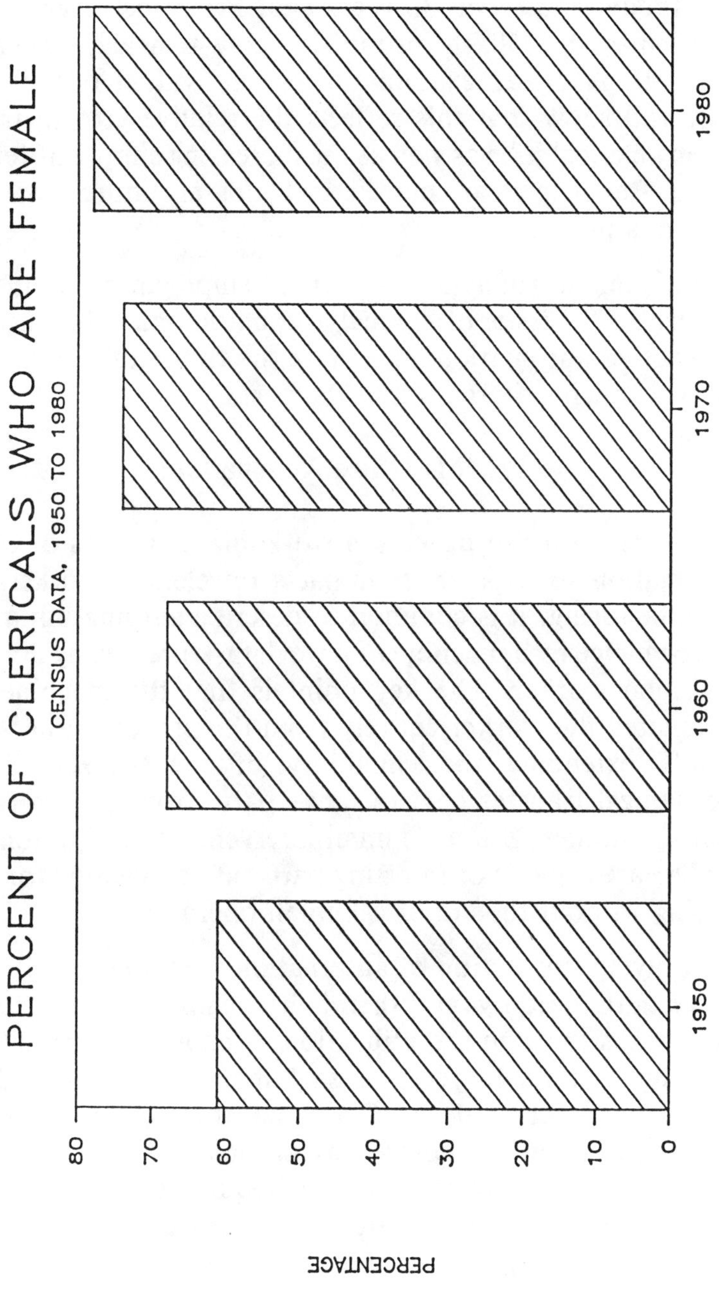

PERCENT OF CLERICALS WHO ARE FEMALE

CENSUS DATA, 1950 TO 1980

PERCENTAGE

true today than it was 30 years ago! From just over 60 percent female in 1950, the proportion grew to nearly 80 percent by 1980. A closer examination of individual occupations later will show that this reflects the relative growth trends among clerical jobs as well as the increasing supply of female labor. But it is clear that clerical jobs are more than ever women's jobs.

With this introduction to clerical employment trends, let us turn to the issue of clerical automation and the question of whether automation may cause the future of clerical jobs to look much different from the past.

What is Office Automation?

It is necessary to develop a workable definition of office automation to explore its impacts on clerical workers. In manufacturing, it is common to describe automation as the performance by a machine of a work task previously done by a human worker. The key point is that the machine has eliminated the worker entirely from the process rather than simply extending the capability of the worker. Thus, mechanical transfer devices move parts from one workstation to another without human intervention, and automatic feeders are capable of inserting parts into a machine for processing without the aid of a human operator.

Applying this notion of automation from manufacturing, office automation would then be the elimination of clerical work tasks through the utilization of capital equipment. In fact, in the past 40 years or so hundreds of thousands of clerical jobs have been eliminated through automation, telephone operators replaced by automatic switching units, stenographers by office dictation equipment, and so on. More recently, computer software is being used to determine the appropriate price for an insurance policy, a job task which was once done manually by a clerical specialist called a rater, and automatic mail sorting devices are reducing the need for mail clerks. There is no doubt that automation is eliminating some kinds of clerical jobs.

Although this notion of office automation provides a useful beginning and certainly constitutes one aspect of office automation, it is much too narrow a perspective. In broader terms automation is the process of substitution of capital for labor, which ultimately results in higher labor productivity. From an analytical viewpoint there appears to be no justification to limit the idea of office automation to fully automatic devices. As one example, word processors do not eliminate the manual keystrokes entered by a human operator. However, they may improve the efficiency of the process and thereby eliminate the need for some clerical workers, all other things equal.

In this monograph, office automation will be interpreted broadly as any technological change which enhances the productivity of clerical workers. There are many reasons for utilizing such a broad definition of office automation. First, clerical jobs encompass a wide variety of positions, many of which are not located in offices. This implies a tremendous number of different kinds of capital equipment that may be used by clerical workers as a group. Therefore, it would be a mistake to define office automation narrowly, in terms of particular machinery. Clerical jobs and the machinery and equipment that are used in those jobs are very diverse.

Second, this broad definition of office automation facilitates the examination of the overall results which have been achieved by the utilization of office hardware. This approach is the most consistent with the historical review of employment trends in clerical occupations. It will be seen later that precious little hard data are available on office automation equipment, so it is extremely important to make the maximum use of the employment data which are available. The broadest possible perspective on office automation is therefore encouraged.

Finally, even if detailed data were available on office automation, it would still be critical to examine actual outcomes rather than intentions or the technical potential of the equipment. Many clerical jobs tend to be relatively unstructured, and there is no reason to think that the absolute technical potential will be realized. It is also well known that vendors and those responsible for implementation decisions within firms have a self-interest in being optimistic about the capabilities of office automation.[6]

Technological change in the office has been occurring for a long time and has involved numerous types of capital equipment. Nevertheless, an assessment of the overall trends in clerical employment should reveal the impacts of recent improvements in office automation, provided they are sufficiently dramatic and adequately diffused. If this technology is truly revolutionizing the productivity of the office, some employment impacts should be apparent in the last few years. According to one survey, nearly one-fourth of secretaries may have had direct access to a word processor by late 1982, while just over one-sixth may have had access to a personal computer in the office.[7] Clearly the continued diffusion of office automation equipment since 1982 should have begun to impact employment levels significantly if such dramatic effects actually exist.

The popular press is full of the wonders of current office automation technologies. Taking some of these treatments at face value, the "paperless" office is just around the corner. Fully automatic correspondence systems that can take raw dictation and turn it into finished text, properly formatted and polished, seem only a matter of months away. In fact, the capabilities of current office automation *are* impressive, but nowhere near what the futurists would have us believe.

There are two key aspects of today's office automation systems: computing power and communications. At the heart of these systems is the computer, including the peripheral devices for input and output as well as the software which makes the system operate. The computer is not a new piece of technology, but it has become radically smaller and more powerful over the years and definitely much less expensive. Thus, in contrast to the mainframe computer revolution of the 1960s, the excitement today is about the minicomputers and microcomputers which are invading both our offices and homes. There is no doubt that the diffusion of computers beyond centralized data processing centers is putting enormous computational power in the hands of more and more people.

Adequate data on computer sales, as in other areas of office automation, are hard to come by. Some consulting firms maintain such data bases. But the reliability of the data is unknown, it tends to be expensive to access, and even when access is granted, the user is generally not permitted to publicly disseminate the data for proprietary reasons. Another potential source of data on computers is the current industrial reports program of the U.S. Department of Commerce. They maintain data on computer *sales* but it is limited to the shipments of domestic manufacturers.

The ideal data base on computers would contain information about the actual population of computers *in use* by industrial sector within the U.S. Unfortunately, that type of data is not available at all. The Computer and Business Equipment Manufacturers Association (CBEMA) does publish data about the domestic consumption of computers. The data are maintained separately for microcomputers, minicomputers, and mainframe computers, where the distinctions are a function of price and computational power. Microcomputers are those priced from $1,000-$20,000, minicomputers from $20,000-$250,000, and mainframes $250,000 and above. Although the specific computational power parameters are not reported and the reliability of the data is unknown, the CBEMA data appear to be the best available for our purposes.

The domestic consumption of micro-, mini-, and mainframe computers from 1960-1984 is reported in table 1.1. Domestic consumption includes all sales, foreign and domestic, made to U.S. users. It attempts to capture import sales of foreign firms but excludes the export sales of U.S. manufacturers, i.e., it is the U.S. market for computers. The data are reported in unit terms rather than dollar terms because that may be the best indicator of the impact of computers on the workforce.[8]

According to table 1.1, the growth of mainframes (price of over $250,000) has averaged a little under 8 percent per annum for the entire 24-year period. It is interesting to note that this category of computer, which remains the backbone of the industry, has proven quite susceptible to the vagaries of the business cycle. Unit sales declined in 11 of the 24 years. There were peak years in 1967, 1973, and 1981. Moreover, the absolute sales of 14,000 units in 1972 outdistanced the 1981 peak of 10,700 units by some 30 percent.

In contrast, the sales of minicomputers (priced from $20,000 to $250,000) have increased in every year that CBEMA reports the data except 1983. The annual growth rate exceeds 33 percent. However, the decline in 1983 certainly seems to demonstrate the cyclical sensitivity of minicomputer sales as well. But it is the sales of microcomputers (priced under $20,000) that have been truly astounding. The annual growth in unit sales from 1975 to 1984 was just under 100 percent. Of course, that growth rate is partly a result of the small base of micros in 1975. Nonetheless, the overall sales gain from 1981 to 1984 was still a very healthy 77 percent annually, bringing the size of the total market to 2,140,000 units. It is not known how many of these microcomputers were sold to business firms and how many to the home market.

The data in table 1.1 raise the interesting question of the susceptibility of the microcomputer market to the business cycle. This may be important in terms of office automation because it is these smaller, cheaper computer systems which are the focus of the current interest in office automation. This question is extremely apropos today because the popular media currently are rife with reports about the slowdown in computer sales.[9] In fact, one popular business magazine expects that 1985 sales of computers to business firms will exceed 1984 sales by a meager 3 percent, and it is projecting 1986 sales growth of only 5 percent (*Fortune* 1985).

There are no hard data about which sectors of the computer market are being affected by the current slowdown in sales, but it appears that the slowdown is relatively broad-based. According to the CBEMA data, mainframe sales began to decline in 1982 and minicomputers dropped in 1983. A firm such as Wang, which has specialized in the office automation market, actually furloughed workers for the first time in corporate history in 1985. Obviously, it is extremely difficult to hazard a guess about how long the slowdown will last. As early as May 1984, one consulting firm (Stanford Research International 1984) released a study that suggested the long-term market for microcomputers in business had been vastly exaggerated.

Since 1984 and 1985 have been reasonably good years in terms of economic growth generally, this slowdown in computer sales, whatever its magnitude, is occurring during the

Table 1.1
Domestic Consumption of Micro-, Mini-, and Mainframe Computers, 1960-1984

Year	Micros		Minis		Mainframes	
	Units	Percent change	Units	Percent change	Units	Percent change
1960	NR	NR	NR	NR	1,790	
1961	NR	NR	NR	NR	2,700	50.8
1962	NR	NR	NR	NR	3,470	28.5
1963	NR	NR	NR	NR	4,200	21.0
1964	NR	NR	NR	NR	5,600	33.3
1965	NR	NR	260	NR	5,350	-4.5
1966	NR	NR	385	48.1	67,250	35.5
1967	NR	NR	720	87.0	11,200	54.5
1968	NR	NR	1,080	50.0	9,100	-18.7
1969	NR	NR	1,770	63.9	6,000	-34.1
1970	NR	NR	2,620	48.0	5,700	-5.0
1971	NR	NR	2,800	6.9	7,600	33.3
1972	NR	NR	3,610	28.9	10,700	40.8
1973	NR	NR	5,270	46.0	14,000	30.8
1974	NR	NR	8,880	68.5	8,600	-38.6

1975	5,100	NR	11,670	31.4	6,700	-22.1
1976	25,800	405.9	17,000	45.7	6,750	0.7
1977	58,500	126.7	24,550	44.4	8,900	31.9
1978	115,660	97.7	29,550	20.4	7,500	-15.7
1979	160,000	38.3	35,130	18.9	7,200	-4.0
1980	250,500	56.6	41,450	18.0	9,900	37.5
1981	385,100	53.7	44,100	6.4	10,700	8.1
1982	735,000	90.9	47,820	8.4	10,600	-0.9
1983	1,260,000	71.4	45,420	-5.0	9,985	-5.8
1984	2,140,000	69.8	72,130	58.8	9,875	-1.1

SOURCE: Computer and Business Equipment Manufacturers Association, *Computer and Business Equipment Marketing and Forecast Data Book*, 1985, p. 87. Data for 1984 from telephone conversation.

NOTE: Micros, $1,000-$20,000; Minis, $20,000-$250,000; Mainframes, $250,000 and above.

NR - Not reported.

recovery phase of the business cycle. It is happening exactly when most computer industry optimists had expected an explosion in computer and office automation sales. The current situation certainly does not give much credence to the position that the microcomputer revolution is impervious to economic conditions.

The current slump in the computer market demonstrates once again the natural tendencies of firms and individuals to be overoptimistic about the possibilities for and the capabilities of new technologies. It seems that only through experience do we modify our overoptimistic expectations about the future. The lack of hard data and the limited experience with the new technologies also contribute to wide swings in our expectations about these systems.

The second key aspect of office automation technologies today is communications. Within an individual computer system the goal is to be able to input commands, data, or text by voice or by optical scan devices. These changes would, obviously, significantly reduce the keying of data. Across computer systems, the goal is to achieve effective, flexible communications. Users would be able to easily talk with mainframes and access the large data bases which are maintained on those systems. Ideally, users would also be able to interact with other users, regardless of hardware or software selection.

The problem with communications technologies today is that only part of these systems are available now and their capabilities tend to be limited. For example, voice input devices are still in the experimental stages, except for a few specialized applications. Voice input systems can be constructed today that understand a very limited vocabulary, but may only recognize one individual's voice. Today's voice input systems would be particularly inappropriate for the office with its myriad interactive tasks and people. Obviously, it is very difficult to talk about diffusion of systems which are still experimental

Computers today are being interconnected in what are known as local area networks (LANs). That is the buzzword in the trade press in 1985. These systems are not yet very flexible, however. They enable certain makes of computers to communicate with each other, perhaps a micro to a mainframe to access some particular data base or software package, but there is a bewildering array of incompatible computer hardware and software on the market which is hindering these changes. LANs may also support communication between workstations by using electronic mail, but the system may be limited by the lines of text that can be transmitted and it is not likely that it will accept graphics. It should also be remembered that even this level of communication becomes impossible if one is trying to access another computer not on the hard-wired LAN. That is not meant to deny the existence of long distance communication using modems and ordinary telephone lines. These communications are primitive and restrictive, however, compared to the capabilities required to gain wide acceptance by the business community.

It is fair to conclude that the diffusion of the newer communications systems is currently lagging the diffusion of micros and minis by a wide margin. In fact, one of the explanations being offered for the current slowdown in computer sales is that firms are trying to determine how they are going to tie together dissimilar hardware and software systems that were purchased before the potential for interconnectivity was recognized. It remains to be seen when LANs will reach the level of acceptance of the ubiquitous personal computer.

It should not be surprising that some optimists are trumpeting the new communications technologies as finally heralding the paperless office of the future. Others are not so certain. In any event, there seems to be no doubt that thus far computers have created a veritable mountain of paper reports. It is also clear that we have required a growing army of clerical workers to cope with the paper avalanche.

Potential Employment Impacts of Office Automation

Technological change is frequently classified as either a change in process or product technology. Process technology refers to the machinery and equipment and the associated production techniques which are used to produce individual goods and services. Product technology, on the other hand, is that technology which is embedded in the final good or service itself. Thus a given change in knowledge might be applied to changing the nature of the final product, or to changing the way in which the product is produced.

In many cases the distinction between process technology and product technology is artificial. Changes in the nature of a product frequently have important implications for the process used to create it. And changes in the method of manufacture also generally lead to changes in the product itself. These issues are even more complex when dealing with office automation, since the product (office output) is not normally sold on a market. Nevertheless, the distinction is useful analytically.

Office automation is like other process technological change in that it is designed to enable workers to produce more output in a given amount of time (higher labor productivity). When the productivity of labor rises, however, there are a number of possible outcomes with very different consequences for employment levels. The specific outcome is determined by the nature of the technological change itself, but also by the conditions in the firm and industry where the change occurs, the labor market conditions when the technology is applied, the overall economic and regulatory climate, and other factors.

For example, if a new process technology is introduced that significantly increases labor productivity while total output is constrained to a fixed quantity for any reason, obviously some redundancy has been created in the labor input. The desired output can be produced with fewer than the current number of workers. Under these circumstances, one can expect to see workers displaced from these jobs (laid off). However, if the normal voluntary turnover of workers occurs more rapidly than the redundancy created by the technological change, there would be no necessity for displaced workers. Of course, the number of job opportunities in the aggregate might be reduced, but none of the current employees would have to leave their jobs against their will.

On the other hand, output is rarely fixed in an absolute sense either at the firm or industry level. Thus the situation is usually much more complicated than the simple example above. The question of employment impact then depends partly upon the strategy of the firm and the conditions in the market in which the firm's output is sold. If it turns out that the new technology reduces the costs of production (not always obvious), the firm adopting the new technology has derived an advantage over its competitors.

The firm then faces a choice between producing the old output level at lower cost and higher unit profit, or trying to expand output to gain a larger share of the market. If the firm chooses to expand output in a competitive market, it will likely have to either lower the price or in some way offer more value for the same price as other firms. In either circumstance, the firm's profit margin per unit would decline, but the firm would hope to sell enough extra units to more than make up the difference.

If the firm chooses to lower the price and produce more output, clearly the number of workers needed will rise. This will mitigate the original displacement effect of the technological change. Whether more workers or fewer workers are required on balance depends in part on the price elasticity of demand for the output of the firm. If demand is relatively inelastic (not very responsive to price changes), there may still be displaced workers even though the firm's output expands. If demand is elastic, the net effect on employment depends on the relative sizes of the productivity impact and the quantity of output impact. Of course, normal labor turnover still plays a role in determining how likely previous employees are to lose their jobs.

If the firm chooses to try and make its product more attractive in quality or tries to differentiate its product in some way (nonprice competition), the situation is much the same. The number of workers required will rise, although they may not be of exactly the same occupation or skill level if they are producing different products or services. For instance, if the firm chooses to raise the quality of the product, they may require more supervisors, more inspectors, or more highly skilled production people. On the other hand, if they are successful in increasing the demand for their product, the number of workers needed to produce the basic output will rise once again. As before, the net effect depends on whether the productivity impact dominates the output impact.

This general conceptual framework is shown in figure 1.6. Changes in process technology are presumed to lead to increased labor productivity. The net impact on labor input levels is conditioned by changes in the quantity of output, the quality of output, and product changes. Even if there is a net reduction of labor input, the possibility of involuntary layoffs is mediated by normal (voluntary) turnover, and also

Figure 1.6

POTENTIAL EMPLOYMENT IMPACT OF OFFICE AUTOMATION

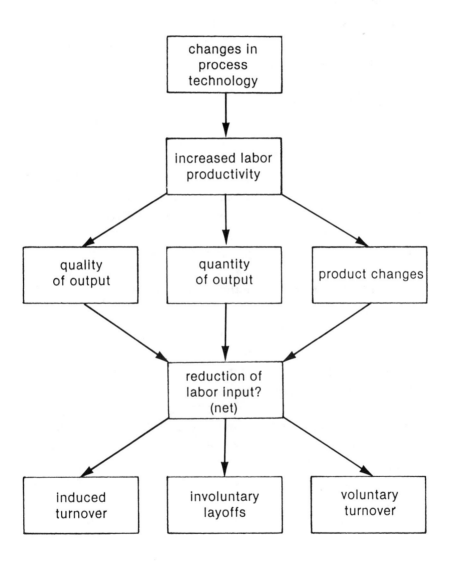

by the possibility of policy initiatives such as early retirement bonuses (induced turnover). Thus the final labor displacement impact (layoffs) of changes in technology are not obvious from the productivity impact.

If a technological innovation confers a substantial economic advantage on the firm, its competitors will adopt the new technology as well. So it is necessary to move up to the industry level to analyze the probable employment impacts in the longer run. At the industry level, the employment level is less affected by interfirm competition than by economic fundamentals. If the average price for the industry is reduced by a process technological innovation, total output can be expected to increase since consumers in the aggregate generally purchase more at a lower price. This is because there are usually opportunities to substitute among different products in competition for the consumer's dollar (the substitution effect). In addition, there is the obvious impact of having more real income if prices decline (the income effect).

But there is another reason to expect that demand for the output of the industry, and therefore employment levels, may increase. Since consumers' incomes tend to rise through time with general economic growth (from rising labor productivity), there is a natural growth in the demand for the output of the industry from income increases. These changes are summarized in the income elasticity of demand for the product. Some types of goods and services tend to have very high income elasticity of demand; that is, the quantity of goods sold rises more rapidly than income. Other kinds of products have low income elasticity of demand and do not increase significantly in sales when incomes rise. Of course, any output increase from rising incomes would also tend to ameliorate the labor displacing effects of technological change in the industry.

A number of these concepts are important in evaluating the probable employment impacts of office automation technology. As discussed in the previous section, office automation can be regarded as the general substitution of capital for labor in the production of office output. Under the assumption that office automation has the potential to significantly increase the productivity of office workers, what employment effects can be expected?

First, it is clear that in the office, output is very hard to measure. Clerical workers do a number of different tasks, and many of them are sufficiently abstract or irregular that it is not a simple matter to count how much was produced at the end of the day. So it is possible that part of the potential increase in labor productivity may simply be lost to task indivisibilities, increased leisure on the job, or other inefficiencies.

Second, quantity of output changes are especially likely in the case of increases in office productivity. The demand for office output appears to be highly elastic, based on the last 25 years of expansion in demand.[10] There is no obvious reason why the microprocessor revolution should not produce the same increased demand for information that has accompanied the mainframe revolution.

Third, quality of output changes are also very likely with new office technologies. This is partly because the relevant decisions are diffused throughout the organization and partly because of the difficulties in measuring output. For example, many organizations have found that word processing technology leads to an increase in the quality standard for typographical errors in routine correspondence.

Fourth, it also seems that the application of new process technology to the office has the potential to change the product substantially. Microprocessor capability in the form of a personal computer may change the nature of office output by putting spreadsheet analysis in the hands of secretaries. The possibility of including graphics and spreadsheets in letters and memos through the use of integrated software may also significantly change the type of correspondence that leaves the office.

In the final analysis, increases in labor productivity made possible by new office technologies will be manifested in higher quality output and in office product changes, as well as in increases in the quantity of output that result from lower costs. The net impact of office automation on the level of clerical employment is very uncertain. This is particularly apparent since the last 25 years appear to demonstrate that the elasticity of demand for information is rather high. As will be shown, clerical employment has grown very rapidly through the first quarter century of the computer age. It is not yet obvious that current office automation initiatives based on microprocessor technology will reverse this pattern.

Problems with Different Data Sources

There is a rather serious data problem that should be discussed before launching into the examination of detailed findings in this book. The problem is that there are a number of data sources that will be used to develop the empirical picture of clerical workers and their employment patterns, and they are not totally consistent with one another.

When the number and type of clerical jobs are described in chapter 2, the 1980 Census will be the primary source of data. As will be shown, because of a massive reorganization of the occupational classification system, the 1980 Census employment data are almost totally incompatible with Census measurements in the past. Thus, adopting the 1980 Census as a base for the description would automatically rule out consistent time series comparisons. When the desire is to show the long-term trends in the employment of clerical workers from 1950 to 1980, the 1970 Census is chosen as the base because that facilitates the translation of dissimilar Census data into roughly comparable terms.

For recent trends in clerical employment, it is necessary to use the Current Population Survey as a data source. This is generally consistent with Census observations, since it is bench-marked to the decennial Census, but that also means that there will be a break in the time series at least every 10 years. For example, there are consistent data available on occupational employment from the CPS from 1972 to 1982, but the change to the 1980 Census occupational classification system in 1983 renders the data noncomparable at that point. This problem is explored in chapter 2. If there are changes in definitions or procedures in the interim, the data are even more problematical, of course.

In chapter 4, when attention turns to the industries in which clerical workers are employed, it is necessary to utilize still another data source from the Bureau of Labor Statistics to maximize the detail that is available. Finally, when the forecasts of future clerical employment levels are evaluated in chapter 5, the special Occupational Employment Statistics (OES) data base developed to support the BLS occupational forecasting effort will be employed.

The intent of this monograph is to describe what is happening to clerical employment and, to the extent possible, why. The goal is not to analyze the sufficiency of the statistics.[11] However, it is important to carefully explain the problems with the data so that the reader can fully appreciate the limitations and reservations that they impose on any conclusions that can be drawn. It is critical that the data not be pushed beyond their capability or it is no longer possible to tell what is fact and what is conjecture.

For the reader who is already steeped in occupational employment data and the problems and uncertainties associated with them, this approach may be tiresome. However, some readers will need the limitations spelled out in detail. Our hope is that this has been done sufficiently well that the reader takes away not only an understanding of what has been happening to clerical employment in recent decades, but also an appreciation for how fragmentary the data are and how difficult it can be to piece together a consistent, accurate picture of clerical employment trends in the face of these limitations. With these introductory thoughts in place, let us get on with the task at hand.

NOTES

1. These data have been adjusted rather extensively for consistency. Thus the figures reported here do not correspond exactly with Census figures from other sources. This issue will be addressed in chapter 2.

2. See Bowen and Mangum (1966) for the policy resolution of the questions raised in the early 1960s.

3. These data from the Current Population Survey are not adjusted for all changes in definitions of occupations over the years. In particular, the change-over to 1970 Census definitions in 1971 shows up as an anomalous absolute decline in clerical employment in 1971. While data for 1983 and 1984 have been adjusted to reflect some changes in Census definitions, this adjustment is not complete. It is not possible to make a complete adjustment of CPS occupational employment due to insufficient detail in published figures. A full explanation of this problem is offered in chapter 2.

4. Again, the apparent drop in 1971 should be ignored as it reflects the conversion to new Census codes rather than any actual change in clerical employment levels.

5. The Panel on Technology and Women's Employment of the National Research Council has been examining these issues for the last two years. Their report, *Technology and Women's Employment,* will be available in 1986.

6. Salerno (1985) for example suggests that computer vendors have so aggressively promoted their products that they have significantly exaggerated their capabilities.

7. Honeywell (1983) survey, Table 24.

8. This is not to deny the incredible increases in computing power over the last 25 years. But prices have come down so rapidly that a unit sales figure gives a better picture of the diffusion of computers in general. There also are no price indices available that correspond to the CBEMA definitions.

9. For an example of the media reporting, the interested reader may wish to look at the cover story entitled "The Computer Slump," *Business Week,* June 24, 1985.

10. To the best of our knowledge, there are no formal estimates of either price or income elasticity of demand for office output.

11. See Hunt and Hunt (1985) for an assessment of the data available to study the employment effects of technological change.

2

Employment Patterns of Clerical Workers

This chapter will provide a general description of clerical jobs and the workers who hold them. First, the difficulties in measuring occupational employment will be discussed. Next, the number and types of clerical jobs will be presented using data from the 1980 Census. The emphasis will be on describing the breadth and variety of clerical jobs that exist. Then the demographic characteristics of clerical workers will be explored. This will be followed by a review of the trends in clerical employment for the last 30 years at the detailed occupational level. Next, the trends in employment of clerical workers in the decade from 1972 to 1982 will be examined. Finally, recent changes in the demographic characteristics of clerical workers will be briefly described.

The period 1950 to 1980 encompasses the introduction of mainframe computers to the office, as well as the beginnings of the microcomputer age. Thus one way to interpret the review is as an indirect search for the employment effects of technological change. If changing office technologies displaced large numbers of clerical workers during the first computer revolution, the evidence should be in the employment record of the 1960s and 1970s. Similarly, if the current office technologies threaten clerical jobs, some evidence of this should be found in the employment figures of the early

1980s. This analysis is presented in the hope that it will aid in assessing the likelihood of significant displacement among current clerical workers accompanying the introduction of the new microprocessor-based office technologies of the 1980s.

The emphasis in this chapter is on the entire population of clerical workers, with individual occupations only briefly highlighted. Chapter 2 also introduces the data sources and discusses some of the problems of comparability across data sources. Chapter 3 takes the individual clerical occupations as a point of departure and examines the employment trends in selected occupations. Both chapters use the same sources of data, but the focus is very different. Chapter 3 looks to the employment trends in individual occupations for illustrations of the impacts of technological change while chapter 2 concentrates on an overview of the broad clerical employment trend with particular occupations noted as exceptions. The reader who wants an overview of clerical employment trends may prefer chapter 2 while the reader interested in a particular occupation or group of occupations would find chapter 3 more suitable.

Difficulties in Measuring Occupational Employment

It is not difficult to look up employment figures in a data source and make comparisons between the number employed in two different years. There are a number of reasons to be cautious about the accuracy of comparisons of employment levels in particular occupations, however. Occupational data are notoriously difficult to deal with, both because the classifications are subjective and the measurements are difficult to quantify. There are at least five independent factors that can produce measured change in the number of people employed in a particular occupation.

First, occupational data are subject to well-known but un-quantifiable reporting biases. Occupational information collected from households is known to reflect some "title exaggeration" due to the ego involvement with occupational status. One example is that the number of accountants reported relative to bookkeepers is higher in household surveys than in employer reports. Presumably this represents the subtle shadings of interpretation that affect measurements of most social characteristics. However, these biases will only cause serious problems in accurately measuring occupational employment if tastes change substantially over time, or if employment totals from different sources of data are compared incautiously.

Second, the yardstick used to measure occupational data inevitably must be changed over time, and this can introduce systematic bias into the reported figures. As new jobs appear and old ones disappear, the classificaiton system used to measure occupational employment is altered gradually to reflect these trends. The desire to capture new occupations is laudable, but when the shift is made the comparability with old measurements in endangered. A recent example of this problem is with word processor operators.

Obviously the occupational classification systems did not have a category for word processing previous to its emergence as a significant category of employment. So when word processors came along, a decision had to be made on how to classify these workers. At first, they were classified as typists since that seemed the most directly comparable in terms of office procedure. But typists represent the old technology that word processing is replacing, so grouping them together would tend to mask this process.

Thus, a decision was made to switch word processor operators from typist to keypunch operator in the Census and CPS classification systems. This change was implemented in 1982 in the CPS data. It goes without saying that this change, whether appropriate for some purpose or not, creates severe problems of comparability of employment figures for both categories involved. While it is possible to get around this by a special study to reconstruct a historical series based on the new definition, such efforts are increasingly rare with the budget pressure being experienced in most statistical programs of the federal government.

Third is the problem of changes in job titles that may or may not reflect changes in job content. Even if it was always clear exactly what one wanted to measure with occupational data (and it is not), the changing usage of job titles could still introduce a significant bias into the measurement. An example of this problem that is related to technological change is the case of stenographers. The number of stenographers has been dropping rapidly for many years. This does not reflect a similar decline in the amount of dictation being done. In fact, the amount of dictation appears to be on the increase. But it does reflect the growing utilization of dictation equipment by executives who formerly needed a human to take dictation directly.

Thus a technological change (the miniaturization of dictation equipment and improvements in magnetic tape technology) combined with changing consumer acceptance of the new methods caused a decrease in the number of stenographers. The people who now serve the same function are called either secretaries or transcription machine operators. Since the skill referenced by the term stenographer is no longer required, the job title is dropped. From the point of view of the skill involved, the job has changed. From the point of view of the function, it may not have changed in the same way or by the same amount. This is a rather common occurrence in a dynamic, growing economy. Technological change and other developments are continually altering the way work is done. These subtle changes cannot be adequately captured in any occupational measurement system.

The same thing can happen when creative managers use "job title inflation" instead of wage or salary increases to reward employees. While this may be an acceptable tradeoff to the employees involved, the semantic changes can cause inappropriate changes in classification of the job, perhaps from clerical to managerial, or from technical to professional. If there is no accompanying change in job duties, this may be inappropriate. The point is that the changing use of the job titles can easily confuse the measurement of occupational employment.

Fourth, as with all sample data, occupational data are subject to sampling variability. Sample statistics generally have known sampling properties and confidence intervals can be calculated, but this is not a factor that is readily apparent to the unsophisticated consumer of occupational information. It is easy to misread the degree of precision in published occupational employment figures. Some of this will become apparent later in the chapter. Since sampling errors are generally small for published statistics, this should not be a problem in interpreting broad occupational trends, but it remains a serious source of variation in reported statistics for smaller occupational groups.

Fifth and last, there are the actual changes in the number of individuals employed in given occupations. Presumably these changes are the intended final product of occupational employment measurement. But what if the incidence of part-time work increases in a particular occupation? In most employment statistics, this would not be recorded. If two individuals are each working half-time rather than one full-time employee, measured employment has increased. Similar reservations apply to dual jobholders. In a household-based employment survey (such as the Census or Current Population Survey), many dual jobholders may be missed. If this bias affects particular occupations systematically, occupational employment will be distorted. Occupational employment is measured imperfectly due to all the intervening biases described above. Faced with a measured change in occupational employment, it is frequently difficult to determine exactly what it means, much less what may have caused it.

Even if the measurements were without error, the problems of determining the occupational impacts of technological change would still be formidable.[1] There are a number of causes of employment changes in a given occupation. In the first place, it is normal that economic growth would tend to lead to an expansion of employment in all categories. Second, it is likely that employment growth will differ systematically by industrial sector. Since industries employ occupations in different proportions, these variations in industry growth rate will produce differences in the employment trends in individual occupations. Third, it is likely that technological change and other factors will, within each industry, cause some occupations to grow faster than others. In chapter 4, each of these influences will be explored and quantified. For now, the discussion will concentrate simply on the measured employment levels for clerical workers.

The Number and Type of Clerical Workers

For descriptive purposes, it is helpful to divide clerical workers into a number of subgroups. Clerical workers as a whole are such a diverse group that they lack any substantial coherency, but the individual clerical occupations are so numerous that general impressions can get submerged in all the detail. Thus, in this monograph, the clerical subgroups used in the 1980 Census will be employed wherever possible to provide an intermediate level of specificity.[2]

Table 2.1 shows the employment in 1980 of administrative support occupations (the 1980 Census replacement for the clerical worker classification) by subgroup. According to the Census Bureau, there were just under 17 million administrative support workers employed in 1980. As shown in the table, the largest single group is that of the *secretaries, stenographers, and typists*. Nearly 4.66 million workers, over one-fourth of all administrative support personnel, are found in these prototypical clerical occupations.[3]

Table 2.1
Employment of Administrative Support Occupations in 1980

Sub-Group	Number employed	Percent
Administrative support occupations..........	16,851,398	100.0
Supervisors	1,056,710	6.3
Computer equipment operators	408,475	2.4
Secretaries, stenos, and typists	4,656,955	27.6
Information clerks	894,178	5.3
Non-financial records processing	965,107	5.7
Financial records processing	2,254,084	13.4
Dupl. and other office machine oper........	58,671	0.3
Communications equipment oper.	308,690	1.8
Mail and message distributing clerks	773,826	4.6
Material recording, sched. & distrib.	1,662,256	9.9
Adjusters and investigators	515,666	3.1
Miscellaneous	3,296,780	19.6

SOURCE: 1980 Census of Population.

Table 2.2 reports the detailed occupational content for each of the clerical subgroups. As an example, table 2.2 provides the information that 3.87 million of the 4.66 million workers in this subgroup are actually secretaries. In the case

Table 2.2
Detailed Administrative Support Occupations in 1980

Occupation	Total employment
Administrative support occupations.................	16,851,398
Supervisors of admin. support workers	1,056,710
Supervisors, general office.......................	631,337
Supervisors, computer equip. oper.	42,142
Supervisors, financial records proc.	157,409
Chief communications oper.	66,765
Supervisors, distr., sched. & adj. clerks	159,057
Computer equipment operators....................	408,475
Computer operators	384,392
Peripheral equip. oper..........................	24,083
Secretaries, stenos & typists	4,656,955
Secretaries	3,870,582
Stenographers	85,785
Typists	700,588
Information clerks	894,178
Interviewers	134,002
Hotel clerks	61,217
Transport. ticket & reserv. agents	99,449
Receptionists	516,498
Information clerks, n.e.c.	83,012
Non-financial records processors	965,107
Classified-ad clerks	13,552
Correspondence clerks	19,309
Order clerks	311,321
Personnel clerks..............................	75,235
Library clerks................................	140,731
File clerks	277,592
Records clerks	127,367
Financial records processors	2,254,084
Bookkeepers & accounting clerks	1,827,890
Payroll clerks................................	159,292
Billing clerks	129,380
Cost and rate clerks...........................	85,855
Billing, posting, calc. mach. oper.................	51,667

Table 2.2 (cont.)

Occupation	Total employment
Duplicating, mail, office machine oper..............	58,671
Duplicating machine oper.......................	18,822
Mail and paper handling machine oper.	7,052
Office machine oper., n.e.c.	32,797
Communications equipment operators..............	308,690
Telephone operators	292,165
Telegraphers	7,604
Comm. equipment oper., n.e.c.	8,921
Mail & message distr. clerks.....................	773,826
Postal clerks.................................	267,035
Mail carriers, postal service	256,593
Other mail clerks	167,973
Messengers..................................	82,225
Material recording, sched. & distributing............	1,662,256
Dispatchers	94,830
Production coordinators	254,625
Traffic, shipping & receiving clerks...............	481,958
Stock & inventory clerks.......................	570,906
Meter readers................................	41,407
Weighers, measurers & checkers	72,040
Samplers....................................	2,542
Expediters	106,146
Material recording, n.e.c.......................	37,802
Adjusters & investigators	515,666
Insurance adjusters, exam, investigators	163,586
Non-insurance investigators & examiners...........	243,616
Eligibility clerks, social welfare	24,128
Bill and account collectors	84,336
Miscellaneous admin. support occupations	3,296,780
General office clerks	1,648,934
Bank tellers	494,851
Proofreaders	27,321
Data-entry keyers	378,094
Statistical clerks.............................	139,174
Teachers' aides	206,695
Admin. support, n.e.c..........................	401,711

SOURCE: 1980 Census of Population.

of the secretaries, stenographers, and typists subgroup, the occupational content is fairly apparent; in other cases it is much less so.

The second largest clerical subgroup is the *financial records processors* with 2.25 million employed in 1980. This group includes such job titles as bookkeepers, accounting clerks, payroll clerks, billing clerks, and billing and posting machine operators. Table 2.1 shows that nearly one clerical worker in seven is employed in the processing of financial records. Table 2.2 demonstrates that most of these workers are in fact bookkeepers and accounting clerks.

Over 1.66 million persons are employed in the *material recording, scheduling and distributing* clerical occupations. This is nearly 10 percent of all clerical workers. They are employed as dispatchers, expediters, production coordinators, shipping and receiving clerks, stock clerks, meter readers, weighers, measurers, checkers and other similar jobs. This group of jobs is clearly more directly identified with the production of goods and services than the office employment of the previous groups. While these may not be prototypical clerical jobs, they are an important part of the clerical workforce.

Supervisors of administrative support workers accounted for just over one million employed in 1980, about one clerical worker in 16. As shown in table 2.2, over 60 percent of these workers are general office supervisors. The treatment of clerical supervisors represents a special departure in the 1980 Census, where efforts were made to separate the clerical supervisors from the general clerical workforce. As a result, many more supervisors were tabulated than in previous measurements. [4]

Non-financial records processors include such occupations as personnel clerks, classified-ad clerks, correspondence clerks, library clerks, file clerks, and order clerks. The primary distinction between these occupations and the financial records processing group discussed above is the nature of the records they work with. As shown in table 2.1, there were nearly one million such workers employed in the U.S. economy in 1980. The largest occupations within this subgroup are the order clerks and file clerks.

The *information clerk* subgroup includes interviewers, receptionists, hotel clerks, and transportation ticket and reservation agents. The main characteristics of these clerical jobs is that they involve interaction with customers or clients. Thus these clerical occupations demand more people-oriented skills than some of the others which are document-oriented. The table shows that there were nearly 900,000 such jobs in 1980, about 6 percent of all clerical workers. As will be discussed later, it is logical to expect that these jobs will be significantly less susceptible to office automation than those that are oriented to processing records.

There were also nearly three-quarters of a million *mail and message distributing clerks* employed in 1980. Table 2.2 demonstrates that this subgroup is dominated by the postal service employees; postal clerks and mail carriers make up almost two-thirds of the employment in this category. However, the growing private competitors with the post office are also represented in this group. So is the traditional clerical position of messenger, which has been making a comeback in urban areas in recent years.

There were just over one-half million people employed as *adjusters and investigators* in 1980 according to table 2.1. This group includes insurance adjusters, examiners, and investigators, bill collectors, social welfare eligibility clerks, and other assorted investigators and examiners. This is a diverse group of clerical workers with a wide range of duties and responsibilities, but they share the characteristic that they tend to deal directly with customers or clients in the course of their duties, as in the case of the information clerks discussed earlier.

In 1980, there were slightly over 400,000 people employed in the *computer equipment operator* subgroup. This category was removed from the general business machine operator group with the 1980 Census and made a subgroup of its own. It now includes only computer operators and peripheral equipment operators: the people who actually operate the equipment in electronic data processing installations. It is important to understand that this does not include programmers, systems analysts, or other professional and technical occupations. While the computer equipment operator occupations have enjoyed spectacular growth over the past 25 years, in 1980 there was still only one computer equipment operator for every 10 secretaries, stenographers, and typists.

The remnants of the office equipment operator group are included in tables 2.1 and 2.2 as *duplicating and other office machine operators*. There are less than 60,000 employed in this subgroup, mostly in the not elsewhere classified category. For that reason, this subgroup will not be analyzed separately here or in chapter 3. When trends in employment are discussed, these office equipment operators will be recombined with the computer equipment operators, as they were before the changes of the 1980 Census.

Table 2.1 reports that there were some 300,000 *communications equipment operators* employed in 1980. These consisted primarily of telephone operators, but also included telegraphers and other similar occupations. Due to automation of the telephone switching system over the past 40 years, there has been a rapid decline in the number of telephone operators. This has not been offset by the employment generated in new communications applications which tend to create technical jobs rather than clerical jobs.

The *miscellaneous administrative support occupations* subgroup is actually the second largest of all, comprising nearly 20 percent of all clerical workers. It obviously includes a considerable variety of occupations, but among the largest are general office clerks, bank tellers, data-entry keyers, teachers' aides, and statistical clerks. The fact that nearly one clerical worker in five ends up in this miscellaneous category illustrates the difficulty in generalizing about clerical occupations. There is tremendous diversity among clerical occupations in the nature of the work, in the characteristics of the people who do the work, in the historical employment trends, and in the future prospects for employment with clerical automation.

Demographics of Clerical Workers

In addition to the question of what kinds of jobs are included under the category of clerical work, there is an interest in the people who hold those jobs. This is particularly true since it will be shown that clerical jobs are not uniformly distributed across the demographic categories of sex and race. Thus it is possible that future changes in clerical employment may impact especially on the job outlook for given race-sex groups.

Figure 2.1 and table 2.3 make it clear that administrative support occupations are the most uniquely female of any occupational group. Over three-fourths of all administrative support personnel are female. The next highest concentration of females in an occupational group is service occupations with 59 percent. Since 35.4 percent of all nonclerical employees in 1980 were female while 77.1 percent of clerical workers were female, administrative support personnel are more than twice as likely as all other employees to be female.

Of course, the obverse side of this fact is that a number of nonclerical occupational groups are male dominated. Table

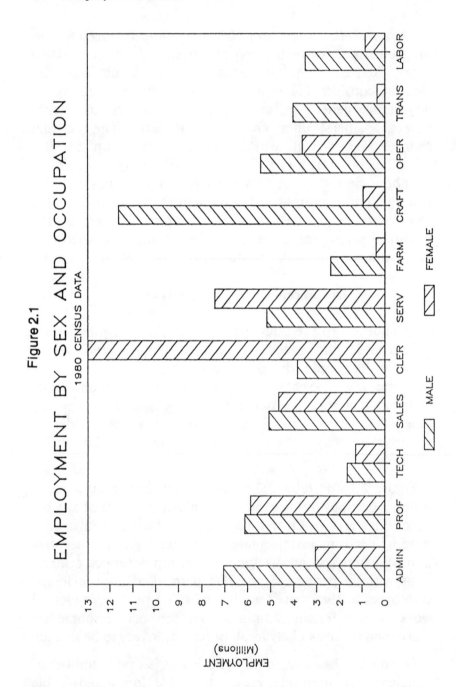

Figure 2.1

EMPLOYMENT BY SEX AND OCCUPATION
1980 CENSUS DATA

Table 2.3
Employment by Occupational Group 1980

Occupational Group	Total male	Percent male	Total female	Percent female	Total
All employed persons 16 years and over	56,004,690	57.4	41,634,665	42.6	97,639,355
Executive, admin., & managerial occ.	7,063,304	69.7	3,070,247	30.3	10,133,551
Professional specialty occ.	6,133,501	51.0	5,884,596	49.0	12,018,097
Technicians and related support occ.	1,679,062	56.3	1,303,889	43.7	2,982,951
Sales occupations	5,088,664	52.1	4,671,493	47.9	9,760,157
Admin. support, occupations	3,854,322	22.9	12,997,076	77.1	16,851,398
Service occupations	5,177,580	41.0	7,451,845	59.0	12,629,425
Farming, forestry, and fishing occ.	2,406,989	85.6	404,269	14.4	2,811,258
Precision prod., craft, and repair occ.	11,616,225	92.2	977,950	7.8	12,594,175
Mach. oper., assemblers, and inspectors....	5,438,751	59.9	3,646,237	40.1	9,084,988
Transportation and material moving occ. ...	4,041,532	92.1	347,880	7.9	4,389,412
Hand, equip. clean., helpers, and labor	3,504,760	79.9	880,183	20.1	4,384,943

SOURCE: 1980 Census of Population.

2.3 shows that the most uniquely male occupational groups (92 percent), are the precision production, craftsman, and repair occupations and the transportation and material moving occupations. The farming, forestry and fishing occupations are over 85 percent male, while handlers, equipment cleaners, helpers and laborers are 80 percent male. So the clerical workers are by no means unique in their close identification with a single sex.

While women are overrepresented among clerical workers, minorities generally are not. Table 2.4 reports that blacks number 9.7 percent of administrative support personnel and 9.6 percent of all employed persons 16 years and older. Those of Spanish origin make up 5.6 percent of all employed, but only 4.9 percent of clerical workers. Asians constitute an identical 1.7 percent of clerical workers and all employed. Thus none of these minority groups are more likely than average to be clerical workers, and Hispanics are actually somewhat underrepresented. The table does reveal substantial differences in minority representation in other major occupational groups.

Because of the high proportion of females among clerical workers, it is worth looking at the occupational distribution of females separately to determine if there is some interaction between sex and race. Figure 2.2 presents the distribution of females among the major occupational groups according to their race of Spanish heritage. In general, there are very marked differences in the proportion of women of different racial or ethnic heritage who work in different occupations. This is apparent in figure 2.2 in the case of service occupations, professional occupations, sales occupations, and operatives.

Black women are particularly likely to be employed as service workers, but are less likely to work in sales occupations than other women. Hispanic women are more likely than

Table 2.4
1980 Employment by Occupational Group, by Race and Spanish Origin

Occupational group	Total	White	Percent	Black	Percent	Hispanic*	Percent	Asian	Percent
Employed persons 16 years and over ..	97,639,355	84,027,375	86.1	9,334,048	9.6	5,456,857	5.6	1,689,070	1.7
Executive, admin. & managerial occ. ..	10,133,551	9,336,266	92.1	487,432	4.8	323,745	3.2	178,893	1.8
Professional specialty occ.	12,018,097	10,731,198	89.3	829,648	6.9	343,180	2.9	308,399	2.6
Technicians & related support occ. ...	2,982,951	2,590,639	86.8	247,834	8.3	111,960	3.8	93,290	3.1
Sales occupations	9,760,157	8,998,463	92.2	468,364	4.8	393,003	4.0	141,120	1.4
Admin. support occ, inc. clerical......	16,851,398	14,561,460	86.4	1,635,881	9.7	829,593	4.9	285,988	1.7
Service occupations	12,629,425	9,765,973	77.3	2,156,194	17.1	888,941	7.0	263,673	2.1
Farming, forestry, & fishing occ.	2,811,258	2,437,307	86.7	182,190	6.5	254,455	9.1	36,046	1.3
Precision prod., craft, & repair occ. ...	12,594,175	11,249,214	89.3	834,947	6.6	764,835	6.1	141,760	1.1
Mach. oper., assemblers, & inspectors	9,084,988	7,242,863	79.7	1,256,932	13.8	870,793	9.6	159,008	1.8
Transportation and material moving occ.	4,389,412	3,665,245	83.5	563,210	12.8	260,724	5.9	28,567	0.7
Hand, equip. clean. helpers, and labor	4,384,943	3,448,747	78.6	671,416	15.3	415,628	9.5	52,326	1.2

SOURCE: 1980 Census of Population.

*Persons of Spanish origin can be of any racial group.

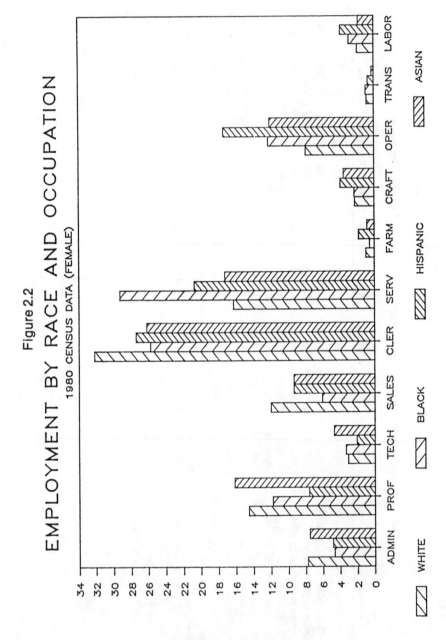

Figure 2.2

EMPLOYMENT BY RACE AND OCCUPATION

1980 CENSUS DATA (FEMALE)

average to work as operatives, but are less likely to be found in professional occupations. Asian women are the most likely of all to be found in professional occupations, but are less likely to work in service occupations or as operatives.

Interestingly, there are not substantial differences in the overall percentage of women of different races who work as clericals. White females are most likely to work in clerical or administative support occupations; some 32 percent of them are so employed. Black females are least likely at 26 percent, with Hispanic and Asian females falling in between. Only among black women does any other occupational group outnumber the clerical workers. So it is generally true for minority women as well as for women as a whole that clerical work is an extremely important source of employment opportunities.

Among individual clerical occupations there are also substantial variations in the sex distribution of workers. Table 2.5 makes it clear that within the administrative support area, the traditional clerical occupations of secretaries, stenographers, and typists are more female (over 98 percent) than any other subgroup. Additional clerical subgroups that are more than three-fourths female are the communications equipment operators, the financial records processing occupations, information clerks, and non-financial records processing occupations. The percentage female among the detailed occupations in table 2.5 also reveal that, with few exceptions, what is true of the subgroups holds for individual clerical occupations as well.

The only clerical subgroups where females are underrepresented relative to their numbers in total employment are mail and message distribution and material recording, scheduling and distributing occupations. Of course, these are also among the least "white-collar" of the clerical occupations. It is very clear that the traditional clerical jobs are predominantly held by women.

Table 2.5
1980 Employment of Administrative Support Occupations, by Sex

Occupation	Total		Percent female
	Male	Female	
Administrative support occupations	3,854,322	12,997,076	77.1
Supervisors, admin. support occupations	559,042	497,668	47.1
Supervisors, general office	276,927	354,410	56.1
Supervisors, computer equip. oper.	29,750	12,392	29.4
Supervisors, financial records proc.	80,237	77,172	49.0
Chief communications oper.	43,867	22,898	34.3
Supervisors, distr., sched. & adj. clerks	128,261	30,796	19.4
Computer equipment operators	167,320	241,155	59.0
Computer operators	158,038	226,354	58.9
Peripheral equip. operator	9,282	14,801	61.5
Secretaries, stenos & typists	77,017	4,579,938	98.3
Secretaries	47,334	3,823,248	98.8
Stenographers	7,944	77,841	90.7
Typists	21,739	678,849	96.9
Information clerks	130,617	763,561	85.4
Interviewers	29,420	104,582	78.0
Hotel clerks	19,461	41,756	68.2
Transport. ticket & reserv. agents	42,288	57,161	57.5
Receptionists	21,698	494,800	95.8
Information clerks, n.e.c.	17,750	65,262	78.6
Non-financial records processing	219,735	745,372	77.2
Classified-ad clerks	3,031	10,521	77.6
Correspondence clerks	3,568	15,741	81.5
Order clerks	101,450	209,871	67.4
Personnel clerks	9,476	65,759	87.4
Library clerks	26,437	114,294	81.2
File clerks	56,242	221,350	79.7
Records clerks	19,531	107,836	84.7
Financial records processing	262,465	1,991,619	88.4
Bookkeepers & accounting clerks	187,657	1,640,233	89.7
Payroll clerks	26,670	132,622	83.3
Billing clerks	14,360	115,020	88.9
Cost and rate clerks	27,124	58,731	68.4
Billing, posting, calc. mach. oper.	6,654	45,013	87.1
Duplicating, mail, office machine oper.	20,209	38,462	65.6
Duplicating machine oper.	7,338	11,484	61.0
Mail and paper handling mach. oper.	2,662	4,390	62.3
Office machine oper., n.e.c.	10,209	22,588	68.9

Table 2.5 (cont.)

Occupation	Total Male	Female	Percent female
Communications equip. oper.	32,542	276,148	89.5
Telephone operators	26,227	265,938	91.0
Telegraphers	4,893	2,711	35.7
Comm. equip. oper., n.e.c.	1,422	7,499	84.1
Mail & message distr. clerks	544,730	229,096	29.6
Postal clerks	171,524	95,511	35.8
Mail carriers, postal service	223,414	33,179	12.9
Other mail clerks	88,548	79,425	47.3
Messengers	61,244	20,981	25.5
Material recording, sched. & distributing	1,090,956	571,300	34.4
Dispatchers	65,262	29,568	31.2
Production coordinators	142,086	112,539	44.2
Traffic, shipping & receiving clerks	368,404	113,554	23.6
Stock & inventory clerks	372,561	198,345	34.7
Meter readers	37,168	4,239	10.2
Weighers, measurers & checkers	45,692	26,348	36.6
Samplers	1,385	1,157	45.5
Expediters	48,904	57,242	53.9
Material recording, n.e.c.	9,494	28,308	74.9
Adjusters & investigators	194,432	321,234	62.3
Insur. adjusters, exam., investigators	65,179	98,407	60.2
Non-insur. investigators & examiners	91,665	151,951	62.4
Eligibility clerks, social welfare	4,384	19,744	81.8
Bill and account collectors	33,204	51,132	60.6
Miscellaneous admin. support occupations	555,257	2,741,523	83.2
General office clerks	295,683	1,353,251	82.1
Bank tellers	43,386	451,465	91.2
Proofreaders	5,711	21,610	79.1
Data-entry keyers	28,617	349,477	92.4
Statistical clerks	34,829	104,345	75.0
Teachers' aides	15,131	191,564	92.7
Admin. support, n.e.c.	131,900	269,811	67.2

SOURCE: 1980 Census of Population.

While it was shown earlier that there is little variation in the overall proportion of minority workers employed in clerical occupations, table 2.6 demonstrates that there is substantial variation among the clerical subgroups. Blacks are much more likely to be employed as mail and message distribution clerks, communications equipment operators, and non-financial records processors when compared to their proportion of all clerical workers. They are slightly more likely to be employed as computer equipment operators, material recording, scheduling and distributing workers, or in miscellaneous clerical occupations. Blacks are significantly less likely to be employed in financial records processing occupations or as secretaries, stenographers, and typists.

Hispanics are somewhat overrepresented among material recording, scheduling and distributing occupations. They are less likely to be employed as financial records processors, or secretaries, stenographers and typists. Asians are more likely to be employed as computer operators and less likely to be employed as communications equipment operators or secretaries, stenographers and typists. It is interesting that only among the secretaries, stenographers, and typists subgroup are minorities uniformly underrepresented.

Once again, it is informative to look at the distribution of females among clerical occupations by race and Spanish origin since combining the sexes tends to conceal some important differences. Table 2.7 shows that black females are more than twice as likely to be mail and message distributing clerks and more than 1.5 times as likely to work as communications equipment operators as their general clerical percentage. They are at least 25 percent more likely to work as computer equipment operators, non-financial records processors, adjusters and investigators, or in miscellaneous clerical occupations. They are only about half as likely to be

Table 2.6
1980 Employment of Administrative Support Occupations by Race and Spanish Origin

Sub-Group	Total	White		Black		Hispanic		Asian	
		Number	Percent	Number	Percent	Number	Percent	Number	Percent
Administrative support occupations..	16,851,398	14,561,460	86.4	1,635,881	9.7	829,593	4.9	285,988	1.7
Supervisors, admin. support occupations	1,056,710	925,019	87.5	97,689	9.2	45,586	4.3	15,582	1.5
Computer equipment operators	408,475	341,018	83.5	47,474	11.6	20,998	5.1	10,728	2.6
Secretaries, stenos & typists	4,656,955	4,179,921	89.8	334,083	7.2	191,016	4.1	57,250	1.2
Information clerks	894,178	777,138	86.9	79,539	8.9	49,770	5.6	14,529	1.6
Non-financial records processing	965,107	797,121	82.6	123,673	12.8	55,867	5.8	18,987	2.0
Financial records processing	2,254,084	2,063,721	91.6	114,530	5.1	82,429	3.7	42,347	1.9
Communications equipment oper.	308,690	254,688	82.5	43,353	14.0	14,790	4.8	3,127	1.0
Mail & message distr. clerks	773,826	600,915	77.7	140,191	18.1	40,480	5.2	13,823	1.8
Material recording, sched. & distributing	1,662,256	1,399,294	84.2	190,582	11.5	106,923	6.4	24,683	1.5
Adjusters & investigators	515,666	440,688	85.5	55,586	10.8	23,679	4.6	9,266	1.8
Miscellaneous admin. support occupations	3,296,780	2,736,304	83.0	399,446	12.1	194,373	5.9	74,168	2.2

SOURCE: 1980 Census of Population.

Table 2.7
1980 Employment of Females in Administrative Support Occupations, by Race and Spanish Origin

Occupation	Total	White		Black		Hispanic		Asian	
		Number	Percent	Number	Percent	Number	Percent	Number	Percent
Administrative support occupations	12,997,076	11,325,716	87.1	1,200,516	9.2	595,461	4.6	205,036	1.6
Supervisors, admin. support occupations	497,668	430,522	86.5	51,481	10.3	20,578	4.1	7,160	1.4
Supervisors, general office	354,410	304,707	86.0	38,027	10.7	15,495	4.4	4,955	1.4
Supervisors, computer equip. oper.	12,392	10,683	86.2	1,248	10.1	530	4.3	253	2.0
Supervisors, financial records proc.	77,172	70,042	90.8	4,868	6.3	2,608	3.4	1,462	1.9
Chief communications oper.	22,898	19,261	84.1	3,243	14.2	714	3.1	141	0.6
Supervisors, distr., sched. & adj. clerks	30,796	25,829	83.9	4,095	13.3	1,231	4.0	349	1.1
Computer equipment operators	241,155	202,392	83.9	28,374	11.8	11,396	4.7	5,272	2.2
Computer operators	226,354	189,858	83.9	26,597	11.8	10,666	4.7	4,980	2.2
Peripheral equip. oper.	14,801	12,534	84.7	1,777	12.0	730	4.9	292	2.0
Secretaries, stenos & typists	4,579,938	4,115,730	89.9	325,679	7.1	186,010	4.1	55,143	1.2
Secretaries	3,823,248	3,507,644	91.7	214,543	5.6	142,531	3.7	39,681	1.0
Stenographers	77,841	67,511	86.7	7,416	9.5	2,871	3.7	1,643	2.1
Typists	678,849	540,575	79.6	103,720	15.3	40,608	6.0	13,819	2.0
Information clerks	763,561	667,984	87.5	65,629	8.6	41,366	5.4	10,901	1.4
Interviewers	104,582	89,229	85.3	10,702	10.2	5,223	5.0	1,572	1.5
Hotel clerks	41,756	37,746	90.4	2,368	5.7	1,620	3.9	897	2.1
Transport. ticket & reserv. agents	57,161	47,982	83.9	6,418	11.2	3,419	6.0	1,785	3.1
Receptionists	494,800	438,214	88.6	37,819	7.6	27,988	5.7	5,865	1.2
Information clerks, n.e.c.	65,262	54,813	84.0	8,322	12.8	3,116	4.8	782	1.2

Occupation	Total		%		%		%		%
Non-financial records processing	745,372	616,397	82.7	96,966	13.0	40,658	5.5	13,579	1.8
Classified-ad clerks	10,521	9,478	90.1	695	6.6	386	3.7	148	1.4
Correspondence clerks	15,741	13,031	82.8	2,321	14.7	552	3.5	152	1.0
Order clerks	209,871	177,969	84.8	24,654	11.7	11,615	5.5	2,670	1.3
Personnel clerks	65,759	54,709	83.2	7,862	12.0	3,490	5.3	1,473	2.2
Library clerks	114,294	97,642	85.4	11,741	10.3	4,324	3.8	2,765	2.4
File clerks	221,350	171,860	77.6	37,927	17.1	14,917	6.7	4,370	2.0
Records clerks	107,836	91,708	85.0	11,766	10.9	5,374	5.0	2,001	1.9
Financial records processing	1,991,619	1,834,478	92.1	96,239	4.8	67,451	3.4	32,936	1.7
Bookkeepers & accounting clerks	1,640,233	1,526,300	93.1	66,061	4.0	52,075	3.2	26,479	1.6
Payroll clerks	132,622	117,420	88.5	10,670	8.0	5,271	4.0	2,002	1.5
Billing clerks	115,020	102,349	89.0	8,772	7.6	5,090	4.4	1,869	1.6
Cost and rate clerks	58,731	51,014	86.9	5,372	9.1	2,481	4.2	1,328	2.3
Billing, posting, calc. mach. oper.	45,013	37,395	83.1	5,364	11.9	2,534	5.6	1,258	2.8
Duplicating, mail, office machine oper.	38,462	30,359	78.9	6,272	16.3	2,170	5.6	762	2.0
Duplicating machine oper.	11,484	8,998	78.4	1,931	16.8	521	4.5	275	2.4
Mail and paper handling mach. oper.	4,390	3,686	84.0	531	12.1	247	5.6	52	1.2
Office machine oper., n.e.c.	22,588	17,675	78.2	3,810	16.9	1,402	6.2	435	1.9
Communications equip. oper.	276,148	228,320	82.7	38,887	14.1	12,493	4.5	2,602	0.9
Telephone operators	265,938	219,230	82.4	38,033	14.3	12,189	4.6	2,495	0.9
Telegraphers	2,711	2,241	82.7	357	13.2	85	3.1	59	2.2
Comm. equip. oper., n.e.c.	7,499	6,849	91.3	497	6.6	219	2.9	48	0.6
Mail & message distr. clerks	229,096	169,374	73.9	51,173	22.3	9,136	4.0	3,617	1.6
Postal clerks	95,511	60,611	63.5	31,459	32.9	3,092	3.2	1,734	1.8
Mail carriers, postal service	33,179	28,638	86.3	3,738	11.3	928	2.8	268	0.8
Other mail clerks	79,425	62,818	79.1	13,035	16.4	4,070	5.1	1,340	1.7
Messengers	20,981	17,307	82.5	2,941	14.0	1,046	5.0	275	1.3

Table 2.7 (cont.)

	Total	White		Black		Hispanic		Asian	
		Number	Percent	Number	Percent	Number	Percent	Number	Percent
Material recording, sched.									
& distributing	571,300	485,198	84.9	64,039	11.2	30,734	5.4	8,493	1.5
Dispatchers	29,568	25,715	87.0	2,908	9.8	1,188	4.0	321	1.1
Production coordinators	112,539	97,423	86.6	11,150	9.9	5,569	4.9	1,672	1.5
Traffic, shipping & receiving clerks	113,554	96,751	85.2	12,130	10.7	7,455	6.6	1,429	1.3
Stock & inventory clerks	198,345	167,381	84.4	23,021	11.6	9,858	5.0	3,479	1.8
Meter readers	4,239	3,546	83.7	553	13.0	193	4.5	21	0.5
Weighers, measurers & checkers	26,348	21,441	81.4	3,791	14.4	1,769	6.7	233	0.9
Samplers	1,157	1,026	88.7	110	9.5	48	4.1	6	0.5
Expediters	57,242	49,058	85.7	6,361	11.1	2,466	4.3	761	1.3
Material recording, n.e.c.	28,308	22,857	80.7	4,015	14.2	2,188	7.7	571	2.0
Adjusters & investigators	321,234	265,850	82.8	42,185	13.1	15,844	4.9	6,334	2.0
Insur. adjusters, exam.									
investigators	98,407	81,382	82.7	13,231	13.4	3,596	3.7	2,283	2.3
Non-insur. investigators									
& examiners	151,951	126,338	83.1	19,665	12.9	7,358	4.8	2,866	1.9
Eligibility clerks, social welfare	19,744	14,565	73.8	3,831	19.4	1,918	9.7	548	2.8
Bill and account collectors	51,132	43,565	85.2	5,458	10.7	2,972	5.8	637	1.2
Miscellaneous admin. support									
occupations	2,741,523	2,279,112	83.1	333,592	12.2	157,625	5.7	58,237	2.1
General office clerks	1,353,251	1,125,866	83.2	167,590	12.4	74,813	5.5	27,181	2.0
Bank tellers	451,465	401,512	88.9	32,136	7.1	22,163	4.9	8,573	1.9
Proofreaders	21,610	19,447	90.0	1,526	7.1	567	2.6	294	1.4
Data-entry keyers	349,477	269,598	77.1	57,126	16.3	21,516	6.2	13,106	3.8
Statistical clerks	104,345	86,019	82.4	14,099	13.5	4,624	4.4	1,871	1.8
Teachers' aides	191,564	147,189	76.8	31,569	16.5	21,780	11.4	2,125	1.1
Admin. support, n.e.c.	269,811	229,481	85.1	29,546	11.0	12,162	4.5	5,087	1.9

SOURCE: 1980 Census of Population.

employed in financial records processing as their general prevalence among the clerical workforce. Finally, black females are 20 percent less likely to be secretaries, stenographers, and typists.

Women of Spanish origin are substantially (more than 25 percent) underrepresented among financial records processors, and overrepresented among miscellaneous clerical occupations. Asian women are more likely to work as computer equipment operators, adjusters and investigators, and in the miscellaneous clerical occupations. They are substantially less likely to work as communications equipment operators or as secretaries, stenographers, and typists.

Among the detailed clerical occupations, table 2.7 demonstrates that black females are more likely than their general clerical proportion would suggest to be employed as telephone operators and chief communications operators, correspondence clerks, file clerks, postal clerks, other mail clerks, messengers, weighers, measurers and checkers, miscellaneous material recording occupations, welfare eligibility clerks, data-entry keyers, and teachers' aides. Black females are less likely than other females to be employed as bookkeepers and accounting clerks or as secretaries.

Females of Spanish origin are more likely than their overall clerical proportion to work in miscellaneous material recording occupations, as welfare eligibility clerks, and as teachers' aides. Hispanic females are less likely to work as proofreaders or postal mail carriers. Asian women are more likely to work as ticket and reservation agents, library clerks, billing, posting, and calculating machine operators, welfare eligibility clerks, and data-entry keyers. They are less likely to be employed as telephone operators, other communications equipment operators, chief communications equipment operators, postal mail carriers, meter readers, and samplers.

These patterns are quite marked and may be very significant. Their investigation is clearly beyond the focus of this study. However, given the diversity of race and gender-specific occupational distribution, there does not appear to be any obvious way in which the job opportunities of a particular racial group will be impacted by clerical automation or any other change. Clerical workers are well represented among each ethnic group examined. In fact, the major differences among clerical occupations seem to be in the extent of female domination.

Clerical Employment Trends

This section will present the historical trends in clerical employment levels. The first part concentrates on the long term, utilizing Census data from 1950 to 1980 adjusted for consistency in occupational classification. The second part of the section examines the short-term trends, using data from the Current Population Survey from 1972 to 1982. Then the recent demographic changes among clerical workers for the same period, 1972 to 1982, are reviewed. Taken as a whole, this data base will provide the raw material for the discussion of particular occupations in chapter 3. This section introduces the data and the occupational categories that will be treated with more depth in the following chapter.

Census Employment from 1950 to 1980

The Decennial Census produces the most detailed occupational employment data that is available from household reporting. This reflects the extremely large number of observations available. Even though the detailed occupational employment data come from a subsample of all Census respondents, the numbers are still very large by normal sampling standards. However, even large numbers of responses cannot obviate the inevitable measurement problems (discussed earlier) when dealing with occupational information.

Comparisons among Census observations are further complicated by the changes in the measuring rod, the Census occupational classification system. In 1950, occupational employment was tabulated in 12 major groups and 469 detailed occupational categories. In 1960 these 12 major groups contained 494 detailed occupations, but in 1970 there were only 417 detailed occupations accumulated into the same 12 major occupational groups. The overall changes in the classification system can be regarded as relatively minor over this period. With regard to individual occupations, there can be major distortions when an occupational category is added or deleted, of course.

When it comes to the 1980 Census data, the magnitude of the changes in the occupational coding system are very troublesome. There are 503 detailed occupations which have been reshuffled into 13 new major groups, and the lack of comparability is very serious indeed. For example, cashiers have always been regarded as clerical workers in the Census occupational classification schema. The 1980 Census system, however, reclassifies them as sales workers, thereby moving 1.65 million workers from one major occupational group to another. Clearly this complicates the task of comparing the employment levels of both sales workers and clerical workers to their historical antecedents. Similar transfers occurred for legal aides and counter clerks among clerical occupations. For the first time, there is a fundamental lack of consistency at the major occupational group level between adjacent Census observations.

To avoid being misled by these measurement problems, it is necessary to convert all occupational employment numbers to a consistent basis. Upon the advice of the U.S.

Bureau of the Census, the classification system of 1970 was chosen as the standard for this analysis. Since the Bureau of the Census always publishes detailed occupational employment for the last Census and the current one using current definitions, the comparison between 1960 and 1970 occupational employment in terms of the 1970 classifications was readily available.[5]

These data are developed by the Bureau of the Census through a dual classification of a sample of all household units. Thus the proportions of those whose occupation would have moved them from any one detailed occupational group to another can be estimated. After each Decennial Census, such a reclassification study is conducted as a part of the benchmarking to Census observations and the results are published in a Technical Paper.[6]

With painstaking effort it is possible to bridge from one Decennial Census to the next using these estimates of the proportions in each occupational category that moved to another category. It should be mentioned that it was also necessary to standardize the treatment of the "occupation not reported" group across the various Census observations. The numbers reported here include allocation of the occupation not reported group to the detailed occupational level as was done by the Census in 1980. Adjustments were *not* made for the deletion of 14- and 15-year olds from the labor force beginning in 1970, nor for the fact that the 1960 to 1970 occupational conversion factors published were based on the experienced civilian labor force rather than the number of individuals employed.[7]

Because of the wide discrepancies between the 1980 occupational classification system and all those that went before, it is not possible to be completely accurate in reclassifying all occupational employment into 1980 terms without special reclassification studies for each pair of Census observations (i.e., 1950-1980, 1960-1980, 1970-1980). However, it is possible to use the Census unpublished numbers to estimate the 1980 employment in terms of 1970 Census categories. Of course, it should be understood that all of the reclassification work is done on the basis of sample results. Thus the reclassified employment figures are subject both to the original sampling error in estimating occupational employment and the secondary sampling error involved in the reclassification study.

The 1950 Census employment could not be converted directly into 1970 categories since no such reclassification study has ever been done. Therefore the 1950 occupational employment figures were first reclassified into 1960 terms; then those numbers were converted to a 1970 basis using the 1960 to 1970 translation. While the numbers reported here were derived as carefully as possible from the information available, it is not clear precisely how accurate they may be nor what hidden biases may remain.

The numbers reported in table 2.8 represent the best derivable estimates of detailed clerical employment on a consistent basis across the 1950 to 1980 time span. Table 2.8 shows that there were just over 19 million clerical workers employed in 1980 (using the consistent 1970 definitions).[8] This is nearly a threefold increase from the level of 1950. Employment levels for 1950, 1960, 1970, and 1980 are indicated for 42 separate clerical occupations. Table 2.9 reports the same data as table 2.8, but the individual clerical occupations are ranked from largest to smallest according to their level of employment in 1980. The largest single category of clerical workers in 1980 was secretaries. There were over 4 million secretaries employed; they represented just over 4 percent of total employment and 21 percent of clerical employment in that year.[9]

Table 2.8

Employment in Clerical Occupations, 1950 to 1980

Occupational title	Employment			
	1950	1960	1970	1980
Total employment	**57,178,206**	**64,639,256**	**76,553,599**	**97,639,355**
Clerical workers	6,875,546	9,575,247	13,856,074	19,119,280
Bank tellers	66,944	139,477	265,197	476,233
Billing clerks	32,357	45,254	112,876	117,943
Bookkeepers	744,053	973,224	1,633,490	1,804,374
Cashiers	252,252	510,179	884,531	1,654,151
Clerical assistants, social welfare....	0	0	1,279	24,128
Clerical supervisors, n.e.c.	44,348	56,887	119,887	340,946
Collectors, bill and account	25,395	34,229	54,728	76,982
Counter clerks, except food	96,313	127,630	243,697	398,029
Dispatchers and starters, vehicle	33,746	49,205	63,699	87,622
Enumerators and interviewers	85,013	118,723	68,697	88,712
Estimators and investigators, n.e.c. ..	112,469	171,901	282,074	442,553
Expediters and production controllers ..	123,277	151,191	217,107	329,621
File clerks	118,211	152,160	382,578	316,419
Insurance adjusters, examiners, and investigators	33,061	58,726	102,043	159,124
Library attendants and assistants	16,235	38,203	133,911	140,808
Mail carriers, post office	164,851	203,116	268,612	258,966
Mail handlers, except post office......	53,563	67,300	133,839	182,223
Messengers and office helpers	111,508	61,303	61,050	82,225
Meter readers, utility	40,696	39,712	35,144	41,407
Office machine operators	146,778	326,521	588,356	890,288
Bookkeeping & billing machine operators ..	26,610	53,914	67,341	37,200
Calculating machine	19,176	38,903	37,153	17,881

Computer & peripheral equipment operators	868	2,023	124,684	391,909
Duplicating machine operator	5,520	14,392	21,682	17,971
Keypunch operators	75,091	169,000	290,119	382,118
Tabulating machine operator	9,725	26,937	8,685	3,345
Office machine, n.e.c.	9,788	21,352	38,669	39,864
Payroll and timekeeping clerks	65,697	112,901	165,815	218,387
Postal clerks	216,164	242,872	321,263	315,111
Proofreaders	12,708	17,171	29,940	27,321
Real estate appraisers	11,754	15,822	22,735	41,343
Receptionists	77,965	164,446	323,552	536,963
Secretaries	1,005,968	1,539,017	2,875,826	4,058,182
Shipping and receiving clerks	323,785	325,307	400,890	483,183
Statistical clerks	109,956	143,922	265,431	297,939
Stenographers	429,424	283,486	136,197	91,593
Stock clerks and storekeepers	274,089	384,115	482,259	580,979
Teachers' aides, except school monitors	6,105	17,804	139,790	207,391
Telegraph operators	34,811	21,064	13,052	7,604
Telephone operators	363,472	374,495	433,739	314,674
Ticket, station, and express agents	69,807	76,994	104,285	152,841
Typists	60,534	547,923	1,041,804	799,561
Weighers	80,915	44,548	41,410	29,717
Misc. clerical workers	253,633	328,399	506,677	1,163,635
Not specified clerical workers	1,185,906	1,610,020	862,394	1,880,102

SOURCE: Decennial Census. Data were adjusted for consistency by the authors.

Table 2.9
Employment in Clerical Occupations, 1950 to 1980
Ranked by Level of Employment in 1980

Occupational title	Employment			
	1950	1960	1970	1980
Total employment	57,178,206	64,639,256	76,553,599	97,639,355
Clerical workers	6,875,546	9,575,247	13,856,074	19,119,280
Secretaries	1,005,968	1,539,017	2,875,826	4,058,182
Not specified clerical workers	1,185,906	1,610,020	862,394	1,880,102
Bookkeepers	744,053	973,224	1,633,490	1,804,374
Cashiers	252,252	510,179	884,531	1,654,151
Miscellaneous clerical workers	253,633	328,399	506,677	1,163,635
Typists	60,534	547,923	1,041,804	799,561
Stock clerks and storekeepers	274,089	384,115	482,259	580,979
Receptionists	77,965	164,446	323,552	536,963
Shipping and receiving clerks	323,785	325,307	100,890	483,183
Bank tellers	66,944	139,477	265,197	476,233
Estimators and investigators, n.e.c.	112,469	171,901	282,074	442,553
Counter clerks, except food	96,313	127,630	243,697	398,029
Computer & peripheral equipment operators	868	2,023	124,684	391,909
Keypunch operators	75,091	169,000	290,119	382,118
Clerical supervisors, n.e.c.	44,348	56,887	119,887	340,946
Expediters and production controllers	123,277	151,191	217,107	329,621
File clerks	118,211	152,160	382,578	316,419
Postal clerks	216,164	242,872	321,263	315,111
Telephone operators	363,472	374,495	433,739	314,674
Statistical clerks	109,956	143,922	265,431	297,939
Mail carriers, post office	164,851	203,116	268,612	258,966

Payroll and timekeeping clerks	65,697	112,901	165,815	218,387
Teachers' aides, except school monitors	6,105	17,804	139,790	207,391
Mail handlers, except post office	53,563	67,300	133,839	182,223
Insurance adjusters, examiners, & investigators	33,061	58,726	102,043	159,124
Ticket, station, and express agents	69,807	76,994	104,285	152,841
Library attendants and assistants	16,235	38,203	133,911	140,808
Billing clerks	32,357	45,254	112,876	117,943
Stenographers	429,424	283,486	136,197	91,593
Enumerators and interviewers	85,013	118,723	68,697	88,712
Dispatchers and starters, vehicle	33,746	49,205	63,699	87,622
Messengers and office helpers	111,508	61,303	61,050	82,225
Collectors, bill and account	25,395	34,229	54,728	76,982
Meter readers, utility	40,696	39,712	35,144	41,407
Real estate appraisers	11,754	15,822	22,735	41,343
Office machine, n.e.c.	9,788	21,352	38,669	39,864
Bookkeeping and billing machine operators	26,610	53,914	67,341	37,200
Weighers	80,915	44,548	41,410	29,717
Proofreaders	12,708	17,171	29,940	27,321
Clerical assistants, social welfare	0	0	1,279	24,128
Duplicating machine operator	5,520	14,392	21,682	17,971
Calculating machine	19,176	38,903	37,153	17,881
Telegraph operators	34,811	21,064	13,052	7,604
Tabulating machine operator	9,725	26,937	8,685	3,345

SOURCE: Decennial Census. Data were adjusted for consistency by the authors.

The second biggest category was bookkeepers, with about 1.8 million employed, followed by cashiers, with 1.7 million. The only other clerical occupation that has approached 1 million employees is typists. All together, these "big four" clerical occupations accounted for 8.5 million jobs, or about 45 percent of all clerical employment in 1980. These same four occupations only accounted for 27 percent of clerical employment in 1950. All four of these occupations have grown substantially in employment during the last 30 years, although typists declined between 1970 and 1980.

On the other end of the scale in terms of size, there were only about 3,300 tabulating machine operators and about 7,600 telegraph operators employed in 1980. These occupations have been declining for some years, as have the next two smallest occupations, duplicating machine operators and calculating machine operators. Each of these occupations has been adversely impacted by changes in technology.

Table 2.10 ranks these same clerical occupations by the annual compound rate of change in employment from 1950 to 1980.[10] Computer and peripheral equipment operators far exceeded all other clerical occupations in their rate of increase over this period. This occupation has grown from an employment level of 868 persons in 1950 at the dawn of the computer age to over 400,000 persons in 1980, an annual rate of growth of over 22 percent. This is the labor market expression of the computer revolution which began to substantially affect employment levels in computer-related occupations in the 1960s.

It is interesting to note that the second fastest growing clerical occupation over the 1950 to 1980 period was teachers' aides; from high-tech to high-touch in one easy step! The number of teachers' aides increased from 6,000 to over 200,000 in this 30-year period, over 12 percent per year. The third fastest growing clerical occupation was typists, even though there was actually a 23 percent decline in employment from 1970 to 1980. The phenomenal growth of typists in the 1950s and 1960s was sufficient to offset the recent reversals when the entire 30-year period is considered. Following in order of rate of growth are library attendants, clerical supervisors, bank tellers, receptionists, and cashiers. Clearly, there is not a high-tech occupation among them, although they have all been impacted in one way or another by technological change as well as many other influences.

There were also a few clerical occupations that showed absolute declines during this 30-year period. The most rapid declines were among stenographers and telegraph operators, declining in employment by about 5 percent annually. Both occupations have been impacted by technology, but not in a direct and obvious way. The telegraph has been all but replaced by superior communication devices, and this has nearly eliminated the jobs of telegraph operators. As discussed earlier, the improvements in dictation equipment and changing habits of users have spurred the decline in the stenographer occupation. In 1950, there were 2.3 secretaries per stenographer while by 1980 the ratio had risen to 44 to 1!

Fairly rapid declines were also shown by tabulating machine operators and weighers. Actually, the tabulating machine operators would have been the most rapidly retreating if 1960 had been taken as the base year. This occupation provides an excellent example of a technology-specific occupation that experiences rapid growth and then decline. Tabulating machines were very popular in the 1950s for analyzing data on punched paper cards. The number of tabulating machine operators nearly tripled between 1950 and 1960. But electronic data processing technology moved rapidly beyond the capabilities of tabulating machines, and the number of employees in this occupation has fallen by nearly 90 percent since 1960. Rounding out the declining oc-

Table 2.10
Employment in Clerical Occupations, 1950 to 1980
Ranked by Relative Change 1950 to 1980

Occupational title	Employment				Annual percent change
	1950	1960	1970	1980	
Computer & peripheral equipment operators	868	2,023	124,684	391,909	22.6
Teachers' aides, except school monitors	6,105	17,804	139,790	207,391	12.5
Typists	60,534	547,923	1,041,804	799,561	9.0
Library attendants and assistants	16,235	38,203	133,911	140,808	7.5
Clerical supervisors, n.e.c.	44,348	56,887	119,887	340,946	7.0
Bank tellers	66,944	139,477	265,197	476,233	6.8
Receptionists	77,965	164,446	323,552	536,963	6.6
Cashiers	252,252	510,179	884,531	1,654,151	6.5
Office machine operators	146,778	326,521	588,356	890,288	6.2
Keypunch operators	75,091	169,000	290,119	382,118	5.6
Insurance adjusters, examiners, & investigators	33,061	58,726	102,043	159,124	5.4
Miscellaneous clerical workers	253,633	328,399	506,677	1,163,635	5.2
Counter clerks, except food	96,313	127,630	243,697	398,029	4.8
Office machine, n.e.c.	9,788	21,352	38,669	39,864	4.8
Secretaries	1,005,968	1,539,017	2,875,826	4,058,182	4.8
Estimators and investigators, n.e.c.	112,469	171,901	282,074	442,553	4.7
Billing clerks	32,357	45,254	112,876	117,943	4.4
Real estate appraisers	11,754	15,822	22,735	41,343	4.3
Mail handlers, except post office	53,563	67,300	133,839	182,223	4.2
Payroll and timekeeping clerks	65,697	112,901	165,815	218,387	4.1
Duplicating machine operator	5,520	14,392	21,682	17,971	4.0
Collectors, bill and account	25,395	34,229	54,728	76,982	3.8
Statistical clerks	109,956	143,922	265,431	297,939	3.4

File clerks	118,211	152,160	382,578	316,419	3.3
Expediters and production controllers	123,277	151,191	217,107	329,621	3.3
Dispatchers and starters, vehicle	33,746	49,205	63,699	87,622	3.2
Bookkeepers	744,053	973,224	1,633,490	1,804,374	3.0
Ticket, station, and express agents	69,807	76,994	104,285	152,841	2.6
Proofreaders	12,708	17,171	29,940	27,321	2.6
Stock clerks and storekeepers	274,089	384,115	482,259	580,979	2.5
Not specified clerical workers	1,185,906	1,610,020	862,394	1,880,102	1.5
Mail carriers, post office	164,851	203,116	268,612	258,966	1.5
Shipping and receiving clerks	323,785	325,307	100,890	483,183	1.3
Postal clerks	216,164	242,872	321,263	315,111	1.3
Bookkeeping and billing machine operators	26,610	53,914	67,341	37,200	1.1
Enumerators and interviewers	85,013	118,723	68,697	88,712	0.1
Meter readers, utility	40,696	39,712	35,144	41,407	0.1
Calculating machine	19,176	38,903	37,153	17,881	-0.2
Telephone operators	363,472	374,495	433,739	314,674	-0.5
Messengers and office helpers	111,508	61,303	61,050	82,225	-1.0
Weighers	80,915	44,548	41,410	29,717	-3.3
Tabulating machine operator	9,725	26,937	8,685	3,345	-3.5
Telegraph operators	34,811	21,064	13,052	7,604	-4.9
Stenographers	429,424	283,486	136,197	91,593	-5.0

SOURCE: Decennial Census. Data were adjusted for consistency by the authors.

cupations are messengers and office helpers, calculating machine operators, and telephone operators. All appear to be office technology-related declines since the communications and computing capabilities of modern offices have rendered these jobs less essential than in the past.[11]

CPS Employment from 1972 to 1982

The long-term Census data do not seem to demonstrate obvious and widespread impact of technology on particular clerical occupations, but it may be instructive to examine recent annual data for detailed occupations from the Current Population Survey. Due to the benchmarking to Census observations, the only time period for which this can be done with CPS data is the decade from 1972 to 1982.[12] If the microprocessor revolution is going to have catastrophic impacts on clerical employment, it should have become apparent by 1982 when the microcomputer population reached the one million unit level (Computer and Business Equipment Manufacturers Association, 1985:87).

While this period would seem to be adequate for analysis, it is complicated by the fact that the recession of 1981-82 occurs right at the end of the period. Although the recession would be expected to distort occupational employment numbers for production workers in manufacturing industries, its impact on the employment of clerical workers is less certain. The results presented in chapter 1 that showed a decline in clerical employment during the last recession make this a significant question.

In addition, the utilization of annual average data from a much smaller household survey such as the CPS will introduce considerable statistical noise into the data. When observations are closely spaced, the inevitable sampling variability becomes all too apparent. Thus, some reservation must be expressed about any particular annual observation.

More confidence can be put in trends that emerge over a period of three or four years.

Table 2.11 reports the CPS employment data for clerical workers by detailed occupation. It is the analogue to table 2.7, except that this table did not require any bridging of data series collected on different occupational classification systems. The table shows the annual average employment estimates for 32 clerical occupations from 1972 to 1982.[13] Table 2.12 shows the same occupational data ranked according to the employment levels in 1982.

As before, secretaries are the largest single clerical occupation with nearly 4 million employed in 1980. Employment of secretaries declined by about 100,000 between 1980 and 1982, apparently reflecting the influence of the recession. Any decline in this series must be considered unusual since secretaries experienced steady growth of about 100,000 jobs per year throughout the 1970s. This downward trend has not continued in 1983 and 1984, however, as will be shown in chapter 3.

Bookkeepers are the next biggest clerical occupation, followed by cashiers and typists. Typists show a stagnant employment level through the decade of 1972 to 1981, with a turn downward in 1982. The latter apparently reflects the reclassification of word processor operators discussed earlier. Recall that the long-term analysis in the last section showed typists to be a declining occupation. Cashiers and bookkeepers do not show employment declines, but their growth patterns are certainly interrupted in 1982, especially in the case of cashiers. For reasons that will become clearer in chapter 3, it appears that these short-term trend data have been seriously disrupted by the deep recession of 1981 and 1982.

Table 2.11
Employment in Clerical Occupations, 1972 to 1982

Occupational Title	Employment (in thousands)										
	1972	1973	1974	1975	1976	1977	1978	1979	1980	1981	1982
Clerical workers	14,329	14,667	15,199	15,321	15,788	16,372	17,207	17,953	18,473	18,564	18,466
Bank tellers	290	329	356	356	378	416	458	503	542	569	561
Billing clerks	149	166	158	145	140	157	170	164	165	153	154
Bookkeepers	1,592	1,673	1,706	1,709	1,712	1,754	1,861	1,945	1,942	1,961	1,968
Cashiers	998	1,060	1,127	1,200	1,280	1,354	1,434	1,512	1,592	1,660	1,683
Clerical supervisors, n.e.c.	200	184	231	228	239	229	207	241	245	250	270
Collectors, bill and account	61	59	64	73	66	73	80	77	81	93	87
Counter clerks, except food	331	352	350	331	359	349	383	369	358	360	373
Dispatchers and starters, vehicle	86	88	92	93	89	99	99	109	105	115	110
Enumerators and interviewers	39	49	53	44	49	55	54	61	87	58	53
Estimators and investigators, n.e.c.	350	334	374	389	423	459	460	506	545	540	570
Expediters and production controllers	196	202	201	214	210	219	228	244	238	254	257
File clerks	274	287	279	268	274	280	279	312	332	315	278
Insurance adjusters, examiners, and investigators	109	114	127	153	159	172	173	178	179	191	200
Library attendants and assistants	138	123	135	146	143	144	174	168	155	152	150
Mail carriers, post office	271	268	268	254	244	244	258	256	247	242	264
Mail handlers, except post office	129	144	148	145	140	149	164	170	168	175	182
Messengers and office helpers	79	85	77	78	83	95	89	95	98	97	115
Bookkeeping and billing machine operators	69	57	59	60	49	53	47	59	52	49	42
Computer and peripheral equipment operators	199	220	251	302	295	311	403	465	535	564	588
Keypunch operators	284	255	251	253	279	284	277	279	271	248	364

Employment Patterns   77

Payroll and timekeeping clerks	185	200	206	202	211	231	245	241	237	231	224
Postal clerks	282	303	295	293	291	271	272	264	291	269	271
Receptionists	439	450	465	468	511	542	600	614	644	675	672
Secretaries	2,964	3,088	3,218	3,281	3,428	3,470	3,646	3,792	3,944	3,917	3,847
Shipping and receiving clerks	453	461	469	433	446	474	469	493	515	525	499
Statistical clerks	301	301	328	331	342	363	384	408	396	370	365
Stenographers	125	107	104	101	101	84	96	78	66	74	66
Stock clerks and storekeepers	513	478	493	479	499	505	516	539	544	528	497
Teachers' aides, except school monitors	208	232	253	292	325	326	348	357	391	381	373
Telephone operators	394	390	393	348	343	347	317	333	323	308	283
Ticket, station and express agents	130	118	123	138	126	132	131	148	144	148	154
Typists	1,025	1,040	1,046	1,035	995	1,020	1,060	1,038	1,043	1,031	942
All other clerical workers	1,329	1,331	1,388	1,375	1,444	1,587	1,705	1,818	1,899	1,956	1,871

SOURCE: Current Population Survey.

Table 2.12
Employment in Clerical Occupations, 1972 to 1982
Ranked by Level of Employment in 1982

Occupational Title	Employment (in thousands)										
	1972	1973	1974	1975	1976	1977	1978	1979	1980	1981	1982
Clerical workers	14,329	14,667	15,199	15,321	15,788	16,372	17,207	17,953	18,473	18,564	18,466
Secretaries	2,964	3,088	3,218	3,281	3,428	3,470	3,646	3,792	3,944	3,917	3,847
Bookkeepers	1,592	1,673	1,706	1,709	1,712	1,754	1,861	1,945	1,942	1,961	1,968
All other clerical workers	1,329	1,331	1,388	1,375	1,444	1,587	1,705	1,818	1,899	1,956	1,871
Cashiers	998	1,060	1,127	1,200	1,280	1,354	1,434	1,512	1,592	1,660	1,683
Typists	1,025	1,040	1,046	1,035	995	1,020	1,060	1,038	1,043	1,031	942
Receptionists	439	450	465	468	511	542	600	614	644	675	672
Computer and peripheral equipment operators	199	220	251	302	295	311	403	465	535	564	588
Estimators and investigators, n.e.c.	350	334	374	389	423	459	460	506	545	540	570
Bank tellers	290	329	356	356	378	416	458	503	542	569	561
Shipping and receiving clerks	453	461	469	433	446	474	469	493	515	525	499
Stock clerks and storekeepers	513	478	493	479	499	505	516	539	544	528	497
Counter clerks, except food	331	352	350	331	359	349	383	369	358	360	373
Teachers' aides, except school monitors	208	232	253	292	325	326	348	357	391	381	373
Statistical clerks	301	301	328	331	342	363	384	408	396	370	365
Keypunch operators	284	255	251	253	279	284	277	279	271	248	364
Telephone operators	394	390	393	348	343	347	317	333	323	308	283
File clerks	274	287	279	268	274	280	279	312	332	315	278
Postal clerks	282	303	295	293	291	271	272	264	291	269	271
Clerical supervisors, n.e.c.	200	184	231	228	239	229	207	241	245	250	270
Mail carriers, post office	271	268	268	254	244	244	258	256	247	242	264
Expediters and production controllers	196	202	201	214	210	219	228	244	238	254	257

	185	200	206	202	211	231	245	241	237	231	224
Payroll and timekeeping clerks	109	114	127	153	159	172	173	178	179	191	200
Insurance adjusters, examiners, and investigators	129	144	148	145	140	149	164	170	168	175	182
Mail handlers, except post office	149	166	158	145	140	157	170	164	165	153	154
Billing clerks	130	118	123	138	126	132	131	148	144	148	154
Ticket, station, and express agents	138	123	135	146	143	144	174	168	155	152	150
Library attendants and assistants	79	85	77	78	83	95	89	95	98	97	115
Messengers and office helpers	86	88	92	93	89	99	99	109	105	115	110
Dispatchers and starters, vehicle	61	59	64	73	66	73	80	77	81	93	87
Collectors, bill and account	125	107	104	101	101	84	96	78	66	74	66
Stenographers	39	49	53	44	49	55	54	61	87	58	53
Enumerators and interviewers	69	57	59	60	49	53	47	59	52	49	42
Bookkeeping and billing machine operators											

SOURCE: Current Population Survey.

Table 2.13 shows the CPS clerical occupations sorted by the annual rate of change over the 1972-1982 decade. This list is remarkably similar to the earlier 1950-1980 rate of change listing in table 2.10. Once again, computer and peripheral equipment operators experienced the most rapid rate of increase of any clerical occupation, although it was only about half the rate shown for the 1950-80 period. Bank tellers and insurance adjusters, examiners and investigators both edged ahead of teachers' aides in growth rates during the more recent decade. This reflects the fall-off in the rate of growth in teachers' aides as employment growth in education as a whole faltered due to funding difficulties and a reduction in the student population.

Other clerical occupations showing relatively rapid growth during the 1972 to 1982 decade include cashiers, estimators and investigators, and receptionists. All three of these occupations involve direct customer contact and probably would fall into the "hard to automate" category. Messengers and office helpers emerge as a relatively rapidly growing clerical occupation in the 1970s, which is in contrast with their declining employment from 1950 to 1980. The number of bill collectors increased at 3.6 percent annually during the decade, and mail handlers except post office increased at 3.5 percent. Once again, there is no obvious interpretation that emerges from the listing of clerical occupations that grew more rapidly than average during this recent decade.

At the other end of the distribution, the declining occupations, stenographers and telephone operators are joined by bookkeeping and billing machine operators in rather rapid decline for the 1972 to 1982 period. Small annual declines were registered for typists, postal clerks, mail carriers, and stock clerks and storekeepers.

Table 2.13
Employment in Clerical Occupations, 1972 to 1982
Ranked by Relative Change 1972 to 1982

Occupational Title	Employment (in thousands)											Annual Percent change
	1972	1973	1974	1975	1976	1977	1978	1979	1980	1981	1982	
Computer and peripheral equipment operators	199	220	251	302	295	311	403	465	535	564	588	11.4
Bank tellers	290	329	356	356	378	416	458	503	542	569	561	6.8
Insurance adjusters, examiners and investigators	109	114	127	153	159	172	173	178	179	191	200	6.3
Teachers' aides, except school monitors	208	232	253	292	325	326	348	357	391	381	373	6.0
Cashiers	998	1,060	1,127	1,200	1,280	1,354	1,434	1,512	1,592	1,660	1,683	5.4
Estimators and investigators, n.e.c.	350	334	374	389	423	459	460	506	545	540	570	5.0
Receptionists	439	450	465	468	511	542	600	614	644	675	672	4.3
Messengers & office helpers	79	85	77	78	83	95	89	95	98	97	115	3.8
Collectors, bill and account	61	59	64	73	66	73	80	77	81	93	87	3.6
Mail handlers, except post office	129	144	148	145	140	149	164	170	168	175	182	3.5
All other clerical workers	1,329	1,331	1,388	1,375	1,444	1,587	1,705	1,818	1,899	1,956	1,871	3.5
Enumerators & interviewers	39	49	53	44	49	55	54	61	87	58	53	3.1
Clerical supervisors, n.e.c.	200	184	231	228	239	229	207	241	245	250	270	3.0
Expediters and production controllers	196	202	201	214	210	219	228	244	238	254	257	2.7
Secretaries	2,964	3,088	3,218	3,281	3,428	3,470	3,646	3,792	3,944	3,917	3,847	2.6
Clerical workers	14,329	14,667	15,199	15,321	15,788	16,372	17,207	17,953	18,473	18,564	18,466	2.6

Table 2.13 (cont.)

Occupational Title	Employment (in thousands)											Annual Percent change
	1972	1973	1974	1975	1976	1977	1978	1979	1980	1981	1982	
Keypunch operators	284	255	251	253	279	284	277	279	271	248	364	2.5
Dispatchers & starters, vehicle	86	88	92	93	89	99	99	109	105	115	110	2.5
Bookkeepers	1,592	1,673	1,706	1,709	1,712	1,754	1,861	1,945	1,942	1,961	1,968	2.1
Statistical clerks	301	301	328	331	342	363	384	408	396	370	365	1.9
Payroll & timekeeping clerks	185	200	206	202	211	231	245	241	237	231	224	1.9
Ticket, station, and express agents	130	118	123	138	126	132	131	148	144	148	154	1.7
Counter clerks, except food	331	352	350	331	359	349	383	369	358	360	373	1.2
Shipping & receiving clerks	453	461	469	433	446	474	469	493	515	525	499	1.0
Library attendants and assistants	138	123	135	146	143	144	174	168	155	152	150	0.8
Billing clerks	149	166	158	145	140	157	170	164	165	153	154	0.3
File clerks	274	287	279	268	274	280	279	312	332	315	278	0.1
Mail carriers, post office	271	268	268	254	244	244	258	256	247	242	264	-0.3
Stock clerks & storekeepers	513	478	493	479	499	505	516	539	544	528	497	-0.3
Postal clerks	282	303	295	293	291	271	272	264	291	269	271	-0.4
Typists	1,025	1,040	1,046	1,035	995	1,020	1,060	1,038	1,043	1,031	942	-0.8
Telephone operators	394	390	393	348	343	347	317	333	323	308	283	-3.3
Bookkeeping and billing machine operators	69	57	59	60	49	53	47	59	52	49	42	-4.8
Stenographers	125	107	104	101	101	84	96	78	66	74	66	-6.2

SOURCE: Current Population Survey.

Bookkeeping and billing machine operators would appear to be another clerical occupation impacted by the microprocessor revolution. As microcomputers have become more widely distributed, increasing attention has been paid to creating accounting software that will run on the micros. This has undoubtedly impacted the number of bookkeeping machine operators. What is not clear is whether it has impacted the number of people doing the bookkeeping work. Since they are not doing it on a special purpose device, it would no longer be appropriate to call them bookkeeping machine operators, however, and the job titles are very likely changed.

The declines in postal service employment reflect a multitude of influences (including considerable technological change) aimed at making the postal service more efficient and competitive, particularly since it was made "independent" of the government. The superior growth in employment of nonpostal mail handlers appears to indicate that the postal service still has a way to go.

The occupations that show near zero growth during the decade are also interesting. File clerks and billing clerks showed almost no growth from 1972 to 1982. Both suffered from recessionary employment declines that wiped out earlier gains. It might be tempting to conclude that these occupations also were adversely impacted by technological change, but it will become apparent in chapter 3 that the truth is not that simple. Let us turn now to the questions of trends in the number of females and minorities employed in these clerical occupations.

Demographic Trends in Clerical Employment

Clerical work has been prototypical "women's work" in recent decades, particularly for certain clerical occupations. Table 2.14 shows the employment of females in clerical oc-

Table 2.14
Female Clerical Employment, 1950 to 1980

Occupational title	Female employment			
	1950	1960	1970	1980
Clerical workers	4,187,825	6,509,421	10,186,279	14,909,130
Bank tellers	31,025	97,796	228,588	430,858
Billing clerks	25,102	36,819	92,851	104,208
Bookkeepers	572,041	812,101	1,338,807	1,638,220
Cashiers	192,872	392,374	738,946	1,373,336
Clerical assistants, social welfare	0	0	1,001	19,744
Clerical supervisors, n.e.c.	18,499	27,096	51,438	139,652
Collectors, bill and account	3,506	6,804	19,705	42,760
Counter clerks, except food	53,126	77,808	162,287	264,502
Dispatchers and starters, vehicle	3,035	5,161	10,610	29,568
Enumerators and interviewers	66,408	97,257	53,279	66,695
Estimators and investigators, n.e.c.	37,895	56,331	108,802	253,939
Expediters and production controllers	13,421	20,199	48,851	147,603
File clerks	99,439	127,580	313,247	251,476
Insurance adjusters, examiners, & investigators	1,013	6,940	27,199	88,556
Library attendants and assistants	11,693	28,967	105,440	114,803
Mail carriers, post office	3,510	4,435	20,828	33,179
Mail handlers, except post office	16,596	24,306	57,075	79,425
Messengers and office helpers	8,309	9,198	11,932	20,981
Meter readers, utility	952	1,394	883	4,239
Office machine operators	120,544	241,840	433,711	634,577
Bookkeeping & billing machine operators	24,445	48,214	60,197	32,543
Calculating machine	18,961	38,199	33,889	15,885
Computer & peripheral equipment operators	653	1,319	36,377	209,524
Duplicating machine operator	2,941	5,928	12,341	10,633

Keypunch operators	61,122	123,157	260,393	336,980
Tabulating machine operator	3,923	7,901	4,297	2,019
Office machine, n.e.c.	8,498	17,122	26,196	26,993
Payroll and timekeeping clerks	28,630	66,818	114,130	162,302
Postal clerks	23,969	41,731	97,586	103,210
Proofreaders	8,063	11,811	22,406	21,610
Real estate appraisers	0	0	895	4,900
Receptionists	68,682	152,886	306,495	510,447
Secretaries	958,357	1,494,311	2,807,147	4,001,211
Shipping and receiving clerks	21,134	25,892	63,530	120,964
Statistical clerks	55,970	81,972	170,605	231,195
Stenographers	413,945	271,289	127,589	83,649
Stock clerks and storekeepers	31,284	58,391	109,619	191,172
Teachers' aides, except school monitors	3,436	8,990	125,805	193,017
Telegraph operators	7,542	4,760	3,777	2,711
Telephone operators	347,025	358,632	409,613	288,447
Ticket, station, and express agents	7,801	16,642	37,901	72,631
Typists	33,622	521,201	980,955	760,582
Weighers	5,219	8,341	12,003	9,786
Miscellaneous clerical workers	116,201	171,938	322,284	871,262
Not specified clerical workers	777,957	1,139,408	648,457	1,541,713

SOURCE: Decennial Census. Data were adjusted for consistency by the authors.

cupations from 1950 to 1980. It has the same structure as table 2.8 except that only women are included. These data have also been carefully adjusted for changes in the classification of jobs in the various Census observations. Note that nearly 15 million of the 19 million clerical workers in the earlier table are accounted for here, since over three-fourths of clerical workers in 1980 were women.

Table 2.15 contains the same data, but the clerical occupations are ranked according to the level of female employment in 1980. Among women workers, secretaries are the largest single clerical occupation, followed by bookkeepers, cashiers, and typists. Since females dominate the clerical employment ranks, it is not surprising that this ranking should be exactly the same as before. The same is true of table 2.16, which shows the detailed occupations ranked by the annual rate of growth from 1950 to 1980. Rapid growth for female clerical workers occurred among computer operators, insurance adjusters, teachers' aides, typists, bank tellers, bill collectors, and expediters. All showed at least a tenfold increase in the number of females employed over the 30-year period. Declining occupations for female clerical workers included stenographers, telegraph operators, tabulating and calculating machine operators, and telephone operators.

Table 2.17 shows the percentage employment of women for each of the 32 clerical occupations in the Current Population Survey from 1972 to 1982. The occupations are ranked according to the percentage female in 1982. As discussed earlier in the chapter, some occupations are almost exclusively female. Over 99 percent of secretaries are women, as are over 97 percent of receptionists and nearly 97 percent of typists. Keypunch machine operators, teachers' aides, bank tellers and bookkeepers are also over 90 percent female. Most important, *none* of these jobs which are dominated by women show any particular decline in the proportion female over the last decade. Thus these jobs will apparently continue to be almost exclusively female.

At the other end of the scale, postal mail carriers were only 17 percent female in 1982, although this proportion nearly tripled during the 1970s. Messengers and shipping and receiving clerks were also less than 25 percent female while postal clerks, stock clerks, and dispatchers were between 35 and 40 percent female. All the clerical occupations with low percentages of female employment have seen increasing numbers of women workers in recent years. Since the occupations where females predominate have not shown contrary trends, it is difficult to argue that this demonstrates lesser sex stereotyping of jobs, however. It may simply reflect the greater availability of women workers for all clerical tasks, combined with the lowering of barriers to entry for female workers in certain jobs. The bulk of clerical jobs are currently held by women workers and this can be expected to continue for the foreseeable future.

Unfortunately, it is not possible to reconstruct completely comparable occupational employment figures for 1950 to 1980 for minorities from Census data. This is because the reclassification studies that the Bureau of the Census conducts do not include separate figures by race. Thus it is necessary to confine the analysis to CPS data in examining minority employment in clerical occupations over time.

Table 2.18 displays the percent minority employment in the CPS clerical occupations from 1972 to 1982, with occupations ranked by the proportion minority at the end of the period. The highest minority percentage is among postal clerks, with over 25 percent minority workers. Note that this does not include postal mail carriers who are listed separately in the table. In fact, mail carriers include only about 14 percent minority workers. Mail handlers, other than in the post office (i.e., private sector), are also over 20 percent minority.

Table 2.15
Female Employment in Clerical Occupations, 1950 to 1980
Ranked by Level of Employment in 1980

Occupational title	Female employment			
	1950	1960	1970	1980
Clerical workers	4,187,825	6,509,421	10,186,279	14,909,130
Secretaries	958,357	1,494,311	2,807,147	4,001,211
Bookkeepers	572,041	812,101	1,338,807	1,638,220
Not specified clerical workers	777,957	1,139,408	648,457	1,541,713
Cashiers	192,872	392,374	738,946	1,373,336
Miscellaneous clerical workers	116,201	171,938	322,284	871,262
Typists	33,622	521,201	980,955	760,582
Receptionists	68,682	152,886	306,495	510,447
Bank tellers	31,025	97,796	228,588	430,858
Keypunch operators	61,122	123,157	260,393	336,980
Telephone operators	347,025	358,632	409,613	288,447
Counter clerks, except food	53,126	77,808	162,287	264,502
Estimators and investigators, n.e.c.	37,895	56,331	108,802	253,939
File clerks	99,439	127,580	313,247	251,476
Statistical clerks	55,970	81,972	170,605	231,195
Computer & peripheral equipment operators	653	1,319	36,377	209,524
Teachers' aides, except school monitors	3,436	8,990	125,805	193,017
Stock clerks and storekeepers	31,284	58,391	109,619	191,172
Payroll and timekeeping clerks	28,630	66,818	114,130	162,302
Expediters and production controllers	13,421	20,199	48,851	147,603
Clerical supervisors, n.e.c.	18,499	27,096	51,438	139,652
Shipping and receiving clerks	21,134	25,892	63,530	120,964
Library attendants and assistants	11,693	28,967	105,440	114,803
Billing clerks	25,102	36,819	92,851	104,208

Postal clerks	23,969	41,731	97,586	103,210
Insurance adjusters, examiners, & investigators	1,013	6,940	27,199	88,556
Stenographers	413,945	271,289	127,589	83,649
Mail handlers, except post office	16,596	24,306	57,075	79,425
Ticket, station, and express agents	7,801	16,642	37,901	72,631
Enumerators and interviewers	66,408	97,257	53,279	66,695
Collectors, bill and account	3,506	6,804	19,705	42,760
Mail carriers, post office	3,510	4,435	20,828	33,179
Bookkeeping & billing machine operators	24,445	48,214	60,197	32,543
Dispatchers and starters, vehicle	3,035	5,161	10,610	29,568
Office machine, n.e.c.	8,498	17,122	26,196	26,993
Proofreaders	8,063	11,811	22,406	21,610
Messengers and office helpers	8,309	9,198	11,932	20,981
Clerical assistants, social welfare	0	0	1,001	19,744
Calculating machine	18,961	38,199	33,889	15,885
Duplicating machine operator	2,941	5,928	12,341	10,633
Weighers	5,219	8,341	12,003	9,786
Real estate appraisers	0	0	895	4,900
Meter readers, utility	952	1,394	883	4,239
Telegraph operators	7,542	4,760	3,777	2,711
Tabulating machine operator	3,923	7,901	4,297	2,019

SOURCE: Decennial Census. Data were adjusted for consistency by the authors.

Table 2.16
Female Employment in Clerical Occupations, 1950 to 1980
Ranked by Relative Change 1950 to 1980

Occupational title	Female employment				Annual percent change
	1950	1960	1970	1980	
Computer & peripheral equipment operators	653	1,319	36,377	209,524	21.2
Insurance adjusters, examiners, & investigators	1,013	6,940	27,199	88,556	16.1
Teachers' aides, except school monitors	3,436	8,990	125,805	193,017	14.4
Typists	33,622	521,201	980,955	760,582	11.0
Bank tellers	31,025	97,796	228,588	430,858	9.2
Collectors, bill and account	3,506	6,804	19,705	42,760	8.7
Expediters and production controllers	13,421	20,199	48,851	147,603	8.3
Library attendants and assistants	11,693	28,967	105,440	114,803	7.9
Dispatchers and starters, vehicle	3,035	5,161	10,610	29,568	7.9
Mail carriers, post office	3,510	4,435	20,828	33,179	7.8
Ticket, station, and express agents	7,801	16,642	37,901	72,631	7.7
Clerical supervisors, n.e.c.	18,499	27,096	51,438	139,652	7.0
Miscellaneous clerical workers	116,201	171,938	322,284	871,262	6.9
Receptionists	68,682	152,886	306,495	510,447	6.9
Cashiers	192,872	392,374	738,946	1,373,336	6.8
Estimators and investigators, n.e.c.	37,895	56,331	108,802	253,939	6.5
Stock clerks and storekeepers	31,284	58,391	109,619	191,172	6.2
Shipping and receiving clerks	21,134	25,892	63,530	120,964	6.0
Payroll and timekeeping clerks	28,630	66,818	114,130	162,302	6.0
Keypunch operators	61,122	123,157	260,393	336,980	5.9
Office machine operators	120,544	241,840	433,711	634,577	5.7
Counter clerks, except food	53,126	77,808	162,287	264,502	5.5

Mail handlers, except post office	16,596	24,306	57,075	79,425	5.4
Meter readers, utility	952	1,394	883	4,239	5.1
Postal clerks	23,969	41,731	97,586	103,210	5.0
Secretaries	958,357	1,494,311	2,807,147	4,001,211	4.9
Billing clerks	25,102	36,819	92,851	104,208	4.9
Statistical clerks	55,970	81,972	170,605	231,195	4.8
Duplicating machine operator	2,941	5,928	12,341	10,633	4.4
Office machine, n.e.c.	8,498	17,122	26,196	26,993	3.9
Bookkeepers	572,041	812,101	1,338,807	1,638,220	3.6
Proofreaders	8,063	11,811	22,406	21,610	3.3
File clerks	99,439	127,580	313,247	251,476	3.1
Messengers and office helpers	8,309	9,198	11,932	20,981	3.1
Not specified clerical workers	777,957	1,139,408	648,457	1,541,713	2.3
Weighers	5,219	8,341	12,003	9,786	2.1
Bookkeeping and billing machine operators	24,445	48,214	60,197	32,543	0.9
Enumerators and interviewers	66,408	97,257	53,279	66,695	0
Calculating machine	18,961	38,199	33,889	15,885	-0.6
Telephone operators	347,025	358,632	409,613	288,447	-0.6
Tabulating machine operator	3,923	7,901	4,297	2,019	-2.2
Telegraph operators	7,542	4,760	3,777	2,711	-3.5
Stenographers	413,945	271,289	127,589	83,649	-5.2

SOURCE: Decennial Census. Data were adjusted for consistency by the authors.

Table 2.17
Percent Female Employment in Clerical Occupations

Occupational title	Percent female employment										
	1972	1973	1974	1975	1976	1977	1978	1979	1980	1981	1982
Secretaries	99.1	99.1	99.2	99.1	99.0	99.1	99.2	99.1	99.1	99.1	99.2
Receptionists	97.0	96.9	97.4	96.7	96.2	96.8	96.9	97.2	96.3	97.3	97.5
Typists	96.1	96.6	96.2	96.6	96.7	96.3	96.6	96.7	96.9	96.3	96.6
Keypunch operators	89.8	90.9	93.2	92.8	93.5	93.2	95.6	95.3	95.9	93.5	94.5
Teachers' aides, except school monitors	89.3	90.4	90.4	91.3	90.9	93.4	92.1	93.4	93.7	92.9	92.5
Bank tellers	87.5	89.9	91.5	91.1	91.1	90.0	91.5	92.9	92.7	93.5	92.0
Telephone operators	96.7	95.9	93.8	93.3	94.4	95.3	94.2	91.7	91.8	92.9	91.9
Bookkeepers	87.9	88.3	89.2	87.8	90.0	90.0	90.7	91.1	90.5	91.1	9.18
Billing clerks	84.6	83.0	87.3	86.8	87.1	87.8	88.1	90.1	90.2	88.2	87.7
Cashiers	86.6	86.7	87.7	87.1	87.7	87.0	87.1	87.9	86.6	86.2	86.8
Bookkeeping & billing machine operators	91.3	92.9	87.9	91.5	93.8	92.3	86.7	89.5	90.0	87.8	85.7
Stenographers	90.4	92.5	93.2	93.0	89.0	91.6	90.4	93.4	89.1	85.1	84.8
File clerks	84.9	86.3	85.1	86.4	85.5	84.7	85.7	86.6	86.4	83.8	84.5
Enumerators and interviewers	82.1	79.6	81.1	81.4	83.3	79.6	75.5	76.7	76.7	75.9	83.0
Payroll & timekeeping clerks	71.7	72.2	77.5	74.9	73.6	76.2	75.5	81.4	81.0	81.0	82.1
Statistical clerks	70.9	68.5	73.1	74.5	75.4	75.6	76.1	78.8	78.0	80.3	81.6
Library attendants and assistants	75.2	77.9	79.1	80.6	81.6	80.3	80.8	79.4	77.6	82.2	81.3
All clerical workers	75.6	76.6	77.6	77.8	78.7	78.9	79.6	80.3	80.1	80.5	80.7
All other clerical workers	70.3	70.4	72.8	74.1	76.9	75.3	76.0	76.4	77.1	76.9	77.9
Counter clerks, except food	73.9	76.2	77.8	75.8	75.4	77.8	77.2	77.9	73.4	76.4	76.4
Clerical supervisors, n.e.c.	57.8	61.2	65.1	66.4	67.1	65.9	63.2	71.3	70.5	70.8	72.2
Computer & peripheral equipment operators	37.8	40.3	43.1	44.4	52.6	54.6	58.3	61.6	59.8	63.8	63.3
Collectors, bill and account	48.3	37.9	46.0	52.1	51.6	47.9	57.7	59.5	56.4	63.4	62.1
Estimators & investigators, n.e.c.	43.4	49.5	47.2	44.9	48.6	51.0	53.4	55.8	56.2	54.6	58.4

Insurance adjusters, examiners, and investigators	34.3	40.2	45.6	48.0	51.3	50.6	51.5	55.5	57.5	58.1	56.5
Ticket, station, & express agents	31.8	35.0	38.0	39.0	42.7	42.6	40.6	44.4	45.7	47.3	47.4
Mail handlers, except post office	43.8	43.4	44.5	46.2	50.7	49.7	49.4	50.3	47.3	47.4	47.3
Expediters and production controllers	23.1	26.5	30.2	28.0	30.0	34.0	32.1	38.1	40.3	40.9	42.4
Dispatchers and starters, vehicle	16.3	19.5	24.2	18.5	21.6	20.2	30.9	35.5	34.0	38.3	38.2
Stock clerks and storekeepers	22.9	25.3	25.2	30.2	29.1	30.8	31.2	31.9	32.5	34.8	36.8
Postal clerks	26.7	26.9	28.0	30.0	31.7	31.8	32.2	34.4	35.4	37.9	35.1
Shipping and receiving clerks	14.9	14.4	15.9	17.1	17.3	19.5	22.8	21.3	21.6	22.5	24.8
Messengers and office helpers	15.4	20.2	23.7	26.3	29.6	28.0	28.7	31.5	27.6	26.8	23.5
Mail carriers, post office	6.7	6.4	7.5	8.7	9.1	9.5	11.4	10.3	11.1	15.7	17.0

SOURCE: Current Population Survey.

Table 2.18
Percent Minority Employment in Clerical Occupations

Occupational title	Percent minority employment										
	1972	1973	1974	1975	1976	1977	1978	1979	1980	1981	1982
Postal clerks	19.6	21.6	21.8	25.2	26.5	26.2	24.7	23.9	24.2	26.4	26.9
File clerks	18.0	19.7	21.0	20.8	20.4	20.4	23.4	21.0	21.6	22.9	21.2
Mail handlers, except post office	19.5	16.1	21.1	18.9	20.3	21.1	19.1	18.6	23.0	20.6	20.9
Keypunch operators	15.5	17.0	17.3	16.0	18.1	17.9	18.3	23.0	21.8	19.4	20.3
Teachers' aides, except school monitors	21.8	23.6	22.8	19.4	19.4	16.9	18.1	17.1	19.6	19.2	20.1
Messengers and office helpers	17.9	17.9	15.8	18.4	16.0	17.2	20.7	18.5	16.3	19.6	19.1
Typists	12.0	13.4	13.8	13.8	13.9	14.5	16.2	17.2	15.5	17.8	17.4
Telephone operators	12.8	12.4	12.6	13.4	13.9	14.0	12.5	16.8	15.8	17.2	17.3
Stock clerks and storekeepers	12.5	11.6	11.5	11.6	12.4	12.3	12.8	14.4	12.4	13.1	16.1
Library attendants and assistants	11.7	10.7	13.4	10.4	14.2	16.2	11.0	12.7	13.2	14.5	16.0
Computer & peripheral equipment operators	10.2	11.6	11.8	10.5	11.8	11.6	13.2	13.0	14.0	15.8	15.5
Bookkeeping & billing machine operators	8.7	7.1	13.8	10.2	8.3	11.5	13.3	10.5	14.0	14.3	14.3
Mail carriers, post office	14.1	12.4	12.4	14.3	12.4	10.3	9.4	10.7	11.5	13.6	14.0
Statistical clerks	8.4	11.1	10.5	10.1	12.5	11.2	11.7	12.3	14.0	15.1	14.0
Shipping and receiving clerks	13.7	14.4	14.0	11.7	13.2	13.7	14.8	13.6	14.1	14.7	13.8
Stenographers	8.0	11.3	9.7	8.0	10.0	12.0	10.6	13.2	15.6	13.5	13.6
All other clerical workers	9.2	13.6	10.8	10.9	11.1	11.7	14.3	12.7	13.3	13.5	13.1
Ticket, station, & express agents	6.2	6.0	9.9	10.3	11.3	10.9	11.7	9.7	9.3	9.5	13.0
Estimators and investigators, n.e.c.	4.9	7.3	8.4	8.6	8.7	9.3	10.6	10.1	10.7	10.6	12.8
Cashiers	8.0	7.8	7.9	8.5	9.2	8.8	10.6	10.5	10.8	11.8	12.8
All clerical workers	8.7	9.3	9.4	9.4	9.8	9.8	10.5	11.0	11.1	11.6	11.8
Collectors, bill and account	5.0	5.2	6.3	11.3	7.8	8.5	11.5	8.1	7.7	10.8	11.5
Enumerators and interviewers	7.7	12.2	13.2	11.6	10.4	9.3	15.9	10.0	15.1	15.5	11.3
Clerical supervisors, n.e.c.	10.1	9.3	7.4	8.8	10.5	9.7	11.3	11.8	12.0	10.8	10.7

Insurance adjusters, examiners, and investigators	6.5	7.1	8.8	10.0	10.3	10.1	11.2	12.7	10.9	9.9	10.0
Counter clerks, except food	6.4	7.4	7.2	8.9	8.5	9.6	10.1	11.0	9.4	10.3	9.7
Payroll and timekeeping clerks	6.0	6.6	6.9	7.0	7.2	7.5	7.1	8.5	8.6	9.5	8.9
Expediters and production controllers	6.7	6.0	7.5	8.1	9.2	8.8	8.0	9.6	9.4	8.3	8.9
Receptionists	7.6	8.1	7.8	8.9	8.2	8.1	9.5	8.7	8.1	8.6	8.3
Bank tellers	4.9	4.6	6.8	7.1	6.7	7.6	8.0	9.3	8.7	7.6	8.0
Secretaries	5.2	5.7	5.1	4.9	5.7	5.4	6.2	6.6	6.7	7.2	7.4
Dispatchers and starters, vehicle	3.5	6.9	7.7	10.9	9.1	9.1	9.3	6.5	11.7	8.7	7.3
Bookkeepers	3.6	4.1	4.4	4.3	4.1	4.4	5.0	5.4	5.5	6.3	6.6
Billing clerks	6.7	6.7	7.0	6.9	6.5	5.8	7.7	8.6	8.0	10.5	6.5

SOURCE: Current Population Survey.

Other clerical occupations showing 20 percent minority participation include file clerks, keypunch machine operators, teachers' aides, and messengers. In general, the clerical occupations with heavy minority employment are not the strong growth occupations.

Occupations with relatively low percentages of minority employment include billing clerks, bookkeepers, dispatchers, secretaries, bank tellers, and receptionists. However, the general trend in the minority proportion of clerical workers over the last decade is clearly upward. For most of the occupations in table 2.18, the percent minority in 1982 is higher than it was in 1972.

After this brief review it is surprisingly hard to come to any firm general conclusions about the potential impacts of clerical automation on the employment outlook for women and minorities in clerical jobs. It is clear that both women and minorities have made "gains" in recent years in the sense that they are taking a higher proportion of clerical jobs than in the past. But the rumored impacts of technological change on clerical employment have not emerged from the analysis of historical employment data. It is apparent that the analysis of aggregate data is not sufficient to identify the employment impacts of technological change, except in cases of truly declining occupations. We shall see in chapter 4 that there are some good reasons for this disappointing result.

With this data base in place, we turn in chapter 3 to a focus on trends in the employment levels of individual clerical occupations. The data from this chapter will be applied in a more rigorous fashion, as employment levels and demographic characteristics are examined in more detail.

NOTES

1. See Hunt and Hunt (1985) for a full discussion of this issue.

2. Note that this treatment will not be strictly correct because of the marked differences between the 1980 Census occupational classification system and those based on the 1970 and earlier Census systems.

3. For convenience, the terms administrative support personnel and clerical workers will be used interchangeably in this monograph. While the differences in classification are widespread and significant, the discussion will be much improved if this point is ignored except when it is vital to understanding.

4. This will become clear later in the chapter when the trends in employment of clerical workers are presented.

5. See 1970 Census of Population, Detailed Characteristics, United States Summary PC(1)-D1, Table 221, pp. 718-724.

6. See John A. Priebe, Joan Heinkel, and Stanley Greene, "1970 Occupation and Industry Classification Systems in Terms of Their 1960 Occupation and Industry Elements," Technical Paper No. 26, issued July 1972, Washington, D.C.: U.S. Department of Commerce, Bureau of the Census. The 1950 to 1960 conversion was published as Technical Paper No. 18. Unfortunately, the 1970 to 1980 conversion has not yet been published. The Bureau of the Census was good enough to make preliminary unpublished results available for this study.

7. Neither of these factors is thought to introduce serious distortions in clerical worker employment figures. In any event, there is no information available with which to make the adjustments at the specific occupational level.

8. Note that this is some 2.2 million more than reported in the earlier section of this chapter. The major discrepancy is the omission of cashiers from the earlier figures.

9. This differs only slightly from the 3.9 million reported earlier.

10. The category of clerical assistants, social welfare was omitted since it was added in 1970.

11. Later in the chapter, it will be shown that messengers appear to be making a strong comeback.

12. It is frustrating to stop the analysis in 1982. However, the massive reorganization of the occupational classification system introduced to the CPS in 1983 prevents the development of consistent data for all occupations after 1982.

13. There are some differences in aggregation from the Census data that result in only 32 rather than 42 occupations reported. This makes it impossible to use the bridging technique to try to overcome the effects of conversion to 1980 Census titles in 1983 CPS data.

3

Analysis of Employment Trends in Clerical Occupations

This chapter will apply a narrower focus to the data presented in chapter 2. The analysis will concentrate on individual clerical occupations rather than the entire population of clerical jobs. This will make it possible to pull together the trends in employment, the demographic composition, and speculation on the past impact of clerical automation on each occupation. The clerical subgroups from the 1980 Census will be used to organize the occupations, but it is important to realize that there will not usually be a one-to-one correspondence between the subgroup and the occupations discussed.[1] In essence, the analysis will involve selected occupations within each clerical subgroup.

This chapter will draw freely on results that have been presented earlier, especially on the race and sex characteristics of those employed in particular occupations. In the interest of readability, however, the tables from which the results are taken will not be referenced. For some occupations, CPS data will be presented for 1972 to 1982 as in chapter 2, while for others the data will include 1983 and 1984. It is true that the conversion to 1980 Census occupational titles in 1983 rendered the CPS observations incom-

patible with the earlier years. However, there are some occupations where the changes are minimal or nil. The authors
have used their own judgment in deciding which individual
occupations were consistent enough to be presented without
misleading the reader. Also, Census data for 1950 to 1980
and CPS data for 1972 to 1982 or 1984 will be presented
together without too much concern for whether the employment levels are exactly consistent between the two.[2] This is
done in the interest of deriving maximum impact from the
numbers that exist. The interest is in establishing the trend
rather than in getting a precise measurement of the number
of people employed at a given point. This is also the motiva-
tion for presenting the occupational trends in graphical format in this chapter.

Employment Trends

Table 3.1 provides an overview of the rates of increase of
the components of administrative support employment between the 1970 and 1980 Census observations.[3] Since it uses
the 1980 Census occupational classification system, the
numbers are not exactly consistent with those presented
earlier in this monograph. The indication is that there was a
very wide range of employment change between 1970 and
1980 among the clerical subgroups. Aggregate rates of
change vary from the 24 percent reduction in employment of
communication equipment operators over the decade to the
147 percent increase among computer equipment operators.
It will be shown shortly that the increase in supervisors is
clearly a statistical anomaly.

The overall rate of expansion among clerical jobs during
the decade of the 1970s was 32 percent. Other subgroups
growing faster than this rate include the nonfinancial records
processors, information clerks, adjusters and investigators,
and miscellaneous. Those growing more slowly than average

Table 3.1
Employment of Administrative Support Occupations

	Employment from census in 1970			Employment from census in 1980			Percent change
	Male	Female	Total	Male	Female	Total	
Administrative support occupations..	3,448,507	9,350,856	12,799,363	3,854,322	12,997,076	16,851,398	32
Supervisors.................	177,350	221,478	398,828	559,042	497,668	1,056,710	165
Computer equipment operators.....	97,065	68,046	165,111	167,320	241,155	408,475	147
Secretaries, stenos, & typists	121,386	3,783,036	3,904,422	77,017	4,579,938	4,656,955	19
Information clerks	118,633	484,967	603,600	130,617	763,561	894,178	48
Non-financial records processing ...	147,287	535,147	682,434	219,735	745,372	965,107	41
Financial records processing	413,446	1,667,463	2,080,909	262,465	1,991,619	2,254,084	8
Dupl. & other office machine oper...	21,653	38,776	60,429	20,209	38,462	58,671	-3
Communications equipment oper...	32,965	375,132	408,097	32,542	276,148	308,690	-24
Mail and message distributors	575,383	184,521	759,904	544,730	229,096	773,826	2
Material scheduling & distrib.	1,089,228	288,492	1,377,720	1,090,956	571,300	1,662,256	21
Adjusters and investigators	211,417	134,987	346,404	194,432	321,234	515,666	49
Miscellaneous	442,694	1,568,811	2,011,505	555,257	2,741,523	3,296,780	64

SOURCE: 1980 Census, PC80-1-D1-A, Table 276.

(or decreasing) include material scheduling and distributing occupations, secretaries, stenographers and typists, financial records processors, mail and message distributors, and duplicating and other office machine operators. One or more occupations from each subgroup will be examined in order to gain an appreciation for the clerical employment trends at the detailed occupational level.

Clerical Supervisors

Table 3.1 indicated an increase of 165 percent in clerical supervisors between 1970 and 1980, but this is undoubtedly a statistical artifact rather than a real change in the employment of supervisors. One of the major changes introduced in the 1980 Census occupational classification system was the separation of supervisors from the body of clerical workers. Thus the supervisors of computer equipment operators are now regarded as clerical supervisors whereas before they were likely to have been considered as simply computer equipment operators.

When the Bureau of the Census did their reclassification study to make the two distributions comparable, they obviously were forced to use the information that was gathered at the time of the original response. So the reclassification study takes the original job title given by the respondent and classifies it according to the two different systems. But when the classification system changes in such a way that a whole new category of supervisors is created, it is difficult or impossible to impose that on the original data. It seems clear that this accounts for a major share of the apparent increase in clerical supervisors.

Figure 3.1 shows the data presented in chapter 2 (in tables 2.8 and 2.11) in a graphical format. The upper panel of the figure displays the long-term employment trend according to Census data as adjusted. The lower panel of the figure shows

Figure 3.1
EMPLOYMENT OF CLERICAL SUPERVISORS

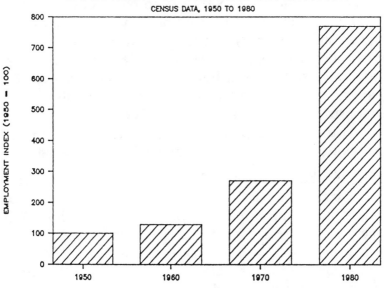

EMPLOYMENT OF CLERICAL SUPERVISORS

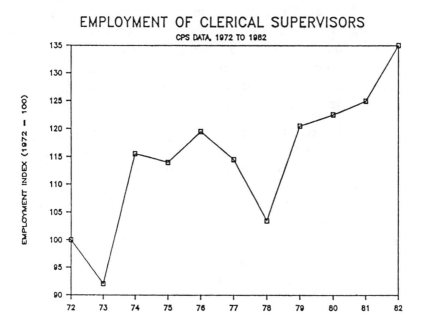

the CPS estimates of annual average employment of clerical supervisors from 1972 to 1982, also on a consistent definitional basis. Since the CPS data only show an increase of 35 percent in the employment of clerical supervisors over a nearly identical span of years, the Census figures clearly represent a statistical artifact that is a consequence of the changes in the measurement system. This is also demonstrated by the fact that the CPS shows that clerical supervisors were 70 percent female in 1980 while the 1980 Census reports that they were only 47 percent female.

On the basis of these data, it would appear that the employment of clerical supervisors has been increasing only slightly more rapidly than clerical workers as a whole. While supervisors increased by 35 percent over the 1972 to 1982 period, all clerical workers increased by 29 percent for the term according to CPS data. The proportion female among clerical supervisors showed a strong positive trend during the 1970s, increasing from 58 percent in 1972 to 72 percent in 1982. Thus at the end of the period, females were approaching a representation among clerical supervisors equal to their proportion of all clerical workers (77 percent). However, the 1980 Census data presented in chapter 2 demonstrated that females were not distributed equally across all supervisory categories.

If females advanced among the ranks of clerical supervisors during the past decade, the proportion of minority employment was relatively constant. While data on race from the CPS are subject to large sampling errors, the data appear to show that the proportion of minority workers among clerical supervisors was roughly the same as their proportion of all clerical workers throughout the '70s. The 1980 Census data for supervisors of administrative support personnel, however, showed that blacks, Hispanics, and Asians were all slightly less likely to be supervisors.

It may not be very satisfying, but clerical supervisors provide a good object lesson on the dangers of putting too much faith in the raw numbers without checking against other data sources. The differences between the 1970 and 1980 Census numbers are so great as to make comparisons between these two data sources meaningless. Yet when we turn to the alternative, the Current Population Survey, we find that the differences in definitions make for noncomparability here as well. Fortunately, all the occupations examined here will not prove so troublesome.

Computer Equipment Operators

As indicated repeatedly in this monograph, computer equipment operators had the fastest growth rate of any clerical subgroup during the decade of the 1970s. This is reflected in figure 3.2 as well. The employment of computer and peripheral equipment operators nearly tripled between 1972 and 1982. The observations for 1983 and 1984 are not entirely consistent with earlier years, since they omit some supervisors of computer equipment operators, but it is clear that the strong employment growth continued in these occupations in 1983 and 1984.

It was reported in chapter 2 that the proportion of females employed as computer and peripheral equipment operators rose from 38 percent to 63 percent between 1972 and 1982, a very considerable rise. Table 3.1 showed that while male employment levels in these occupations increased by 72 percent, female employment increased by over 250 percent between 1970 and 1980. Female workers have obviously made substantial inroads in the most rapidly growing of all clerical occupations.

Minorities also managed to increase their proportion of computer and peripheral equipment operators from 10 percent to 15 percent between 1972 and 1982. The discussion in

Figure 3.2

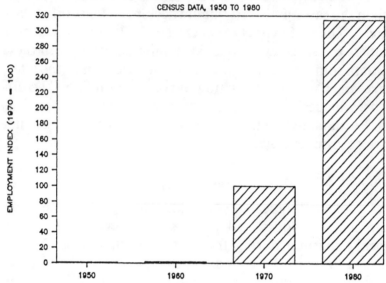

EMPLOYMENT OF COMPUTER OPERATORS

CENSUS DATA, 1950 TO 1980

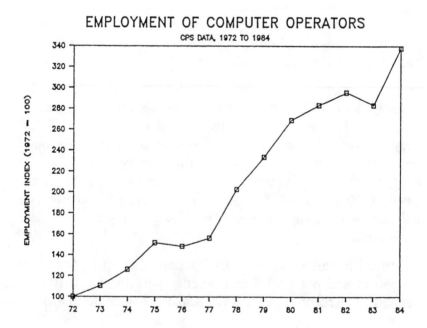

EMPLOYMENT OF COMPUTER OPERATORS

CPS DATA, 1972 TO 1984

chapter 2 showed that blacks, Hispanics, and Asians all were overrepresented among computer equipment operators relative to their share of all clerical employment. Female minorities also were doing well in these occupations. Only female Hispanics were not overrepresented among computer equipment operators. The conclusion is that this rapidly growing clerical occupation has been a real opportunity generator for minorities in the labor force. The extent to which these occupations continue to expand in the future may play an important role in determining the adequacy of female and minority job achievement.

There is considerable uncertainty about how technological change in the office might impact the employment opportunities for computer and peripheral equipment operators. To the extent that electronic mail, data base management systems, word processing systems, and other innovations depend on mainframe or minicomputer installations for their processing power, the number of computer operators would be enhanced by the spread of these services. On the other hand, since microcomputers allow direct hands-on operation by end users, the microcomputer domination of these areas could cause job opportunities for computer operators to be constrained. So the key is the way in which centralized computer systems evolve in the face of decentralized microprocessing capability. If the strong growth in mainframes and minicomputers continues in the future, it is reasonable to expect continued job creation and continued opportunities for minorities.

Miscellaneous Clerical Occupations

It is very illuminating that the second fastest growing clerical subgroup should be a miscellaneous collection of occupations. Table 3.1 showed that this group's employment advanced by 64 percent from 1970 to 1980. The individual occupations that are available for analysis in this subgroup include bank tellers, teachers' aides, and statistical clerks. In addition, cashiers will be discussed here even though they are no longer classified as clerical workers by the Census.

Figure 3.3 shows the strong positive trend in employment of bank tellers from 1950 to 1980 and from 1972 to 1981. The leveling off in 1982 could be permanent in this instance. While data for 1983 and 1984 are not consistent with data presented here, there was no increase in tellers between 1983 and 1984 in the CPS either.

Bank teller is one of the traditional clerical occupations dominated by the employment of white females. Over 90 percent of bank tellers in 1980 were female and 89 percent of these were white. Black females are particularly unlikely to be employed as bank tellers, while Hispanic and Asian women are slightly more likely to be tellers than their numbers would suggest. The conclusion, however, is that the future prospects for employment of bank tellers will impact most directly on jobs traditionally filled by white women.

Figure 3.4 shows the trend in employment for teachers' aides from 1950 to 1980 and 1972 to 1984. This is one of the few occupations where there are no known discrepancies with the move from 1970 Census categories to those of 1980, so the time series should be entirely consistent.[4] The main growth in teachers' aides occurred during the decade of the 1960s when they expanded enormously. This was partly in response to the demand for teachers and partly due to the desire to introduce cultural diversity into the schools. Since fully qualified minority school teachers were more difficult to find, the paraprofessional category of teachers' aides filled the bill. In fact, it was shown in chapter 2 that teachers' aides were one of the occupations with the highest minority employment ratios, over 20 percent in 1982.

Figure 3.3
EMPLOYMENT OF BANK TELLERS
CENSUS DATA, 1950 TO 1980

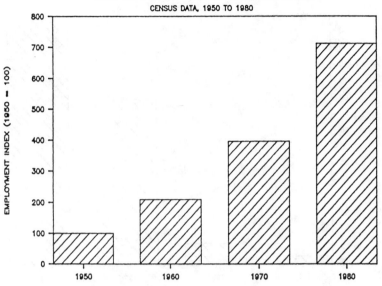

EMPLOYMENT OF BANK TELLERS
CPS DATA, 1972 TO 1982

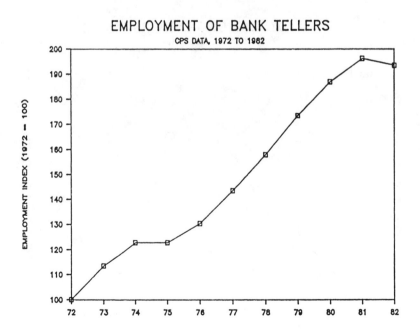

Figure 3.4

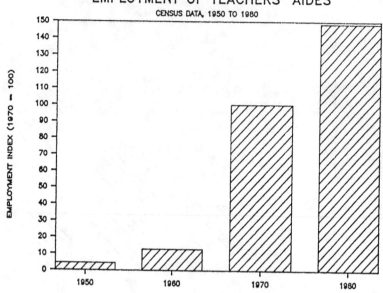

EMPLOYMENT OF TEACHERS' AIDES

CENSUS DATA, 1950 TO 1980

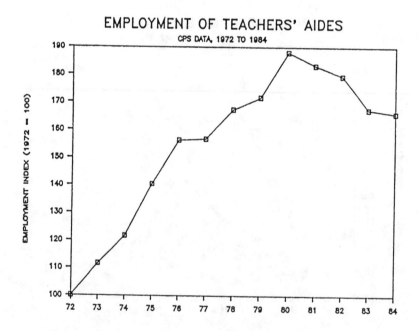

EMPLOYMENT OF TEACHERS' AIDES

CPS DATA, 1972 TO 1984

This occupation is also highly female at over 92 percent in 1982, so clearly many of the job opportunities that were created tended to go to minority females. In the 1980 Census it was reported that 16.5 percent of female teachers' aides were black and 11.4 percent were Hispanic. This is nearly double the black proportion of all female clericals and nearly triple that for Hispanics.

It is doubtful that the decline in teachers' aides employment beginning in 1981 has anything to do with office automation. It is a consequence of the decline in student populations, the increasing supply of accredited minority teachers, and the escalating pressure on school budgets occasioned by the taxpayer revolts of the last few years. Nonetheless, the trend does not augur well for the minority females who found desirable paraprofessional employment opportunities in this occupation.

Figure 3.5 shows the employment trend for statistical clerks from 1950 to 1980 and for the decade from 1972 to 1982. This occupation showed relatively strong growth from 1973 to 1979, but a substantial deterioration beginning in 1980. While consistent data are not available for 1983 and 1984, the indications are that the decline continues. The net result is that statistical clerks grew only about two-thirds as fast as all clerical workers during the period.

It was shown in chapter 2 that this occupation became more female over the decade of 1972 to 1982, rising from about 70 percent to about 80 percent female. The percentage minority also increased over the period. The connection of this occupation to office technology would appear to be through the microcomputer applications of spreadsheet analysis and through statistical and data base management packages of various types. It is frankly not known whether the decline in the employment of statistical clerks is the result of the growth in microcomputers or not, since there is no

Figure 3.5

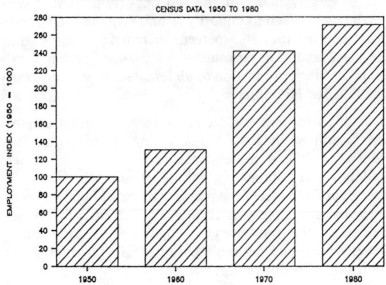

EMPLOYMENT OF STATISTICAL CLERKS

CENSUS DATA, 1950 TO 1980

EMPLOYMENT OF STATISTICAL CLERKS

CPS DATA, 1972 TO 1982

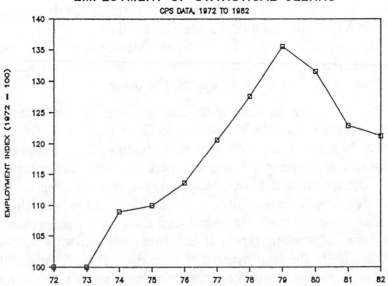

way to make a direct link between the two developments. It would seem likely, however, that this decline might be linked to technological change in the insurance industry and other similar intensive data manipulation situations.[5]

The last miscellaneous clerical occupation to be considered is the category of cashiers. Figure 3.6 shows the trends in the employment of this occupation. It is apparent that it has been a growth occupation for a long time, with the growth accelerating during the 1970s. The observations for 1983 and 1984 may not be 100 percent consistent with the earlier ones, but they serve to demonstrate that this occupation continues to enjoy very strong growth in employment.

Cashiers were not discussed in the first section of chapter 2 since they are no longer included among clerical workers according to the Census. But they were about 85 percent female in 1980, slightly above average among clerical occupations. Cashiers were also shown to have a rising proportion of minority workers, increasing from 8 to 12 percent during the period 1972 to 1982. Cashier jobs might be at risk from clerical automation, particularly in the form of automatic or customer-operated checkout systems. However, the diffusion of these point-of-sale computer devices through 1984 does not appear to have had a marked impact on the employment levels in this occupation since it has had one of the fastest growth rates among clerical occupations in recent years.

Adjusters and Investigators

The subgroup of adjusters and investigators was shown in table 3.1 to have increased in employment by 49 percent over the decade of the 1970s. However, the employment of males in this subgroup actually declined, whereas the level of female employment increased by 138 percent. Thus, this occupational subgroup was one of rapidly increasing job op-

Figure 3.6
EMPLOYMENT OF CASHIERS
CENSUS DATA, 1950 TO 1980

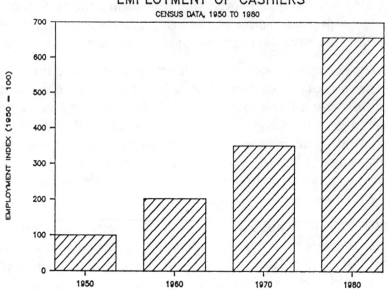

EMPLOYMENT OF CASHIERS
CPS DATA, 1972 TO 1984

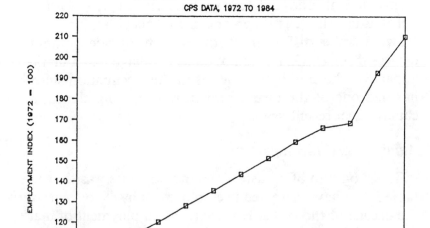

portunities for female clerical workers. The opportunities for minority women were also good as black, Hispanic, and Asian women all were overrepresented in this clerical subgroup in 1980 (see table 2.7). The individual occupation chosen for analysis in this subgroup is that of insurance adjusters.

Figure 3.7 shows the trend in employment of insurance adjusters. It indicates that there has been very strong growth in this occupation for the last 30 years. Table 2.5 reported that employment in this occupation was about 60 percent female in 1980. Furthermore, the analysis of demographic groups showed that black and Asian females were proportionately more likely to hold these jobs, whereas white females and those of Spanish origin were less likely to be employed here. While there is a problem with the consistency of the later observations, it appears that the growth of insurance adjusters continued from 1983 to 1984.

This would seem to be a good example of an occupation that might be a user of clerical automation, but would not be impacted directly without major changes in the way the job is organized. Computerized systems support the work of insurance adjusters and they have more data available to them than ever before. Yet a major portion of their job obviously involves interaction with clients and providers. Thus it is the type of function that is hard to automate unless somehow the job can be reorganized to involve less direct customer contact. In any event, there is no evidence of a slackening of the growth in employment of insurance adjusters to date.

Information Clerks

The subgroup of information clerks includes such occupations as interviewers, receptionists, ticket and reservation agents, and hotel clerks. Table 3.1 showed that the employment of these occupations increased by 48 percent between

Figure 3.7

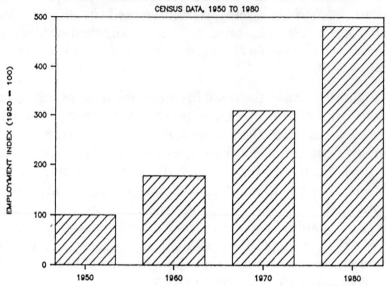

EMPLOYMENT OF INSURANCE ADJUSTERS

CENSUS DATA, 1950 TO 1980

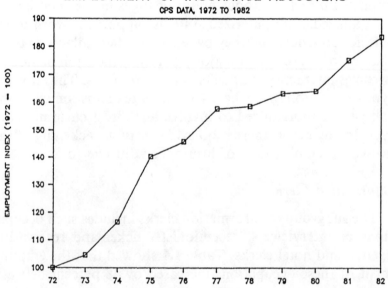

EMPLOYMENT OF INSURANCE ADJUSTERS

CPS DATA, 1972 TO 1982

1970 and 1980, about one-and-one-half times the average for all clerical workers. The results in chapter 2 showed this group to be 85 percent female, with the occupation of receptionists over 95 percent female. Black women and Asian women were slightly less likely to be employed as information clerks than other clerical occupations. Hispanic women were slightly more likely to work in this subgroup. The occupations to be examined here are receptionists and ticket and reservation agents.

Figure 3.8 shows the long-term and recent trends in employment of receptionists, one of the traditional office occupations. The upper panel shows that the employment of receptionists has expanded throughout the last 30 years while the lower panel demonstrates very strong growth in the late 1970s. It would appear that receptionist employment was hurt by the 1981-82 recession, but the inconsistency of later data makes it difficult to determine whether this is a more permanent trend.

In any event, it is doubtful that office automation will have a substantial impact on this occupation because of the public interaction element. If an office needs a receptionist, it indicates that there is some degree of public or customer interface required. Office automation may increase the productivity of the receptionist significantly, but it is doubtful that the position would be eliminated. Thus this occupation provides another example of a clerical occupation which is likely to benefit from office automation by making the job more valuable and productive. If there is an employment impact due to more aggressive automation of clerical functions, it is likely that it will be felt in other less visible occupations.

Figure 3.9 reports the trends in employment of transportation ticket and reservation agents. This occupation shows a much slower growth than that for receptionists, both long-term and short-term. There was very little growth in this oc-

Figure 3.8

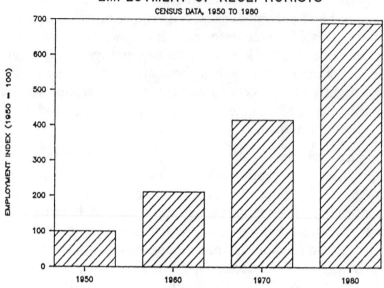

EMPLOYMENT OF RECEPTIONISTS

CENSUS DATA, 1950 TO 1980

EMPLOYMENT OF RECEPTIONISTS

CPS DATA, 1972 TO 1982

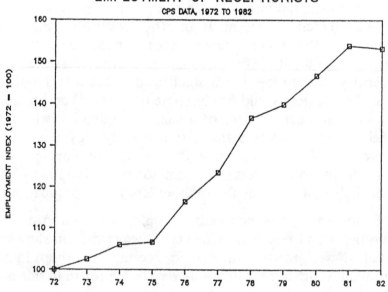

Figure 3.9

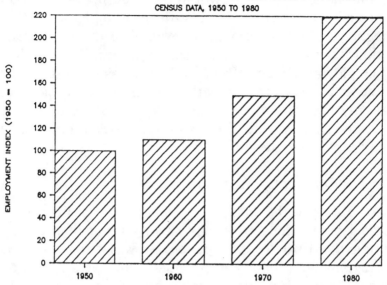

EMPLOYMENT OF TICKET & EXPRESS AGENTS

CENSUS DATA, 1950 TO 1980

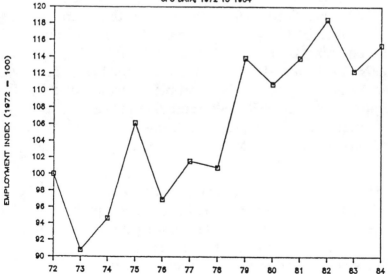

EMPLOYMENT OF TICKET & EXPRESS AGENTS

CPS DATA, 1972 TO 1984

cupation from 1950 to 1970, but it did expand substantially during the 1970s. The growth in travel during this period is well known, but so is the growth in automation of these functions. The most prominent example is the airline reservation system, but others show similar trends. Thus, the level of employment here reflects both increasing consumer demand and increasing automation to improve efficiency. Apparently the level of consumer demand has been stronger since the employment of transportation ticket and reservation agents continues to expand.

Records Processors, Nonfinancial

According to the data presented earlier, this subgroup of clerical occupations grew only slightly faster than average during the 1970 to 1980 period. It was also just about average in the proportion of female employees and above average in the proportion of minority female employees. Included in this subgroup are detailed occupations such as file clerks, order clerks, library clerks, and personnel clerks.

Figure 3.10 shows the interesting trends in the employment of file clerks. The upper panel indicates that there was very little growth in this occupation from 1950 to 1960, but that it was booming during the first computer revolution in the 1960s. A substantial decline followed in the 1970s. The lower panel shows possible data problems with basically flat employment until 1978 followed by an increase of 50,000 in two years. Next the employment drops back to the base level, and then increases by 50,000 once again. The credibility of these recent numbers is uncertain.

The employment of library attendants is shown in figure 3.11. This is an occupation that expanded rapidly from 1960 to 1970 and then stagnated. The lower panel shows that there was a sharp rise during the mid-1970s in employment of library clerks, followed by a gradual decline. Data for 1983

Figure 3.10
EMPLOYMENT OF FILE CLERKS
CENSUS DATA, 1950 TO 1980

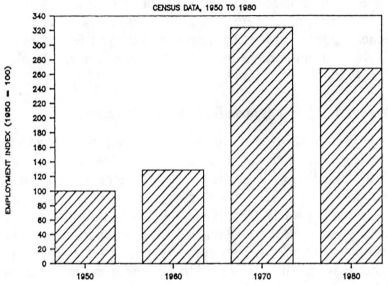

EMPLOYMENT OF FILE CLERKS
CPS DATA, 1972 TO 1984

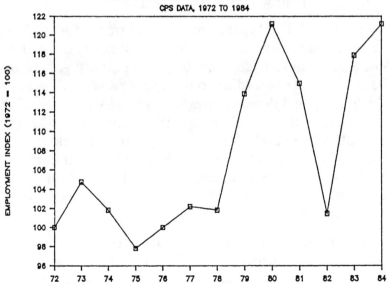

and 1984 indicate that this decline is continuing. While there have been advances in automation that bear on library clerical routines, there has also been a reduction in the general public support for libraries in the last few years. It is likely that both have impacted the employment levels of library clerks.

Material Scheduling and Distributing Occupations

This clerical subgroup includes such occupations as stock and inventory clerks, shipping and receiving clerks, production coordinators, expediters, dispatchers, and meter readers. As a group these clerical occupations expanded by 21 percent from 1970 to 1980, only about two-thirds as fast as all clerical workers. Many of these occupations involve a factory or warehouse environment and whether for this or other reasons, these jobs tend to be held by males. In chapter 2 it was shown that this group was only 34 percent female. However, it was also reported that black females and females of Spanish origin were more likely to work in these occupations than white or Asian females.

Figure 3.12 displays the employment trends for stock and inventory clerks, the single biggest occupation in the group. Stock clerks have had a slow but rather steady growth over the last 30 years according to the upper panel of figure 3.12. The lower panel demonstrates the cyclical sensitivity of this occupation with the declines in employment during the recessions of 1973-75 and 1981-82 very apparent. Employment of stock clerks appears to have dipped by 10 percent during the severe 1981-82 recession. This is atypical for clerical occupations, but would not be remarkable for operatives in manufacturing.

Shipping and receiving clerks are represented in figure 3.13. The same general cyclical pattern can be seen in the lower panel of this figure. The declines are roughly coinci-

Figure 3.11
EMPLOYMENT OF LIBRARY ATTENDANTS
CENSUS DATA, 1950 TO 1980

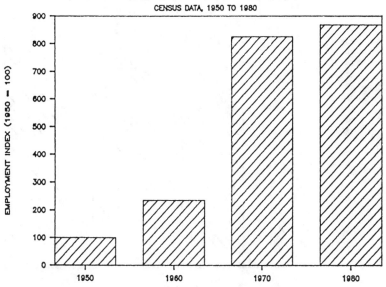

EMPLOYMENT OF LIBRARY ATTENDANTS
CPS DATA, 1972 TO 1982

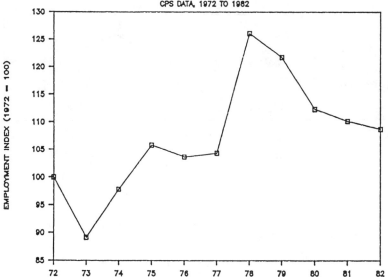

Figure 3.12
EMPLOYMENT OF STOCK CLERKS
CENSUS DATA, 1950 TO 1980

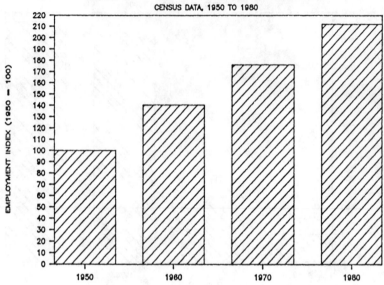

EMPLOYMENT OF STOCK CLERKS
CPS DATA, 1972 TO 1984

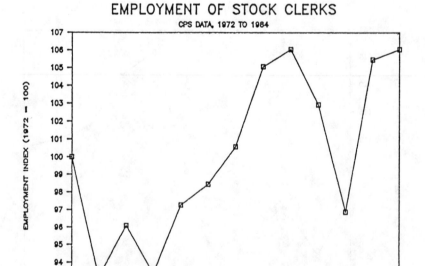

dent with the general business cycle pattern. It is also apparent from the upper panel that shipping and receiving clerks did not show any growth during the decade of the '50s. The message from these occupations is that it is very difficult to perceive long-term trends in employment levels based on a few years of observation, particularly if a recession has clouded the picture.

Secretaries, Stenographers, and Typists

This subgroup is made up of the prototypical clerical workers. They are the single largest subgroup, accounting for over one-fourth of all clerical workers in 1980. They also have been growing much less rapidly than the average for all clerical workers, at only 19 percent from 1970 to 1980. As described in chapter 2, this subgroup is over 98 percent female and almost 90 percent white females.

Even more dominated by white females is the occupation of secretaries. Secretaries are almost 99 percent female and 92 percent of those females are white. The employment trends for secretaries are displayed in figure 3.14. The upper panel reveals a strong long-term growth pattern, particularly during the 1970s. The lower panel shows that this strong growth pattern was interrupted by the 1981-82 recession and has resumed at a somewhat slower pace thereafter. This is another occupation where 1982 appears to be a critical year for observation. The addition of observations in 1983 and 1984 makes the downturn in employment between 1980 and 1982 appear much less ominous. Nevertheless, it is apparent that secretarial employment growth has slowed dramatically in the early 1980s.

Figure 3.15 shows the employment trends from 1950 to 1980 and from 1972 to 1984 for stenographers, one of the declining clerical occupations. It is apparent that this decline has continued for at least the last 30 years. As discussed

Figure 3.13

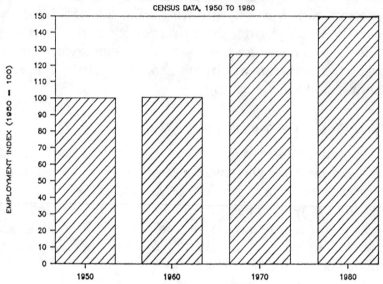

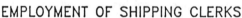

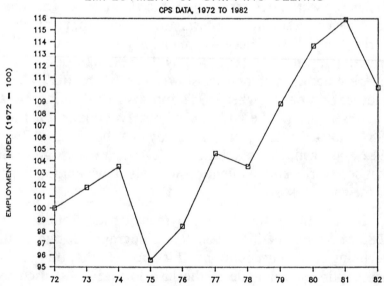

Figure 3.14
EMPLOYMENT OF SECRETARIES
CENSUS DATA, 1950 TO 1980

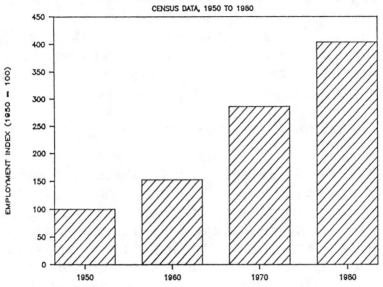

EMPLOYMENT OF SECRETARIES
CPS DATA, 1972 TO 1984

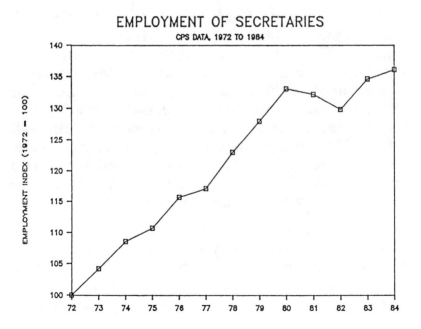

earlier, this decline is due to changes in dictation equipment and procedures. It also probably reflects changing job titles to some degree since it seems clear that there is actually more dictation being done than ever before. However, the operators in a word processing center who transcribe dictation are not likely to be called stenographers, even though they are performing the same basic function.

Financial Records Processing Occupations

Financial records processors include bookkeepers, billing clerks, payroll clerks and others. These occupations only increased by 8 percent over the 1970 to 1980 period, making them one of the slowest growing subgroups among clerical workers. In chapter 2 it was shown that these occupations were 88 percent female in 1980 and that black females were particularly underrepresented among this subgroup of clerical workers. Only 4.8 percent of females employed in these occupations in 1980 were black.

Figure 3.16 reports the employment trends for the dominant occupation in this subgroup, bookkeepers and accounting clerks. This occupation represents over 80 percent of the total employment in the group. Figure 3.16 shows that bookkeepers enjoyed rather rapid employment growth during the 1960s, but much slower during both the 1950s and 1970s. The lower panel shows a brief growth spurt in the latter half of the 1970s, with stagnation in employment levels since. Later observations suggest that this stagnation has continued up to the present. It is plausible that this trend reflects the growth of microcomputer accounting applications.

A somewhat similar pattern is revealed in figure 3.17 which reports the employment trends for payroll clerks. The employment of this group also peaked in the late 1970s but has headed downward since. As in the example of bookkeepers it would be logical to expect some reduction in

Figure 3.15

EMPLOYMENT OF STENOGRAPHERS

CENSUS DATA, 1950 TO 1980

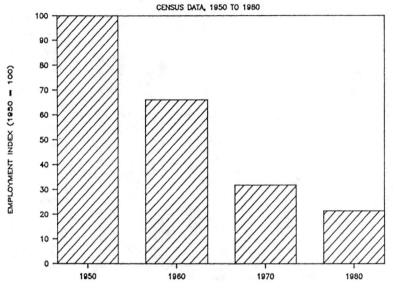

EMPLOYMENT OF STENOGRAPHERS

CPS DATA, 1972 TO 1984

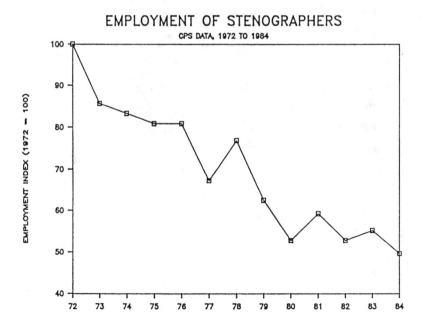

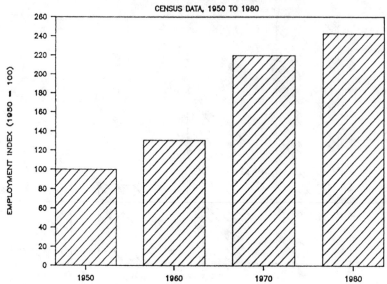

Figure 3.16
EMPLOYMENT OF BOOKKEEPERS
CENSUS DATA, 1950 TO 1980

EMPLOYMENT OF BOOKKEEPERS
CPS DATA, 1972 TO 1982

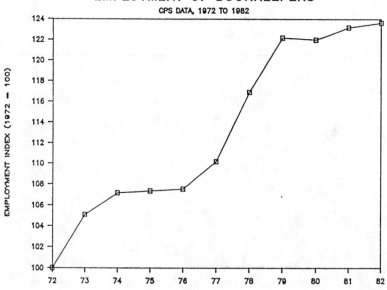

employment with the application of microcomputers and appropriate software to these simple but exacting tasks. Both these trends bear further study.

Mail and Message Distributing Occupations

This group of clerical occupations was virtually flat in employment level from 1970 to 1980, showing only a 2 percent increase over the decade. The group is dominated by employees of the U.S. Postal Service, divided into the occupations of mail carriers and postal clerks. As was shown in chapter 2, these occupations are the least female of any clerical occupations, with only 30 percent of total employment in the subgroup in 1980 consisting of women. However, it was also shown that these occupations have a high proportion of black males and females among their ranks.

Figure 3.18 reports the employment trends for postal clerks from 1950 to 1980 and 1972 to 1984. There was a slow growth in the number of postal clerks from 1950 to 1960 followed by a more rapid expansion between 1960 and 1970. The most recent decade shows a net decrease in employment of postal clerks. The lower panel of figure 3.18 demonstrates considerable instability of employment levels of postal clerks. The same is true of the numbers for mail carriers (not shown). It is possible that some internal changes in the postal service account for this pattern, or it may be due to problems in the data. In any event, in the face of aggressive automation efforts in the postal service, the number of postal clerks is only declining slowly according to figure 3.18.

The competitors to the postal service are represented in figure 3.19, which reports the employment trends for "other mail handlers," i.e., those other than the U.S. Postal Service. It is apparent that the competition has been doing very well over the last 20 years. By all accounts the other mail

Figure 3.17

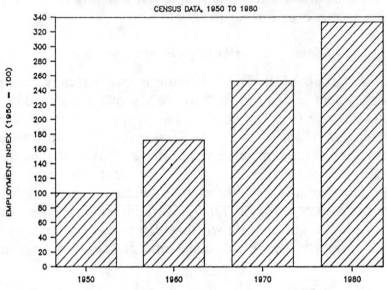

EMPLOYMENT OF PAYROLL CLERKS
CENSUS DATA, 1950 TO 1980

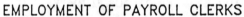

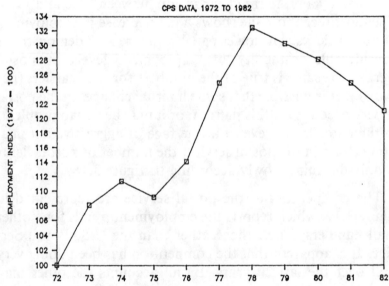

EMPLOYMENT OF PAYROLL CLERKS
CPS DATA, 1972 TO 1982

Figure 3.18

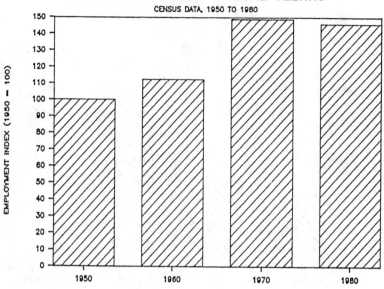

EMPLOYMENT OF POSTAL CLERKS

CENSUS DATA, 1950 TO 1980

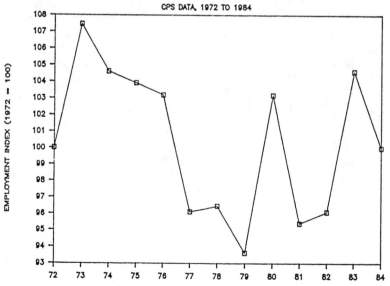

EMPLOYMENT OF POSTAL CLERKS

CPS DATA, 1972 TO 1984

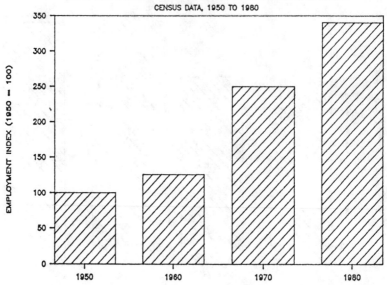

Figure 3.19

EMPLOYMENT OF OTHER MAIL HANDLERS

CENSUS DATA, 1950 TO 1980

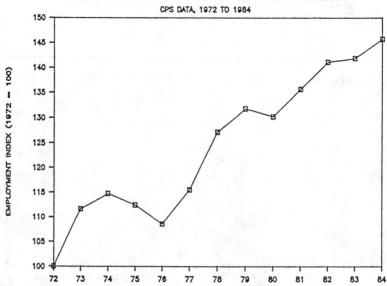

EMPLOYMENT OF OTHER MAIL HANDLERS

CPS DATA, 1972 TO 1984

handling firms (UPS, Federal Express, etc.) are heavily automated, but the employment levels continue to rise as they expand their service levels and move into new markets. This is a pattern that is more characteristic of successful technological change than is declining employment. Of course, the declining employment may show up in other sectors or other occupations as well.

Communications Equipment Operators

The last clerical subgroup to be considered is communications equipment operators. Table 3.1 reported that this subgroup experienced a 24 percent decline in employment between 1970 and 1980. It was the only clerical subgroup to show an actual decline in employment levels. The group was also shown to be 90 percent female with a particularly heavy concentration of black females, some 14 percent of all female employees in the group.

Figure 3.20 displays the employment pattern for telephone operators, who represent 95 percent of the subgroup's employment. The figure shows a pattern of stagnant employment over a long period of time with a decline in recent years. The lower panel confirms this with a relatively steady decline in telephone operators during the 1970s. This is another example of an occupation that has been automated heavily with a consequent decline in employment levels over the long-term. The introduction of automatic switching had a heavy impact in earlier years, and the computerization of information services in recent times has reduced the employment at the telephone operating companies. The advent of modern switching gear among commercial telephone users has also had an impact.

Figure 3.20
EMPLOYMENT OF TELEPHONE OPERATORS
CENSUS DATA, 1950 TO 1980

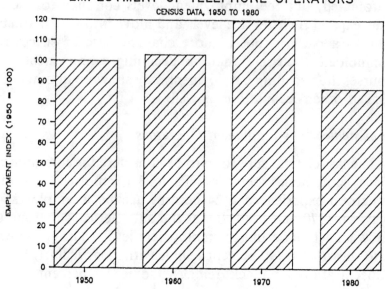

EMPLOYMENT OF TELEPHONE OPERATORS
CPS DATA, 1972 TO 1982

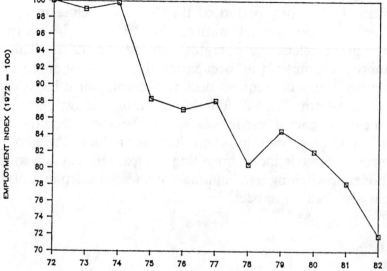

Conclusions

A number of occupations have been examined in some detail now, and it is time for some general conclusions. In the first place, it is surprising how much diversity there is in the employment trends of individual clerical occupations. Of course, there is tremendous variety among clerical jobs as well, so perhaps the diversity of outcomes should have been expected. The last two chapters have demonstrated that there are some clerical occupations that are clearly decreasing in employment, and in some instances it appears to be due to technological change. Examples would include stenographers and telephone operators. There are also clerical occupations that are clearly increasing due to technological change, such as computer operators.

But for the great bulk of clerical occupations, one cannot tell from the aggregate employment data whether technological change has had a significant impact on employment levels, or in which direction! There are simply too many things going on. Some severe measurement problems that arise with occupational employment data have also been discussed. These include theoretical obstacles to measuring occupations as well as practical problems of sampling variability, changing classification systems, and so on. Obviously, the uncertainty over the measured employment trends and their causes is largely because of these problems. Definitive answers require precise measurement. Occupational data do not lend themselves to such precision.

In addition, many occupations are affected by the periodic swings in aggregate economic activity in the economy referred to as the business cycle. The fact that the last consistent year of employment data coincides with the worst recession in the U.S. since the Great Depression of the 1930s does not make the task any easier. Where consistent data are available for 1983 and 1984, they have usually helped to illuminate what went before. Later observations generally will reveal a dip in employment during the recession to have been either a temporary phenomenon or the start of a longer-term trend.

But even where it seems clear that something has changed, it is very difficult to link it to technological change as the causative factor. The level of ignorance about the diffusion of new technologies is very great, and it is nearly impossible to make satisfactory connections between the introduction of a new device or a new process and the resultant employment changes. Macro measurements cannot detect micro adjustments in the production functions of individual firms. There is simply too much noise in the macro measurements to yield meaningful results.

In the following chapter, another attempt will be made to attack this problem. Employment measures at the industry level will be used to explore the determinants of clerical employment levels within a macro environment.

NOTES

1. This reflects the inconsistencies in the data discussed previously. In fact, this chapter will go farther than any other to try to ignore the data problems and concentrate on deriving maximum information from what is available.

2. Actually the employment levels for 1980 from CPS and Census usually do not match exactly. Only where extreme differences were apparent were the occupations excluded from analysis.

3. This table was prepared by the Bureau of the Census itself. It is taken from the summary table they prepare to bridge between any two Census observations. Thus, these figures do not involve any adjustments by the authors.

4. Note, however, that the 1980 employment level in the CPS is nearly double that from the Census. This is due to differences in aggregation.

5. Consistent occupational employment by industry data across time would help explain such trends. Such data do not exist for 1980.

4

Determinants of
Clerical Employment

The trends in occupational employment examined earlier indicated that some clerical occupations were growing while others were declining. In addition, it was shown that the aggregate of all clerical jobs was becoming relatively more important as a proportion of total jobs in the economy, although that growth slowed in the 1970s. It also appeared that the recession of 1980-1982 was unique in that the proportion of clerical jobs did not increase significantly as it has in past recessions. This chapter looks behind the scenes at what might explain the occupational employment movements discussed earlier.

First the role that overall demand and economic growth play in determining employment levels is considered. The groundwork is then laid for understanding two other factors which help determine clerical employment: total industry employment trends and the relative importance of clerical jobs within each industry. An analysis of the industry employment trends in those industries which employ the most clerical workers is followed by a discussion of technological change and clerical employment growth. Much of the earlier analysis of the chapter is synthesized in a mathematical decomposition of occupational employment changes. The chapter ends with a brief conclusions section.

In the broadest terms, aggregate employment is determined by total output and the productivity of the workers who produce that output. Total output is generally measured by Gross National Product (GNP), the value of all final goods and services produced in the economy in a year.[1] If total output rises, employment will rise unless worker productivity increases even faster. On the other hand, if a new technology makes large gains in productivity possible, and if there are no offsetting increases in aggregate demand, technological displacement of labor is a likely result.[2] This simple relationship, although devoid of occupational and industrial content, helps to emphasize two major points relevant to this paper.

First, accepting the notion that productivity is more or less fixed in the short run by the technology of production, then it should be clear that changes in GNP—aggregate demand in the economy—drive any changes in employment. There are many socio-economic factors that affect both the level and rate of growth of GNP. Physical and human resource endowments, societal choices between spending and saving, the amount and type of investment activity, competition in international markets, and many other factors are important. There are also totally unforeseen shocks to the economy, such as the energy crises of the 1970s, which temporarily disrupt the national economic system. The influence of business cycles on employment are also well known, although their length and severity vary tremendously. The point is that all occupations are adversely affected by the failure of GNP to grow sufficiently. Likewise, all occupations tend to benefit from adequate economic growth.

The second factor that influences employment is productivity. Greater labor productivity means fewer jobs for the same aggregate output. If productivity growth outpaces the growth of GNP, total employment will fall. On the other hand, if productivity does not rise, increases in real income per capita are not possible either. What must be emphasized here is that productivity growth and GNP growth are closely intertwined. Thus all workers have a vital stake in productivity gains because that is what allows the *possibility* of economic growth, increasing employment, and rising incomes.[3]

Historically, technological change has not created permanent unemployment for millions of workers. The increases in productivity due to technological change have instead raised the living standards of workers. To be sure, there have been winners and losers in this process, both among firms and individuals, but the net result has been economic growth and increases in real income. No one can guarantee that history will repeat itself with current technological change, but some appear to be too easily persuaded that history will *not* repeat itself, i.e., office automation and other labor-saving technologies will wipe out millions of jobs.[4] Later in this chapter the past and current trends in office automation will be discussed and the impact of clerical workers assessed.

While the general importance of productivity and output in determining employment has been noted, the focus of this chapter is actually on occupational employment trends by industry. The demand for labor is a derived demand based upon the demand for the good or service which that labor produces. In this context the rise and fall of occupational employment is related to the rise and fall of demand for the products and services produced in particular industries. Thus the diversity of goods and services making up GNP is matched by the diversity of occupations that produce that output. Similarly, the factors of productivity and output level that determine employment in the aggregate, also determine employment levels in particular industries.

Unfortunately, the occupational analysis of this chapter is limited to the aggregate of all clerical jobs, rather than the detailed clerical occupations examined in chapter 3. The primary reason is the lack of a consistent time series data base containing industry-specific occupational information. As recounted in earlier chapters, it is a major effort to construct reasonably consistent occupational employment data for the last 30 years. The situation appears hopeless for occupational data by industry. Nonetheless, since occupational employment profiles differ so profoundly by industry, it is important to glean as much information as possible from the limited data which are available.

Clerical Employment by Industry

The analysis of occupational employment by industry begins with the occupational profile of the nation. If GNP is considered to be the nation's output, then this occupational profile represents the relative importance of each occupation in producing that output.[5] The occupational profile of the U.S. for 1982, using the major occupational groups from the Current Population Survey (CPS), is presented in table 4.1.[6] Since occupational structures tend to change slowly, the snapshot presented here will provide an adequate overview of the relative importance of the occupations in the nation.

Table 4.1 makes it clear that clerical jobs are the largest major occupational group in the U.S. In 1982, clerical workers accounted for a little over 18.5 percent of all employment. They are followed closely in importance by professional and technical workers, while service workers are a more distant third. It should be mentioned that these proportions are based on the work in chapter 1-3. Thus they represent the distribution of occupations according to 1970 Census definitions. Both the definition of the major groups and their relative importance have changed substantially with the 1980 Census.

Table 4.1
U.S. Occupational Profile

Occupation	1982 employment (thousands)	Percent of total employment
Professional, technical, and related workers	16,952	17.0
Managers, officials, and proprietors ..	11,494	11.5
Sales workers	6,580	6.6
Clerical workers	18,446	18.5
Craft and related workers	12,271	12.3
Operatives	12,807	12.9
Laborers, except farm	4,517	4.5
Service workers....................	13,736	13.8
Total, all occupations	99,528	100.0

SOURCE: Calculations by the authors based upon data from the *Current Population Survey.*

NOTE: Some occupational detail is omitted. Totals and percentages may not add exactly due to omission of some occupational detail and rounding error.

The relative importance of the various industries in the national employment picture is presented in table 4.2. By far the most important of the individual one-digit industries is the service sector. It accounts for a little over 30 percent of all employment, almost double the size of the next biggest sector, retail trade. Even though 1982 was a recession year, the durable goods sector still holds third place with about 12 percent of total employment.

How important are the clerical jobs in each of these industries? That question is partially answered in table 4.3 which presents the summary staffing ratios for all industries. Occupational staffing ratios measure the relative importance of an occupation in an industry. They are obtained by dividing occupational employment in an industry by total industry employment. Thus the staffing ratios of all occupations within an industry must sum to one as reflected in the bottom row of the table.

Table 4.2
U.S. Industry Profile

Industry	1982 employment (thousands)	Percent of total employment
Agriculture	3,401	3.4
Mining	1,028	1.0
Construction	5,756	5.8
Durables	11,968	12.0
Nondurables	8,318	8.4
Utilities	6,552	6.6
Wholesale trade	4,120	4.1
Retail trade	16,638	16.7
Finance	6,270	6.3
Services	30,259	30.4
Public administration	5,218	5.2
Total	99,528	100.0

SOURCE: Calculations by the authors based upon data from the *Current Population Survey*.

NOTE: Totals and percentages may not add exactly due to rounding.

It should be clearly understood at the outset that the use of terms like industry, occupation, and staffing ratio at the highly aggregated one-digit level of analysis is simply a convenience. These broad groupings are actually very heterogeneous. Industries do not produce durables and nondurables but rather specific products like autos, dishwashers, or soap. The diversity of occupations within the clerical field was illustrated in earlier chapters. Nonetheless, it is convenient to refer to the major occupational and industrial groupings as if they were clearly recognizable occupations and industries.

According to table 4.3, the finance industry shows the greatest concentration of clerical workers, nearly 45 percent of all employees in this industry are clerical workers. In fact, there are twice as many clerical workers in finance as any other occupational group employed in that sector. Public administration is also a heavy employer of clerical workers, about 35 percent of all jobs in this industry are clerical. It is followed by utilities and wholesale trade which utilize slightly above average proportions of clerical workers to produce their output.

The service industry and retail trade show average employment in clerical occupations, although their other occupational needs do not look similar at all. The durable and nondurable manufacturing industries are the home base of the operatives; both show below average employment in clerical occupations. Last is the construction industry which employs relatively few clerical workers, but is the dominant user of skilled craft workers in the economy.

Clearly, different industries use very different mixes of occupations to produce their final output. In other words, the occupational staffing ratios are relatively specific to each type of production. It is this variation in the staffing ratios between industries that makes trends in industry employment an important influence on the distribution of occupations throughout the economy.

The relative importance of the major occupations and industries within the national economy have been described. It is now time to find the absolute number of clerical jobs within each of the industries. The number of clerical jobs in a given industry is obviously the product of the total employment level in the industry and the staffing ratio for clerical workers in that industry. Thus an industry could employ a large number of clerical workers even though it had a relatively low staffing ratio for clerical workers, provided its total employment was large enough.

Table 4.3
Occupational Staffing Ratios by Industry for 1982

Occupation	Construction	Durable goods	Non-durable goods	Utilities	Wholesale trade	Retail trade	Finance	Services	Public administration
Professional and technical......	0.04	0.15	0.10	0.10	0.04	0.02	0.07	0.37	0.20
Managers and administrators	0.13	0.08	0.08	0.11	0.21	0.19	0.20	0.08	0.13
Sales workers ...	0.01	0.01	0.04	0.01	0.24	0.20	0.22	0.01	.00
Clerical workers.	0.08	0.13	0.13	0.22	0.20	0.17	0.44	0.18	0.35
Craft workers...	0.55	0.21	0.17	0.21	0.08	0.07	0.02	0.05	0.06
Operatives	0.04	0.33	0.37	0.02	0.05	0.04	.00	0.03	0.01
Service workers .	0.13	0.04	0.05	0.07	0.06	0.06	0.01	0.02	0.03
Laborers, non-farm	0.01	0.02	0.02	0.03	0.01	0.23	0.04	0.26	0.22
Total.........	1.00	1.00	1.00	1.00	1.00	1.00	1.00	1.00	1.00

SOURCE: Calculations by the authors based upon data from the *Current Population Survey*.

NOTE: Some occupational and industrial detail is omitted. Totals and percentages may not add exactly due to omission of some occupational and industrial detail and rounding error.

The absolute number of clerical jobs in each of the major industries is presented in table 4.4. About 5.5 million clerical workers can be found in the service industry. Just under three million clerical jobs are located in each of two sectors, retail trade and finance. These three sectors combined—services, retail trade, and finance—account for over 11 million clerical jobs, almost 60 percent of total clerical employment. Clerical workers may be dispersed broadly throughout the national economy, but these three sectors are especially important to total clerical employment.

Since this type of matrix will be used to explain occupational employment in this chapter and the next chapter, it is important to understand the various parts of the table. The heart of the table is the occupation by industry employment figures which constitute all of the entries except the last row and column. As stated earlier, these entries can be found by multiplying the occupational staffing ratios of those industries by total employment for each industry.

The row sums of the matrix, depicted in the last column, make up the occupational profile shown in table 4.1, while the column sums are the industry profile shown in table 4.2. It would be highly desirable to track these totals over time in a more detailed fashion. But, as explained earlier, this is currently impossible for most occupations. On the other hand, reasonably consistent and detailed industry employment data are available over time. Detailed industry employment trends are presented in the next section for selected industries that are particularly significant for clerical workers.

Finally, it should be noted that total employment in the economy, the bottom right-hand cell in the table, is the column sum of occupational employment and the row sum of industry employment, presuming that both are measured consistently. This should remind us once again that the overriding determinant of employment outlook is the trend in ag-

Table 4.4
Occupational Employment by Industry for 1982
(in thousands)

Occupation	Construction	Durables	Non-durables	Utilities	Wholesale trade	Retail trade	Finance	Services	Public Administration	Total
Professional and technical	203	1,795	829	679	176	311	418	11,255	1,021	16,952
Managers and administrators	740	981	694	721	880	3,126	1,232	2,294	668	11,494
Sales workers	33	177	335	89	1,009	3,310	1,378	230	4	6,580
Clerical workers	451	1,513	1,074	1,463	844	2,840	2,750	5,473	1,827	18,446
Craft workers	3,167	2,513	1,393	1,373	349	1,110	129	1,643	292	12,271
Operatives	407	4,275	3,428	1,577	564	1,046	17	999	111	12,807
Service workers	33	213	186	199	31	3,898	256	7,750	1,145	13,736
Laborers, non-farm	722	501	379	452	266	997	89	614	148	4,517
Total employment	5,756	11,968	8,318	6,552	4,120	16,638	6,270	30,259	5,218	99,528

SOURCE: *Current Population Survey.*

NOTE: Some occupational and industrial detail is omitted. Totals may not add exactly due to omission of some occupational and industrial detail and rounding error.

gregate demand. The composition of occuptional employment will change slowly over time, as will industry employment levels. But if the trend in total employment is lackluster
or negative, it will pull down the performance of most industries and occupations. If the trend in total employment is
robust, most industries and occupations will benefit from
that growth.

Industry Employment Trends

There are much more employment data by industry in the
U.S. than occupational employment data. The most detailed
data on occupational employment are currently collected in
the Occupational Employment Statistics (OES) program at
BLS. It provides the historical basis for the staffing ratios in
the BLS industry-occupation matrix which is used as the
starting point for the BLS occupational employment projections. The BLS occupational employment projections will be
discussed in chapter 5. This section concentrates on gaining a
better understanding of the way in which occupational
employment is influenced by trends in industry employment.

There are 378 industries tabulated in the OES system. One
of the other components of the BLS economic modeling
system is an input-output model that includes 156 industrial
sectors. Comparisons over time can be made using the latter
model because reasonably consistent time series data are
available from it for 1958 to 1984. However, in order to
build a consistent time series of total industry employment
for this paper which can at least roughly be related to the
OES industry employment totals, it was necessary to find the
lowest common denominator between the two data bases.
Although the match is not perfect in all cases, it turns out
that a 105-industry system was most appropriate for the
present purposes.[7]

It will be necessary to clearly identify the industry employment series which is being used at any point in the text. Basically the choice is dictated by the available data. Only the OES series has any specific occupational detail, so it must be used to discuss occupational employment at a particular point in time. On the other hand, only the BLS input-output industry data are consistent over time, so they must be used to explore industry employment trends. In this analysis, the OES data base will be used to identify the industries with substantial clerical employment, but the BLS input-output series will be used for industry employment trends.

The 20 largest sectoral employers of clerical workers in 1982 are presented in table 4.5. The year 1982 is selected because that is the current base year for the OES occupation by industry employment data. The entries in the table are ranked by the number of clerical employees in each industry. Thus the industry with the largest number of clerical employees is listed first.[8] The clerical staffing ratios and total industry employment are also included to highlight the importance of these variables in determining occupational employment. Finally, the percent of total clerical jobs accounted for by each of the 20 industries as well as the cumulative total is also reported.

The top 10 industries in terms of clerical employment account for about two-thirds of all clerical employment. The top 20 industries account for over 80 percent of all clerical jobs. While clerical jobs are indeed dispersed throughout the economy, none of the top 10 clerical employment industries are from the goods-producing sectors. Furthermore, it is clear how important the federal and state and local government sectors are to clerical employment. Jointly they account for over 3.6 million clerical jobs or almost 20 percent of the total. The importance of banking and insurance, the

Table 4.5
BLS Clerical Employment by Industry, 1982

Industry	Industry employment (thousands)	Employment clerical (thousands)	Clerical staffing ratio (percent)	Percent of total clerical employment	Cumulative percentage of total clerical employment
State and local government and educational services ...	13,068	2,512	19.2	13.4	13.4
Miscellaneous retail trade..............	10,476	2,496	23.8	13.3	26.8
Wholesale trade.......................	5,294	1,531	28.9	8.2	34.9
Banking..............................	1,650	1,180	71.5	6.3	41.2
Federal government	2,739	1,138	41.5	6.1	47.3
Insurance	1,700	911	53.6	4.9	52.2
Miscellaneous business services	3,139	896	28.5	4.8	57.0
Hospitals	4,166	666	16.0	3.6	60.5
Social services, museums, and membership organizations	2,755	587	21.3	3.1	63.7
Credit agencies, security and commodity brokers	1,015	577	56.9	3.1	66.8
Legal and miscellaneous services	1,628	560	34.4	3.0	69.7
Telephone and other communication	1,174	529	45.1	2.8	72.6
Physician and dental offices...........	1,309	394	30.1	2.1	74.7
Construction.........................	3,913	324	8.3	1.7	76.4
Eating and drinking places............	4,781	224	4.7	1.2	77.6
Electric services and gas distribution....	792	207	26.2	1.1	78.7
Trucking and warehousing.............	1,206	199	16.5	1.1	79.8
Miscellaneous printing and publishing ...	846	192	22.8	1.0	80.8
Real estate	986	188	19.1	1.0	81.8
Miscellaneous personal services.......	1,219	186	15.3	1.0	82.8

SOURCE: Calculations by the authors based upon data tape from the 1982-1995 OES/BLS occupational employment projections.

NOTE: The 378 OES industries were first aggregated to 105 industries. The OES data tape includes wage and salary employment only.

two largest sectors within finance, is also apparent in terms of clerical employment. Finally, clerical jobs are important in a variety of service sector industries from business services to personal services.

Since industry employment is so important in determining occupational employment, the trends over the last 27 years in total industry employment are presented in figure 4.1 and table 4.6. Figure 4.1 aggregates the employment in the top 10 industries, while the table presents the employment trends for each of the 10 industries. The numbers are reported in index number form to make it easier to compare the growth trends in the industries. The average growth in employment for all industries is also reported to facilitate comparisons between the particular industry and the average for all industries.

Figure 4.1 demonstrates a number of important features of the top 10 clerical employment industries. First, these industries have been much less susceptible to the vagaries of the business cycle than all industries. The growth rate of the sum of these 10 sectors has remained positive through two of the three recessions during the period. It was only in 1982, during the worst recession since World War II, that the composite employment growth rate of these 10 sectors turned negative—and then, barely so.

Second, the average employment growth rate of these 10 industries has clearly outdistanced the all-industry average for the entire 27-year period. But this is almost entirely due to the fact that employment in these sectors does not ordinarily retreat during recessionary periods. The conclusion is that employment in these 10 important clerical employment industries has grown faster than employment in the overall economy, but that most of this positive growth differential occurs during recessions.

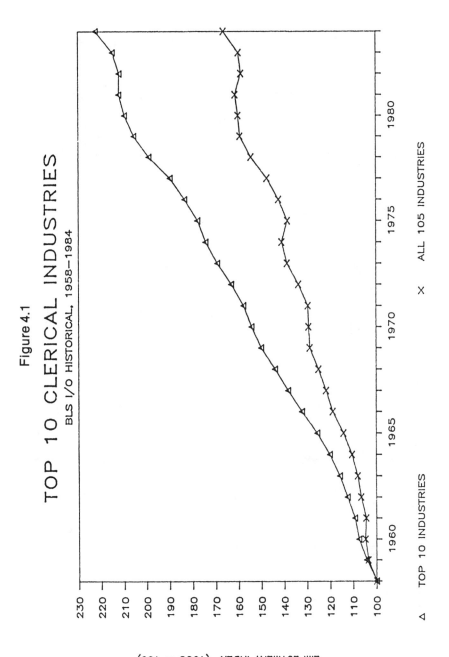

Figure 4.1

TOP 10 CLERICAL INDUSTRIES

BLS I/O HISTORICAL, 1958–1984

Table 4.6
Total Industry Employment Growth of Those Sectors with the Most Clerical Employees

Year	State & local government	Misc. retail trade	Wholesale trade	Banking	Federal government	Insurance	Misc. business services	Hospitals	Credit agencies & commodity brokers	Social services and museums	Top 10 industries	All 105 industries
1958	100	100	100	100	100	100	100	100	100	100	100	100
1959	104	103	103	104	102	101	110	106	109	118	104	104
1960	108	98	105	109	104	103	116	113	116	122	108	105
1961	112	105	105	112	104	105	123	120	124	128	109	105
1962	116	107	107	116	107	106	135	126	129	131	113	107
1963	122	109	109	120	108	109	146	134	132	133	116	108
1964	128	112	112	124	107	111	159	143	138	134	120	111
1965	136	116	116	128	109	112	173	149	142	136	126	114
1966	146	121	121	134	117	114	192	156	149	140	132	119
1967	154	124	124	141	124	119	211	171	156	146	138	122
1968	161	128	127	148	125	122	224	182	171	153	144	125
1969	167	133	131	159	126	125	248	195	186	157	150	129
1970	174	136	134	169	125	129	262	205	182	159	154	129
1971	180	139	134	174	123	131	264	213	184	163	158	130
1972	189	144	138	181	123	133	282	218	194	157	163	134
1973	196	149	144	191	122	135	308	226	202	158	169	139
1974	203	149	149	202	124	139	326	238	202	162	174	141
1975	211	148	148	206	125	140	333	250	202	165	178	139
1976	215	153	153	212	125	142	359	260	210	170	183	142
1977	220	158	158	220	124	148	386	271	222	172	190	148
1978	229	165	167	231	126	154	429	280	238	177	199	155
1979	233	168	175	243	127	160	472	287	256	183	206	159
1980	237	167	177	255	131	164	504	303	268	189	210	160
1981	235	168	180	264	127	167	540	320	284	190	212	161
1982	232	166	177	268	125	168	551	332	291	190	212	159
1983	232	169	176	270	126	169	580	334	317	190	215	160
1984	233	177	185	273	127	172	654	329	343	196	222	167

SOURCE: Calculations by the authors based upon data from the BLS input-output industry series.

By looking at the employment trends in each of the 10 industries in table 4.6, some diversity among the sectors begins to emerge. The most robust employment growth has clearly occurred in banking, miscellaneous business services, hospitals, and the credit agencies and commodity brokers sectors. The growth in employment in miscellaneous business services is particularly striking, more than six times as many workers in this sector in 1984 as there were in 1958, and compares to about a 67 percent increase for all employment. This sector provides a myriad of services to business firms from accounting to customized computer software to consulting advice.

The growth rate of employment in hospitals is also striking. This sector tripled in employment over the period 1958 to 1984. Some of the causes of this growth, such as the aging of the population and the increasing availability of medical insurance for retirees and the indigent through Medicare and Medicaid are well known. In any event, the growth of this sector has not been touched by the business cycle in the past. The real surprise is that hospital employment growth slowed in 1983 and actually turned negative in 1984. Apparently the recent emphasis on cost containment is having an impact on employment in that sector.

It is also clear that the finance sector—especially banking, credit agencies and commodity brokers, and to a lesser extent, insurance—contributed significantly to clerical job growth during these years. All three of these sectors have staffing ratios for clerical workers in excess of 50 percent, the highest of all industries (see table 4.5). Insurance deserves special mention in that its employment growth virtually paralleled that of all industries until about 1974. Then it began to accelerate and outdistanced the national economy in job growth thereafter, except for 1984. The growth of employment in banking, on the other hand, was consistently higher than that for insurance, nearly tripling from 1958 to 1984.

The laggard among the 10 industries with heavy clerical employment was clearly the federal government. The employment trend was very flat from 1965 through the end of the observation period, 1984. Whatever we might hear about swollen federal budgets and the size of the deficit, the federal government has not been a significant source of employment growth for the last 15 years or so. It should also be noted that the growth of state and local government, the largest single employer of clerical workers among the 105 industries in this analysis, was generally above average but actually declined absolutely in employment during the 1980-1982 recession. By the end of 1984, employment in this sector had still not exceeded its peak employment level achieved in 1980. This is significant because it is the first such decline in recent memory for the number one ranking employer of clerical workers.

Of course, the gnawing question is: will these industries continue to show fast employment growth in the future? The question cannot be answered at this point. However, it should be noted that the nation is still experiencing a long run shift from a goods-producing economy to a service-producing economy. This is not to say that the goods-producing sectors such as manufacturing are unimportant, but only that they have not been growing in terms of employment for a long time.

Historically, clerical workers have benefited from this shift since service industries employ much higher proportions of clerical workers. Thus, even if staffing ratios begin to fall for clerical workers (due to office automation or other factors), it is still possible for them to grow at or above the average rate for all jobs because they are concentrated in the nongoods-producing sectors. Clerical workers have a fortunate industry mix in their employment pattern. The next section explores the technological influences on clerical jobs, while the last section measures the contribution of both changing staffing ratios and changing industry mix to the growth of clerical jobs over the last decade.

Technological Change
and Clerical Employment Growth

The introduction to this chapter stressed the importance of demand and productivity in determining employment. It was shown that the overall growth in demand and the changing sectoral composition of that demand, i.e., the rise and fall of particular industries, are important determinants of employment growth. For the sake of exposition, changes in productivity were largely ignored in the earlier discussion. However, when a longer-term perspective is taken, productivity changes are seen to be critical determinants of employment levels. They influence both the number of workers needed to produce a given level of output and the growth of industries, through their influence on cost and price levels for particular products. Many factors affect productivity, but one of the most important of them and the focus of this section is the influence of technological change. More specifically, what role has office automation played in raising the productivity of clerical workers? What impact has clerical productivity had on clerical employment levels?

As in other parts of this study, the available data and selected studies are reviewed in an attempt to answer these questions. However, the review is limited, both in scope and usefulness in addressing the relevant issues. What will be found is that the data are woefully inadequate to assess the impacts of office automation on clerical employment directly. There also is a shortage of systematic studies of the employment impacts of office automation. Forecasts of the employment impacts of office automation are examined separately in chapter 5.

Labor productivity is generally measured as output divided by labor input, although there is not universal agreement about the best empirical approximations for these simple theoretical constructs. One of the most common approaches is to develop a measure of gross output or sales (adjusted for inflation) and divide that by either the number of employees or employee-hours. Labor productivity measures are useful, especially when making comparisons across firms and industries, but it should be mentioned that such simple measures do not isolate the contribution of technology to productivity. They really summarize the joint effect of all input factors on productivity.[9]

The problems in attempting to estimate the gains from office automation are twofold. First, it is impossible to glean from current data any information whatsoever about the relative importance of office automation spending by industry. Investment data are subdivided only into the two broad subcomponents of machinery and equipment and structures. Second, as shown earlier, adequate data about clerical employment are not available over time either. So, even if better investment data were available, it would still be impossible to estimate the productivity gains specifically attributable to clerical workers utilizing various types of electronic office technology. Hunt and Hunt (1985) discuss the many serious data problems in exploring the employment impacts of technological change in another paper.

At the major occupational group level—the aggregate of all clerical workers—there is a limited amount of consistent occupation-by-industry employment data available. If the productivity impact of office automation is sufficiently great, and if the diffusion of such equipment is wide enough, then employment impacts at the major group level should be apparent. It is logical to expect that aggregate staffing ratios for clerical jobs will fall if office automation significantly improves the productivity of clerical workers, all other things equal.[10] This question is examined in the next section.

One simple approach to examining the productivity gains from office automation is to look at those sectors which are significant employers of clerical workers and which are also believed to be the leaders in office automation. It is well known that the finance and insurance industry is the forerunner and recognized leader in the field of office automation. It is also true that more than one-half of the workers in this sector are clerical workers.[11] Therefore, one indicative approach to studying the productivity gains from office automation is to examine the overall productivity gains in finance and insurance.

Finance and insurance is composed of three sectors: (1) banking, (2) insurance, and (3) credit agencies, security and commodity brokers. Recalling the data from table 4.5, these three sectors have clerical staffing ratios of 71.5 percent, 53.6 percent, and 56.9 percent respectively. Thus, if office automation significantly improves clerical productivity, these sectors are logical candidates to demonstrate the effects of such gains.

Figure 4.2 reports the productivity gains for banking, insurance, and credit agencies, security and commodity brokers for the period 1958-1983.[12] The data are reported in index number form to better depict the percent changes in productivity from year to year. The productivity increase for all private nonfarm employment is reported as well to facilitate a comparison of these sectors with a significant segment of the total economy.

The data base utilized for these labor productivity measurements is the BLS time-series data for input-output industries. This same data source has already been used for the industry analysis in this paper and it is one of the key in-

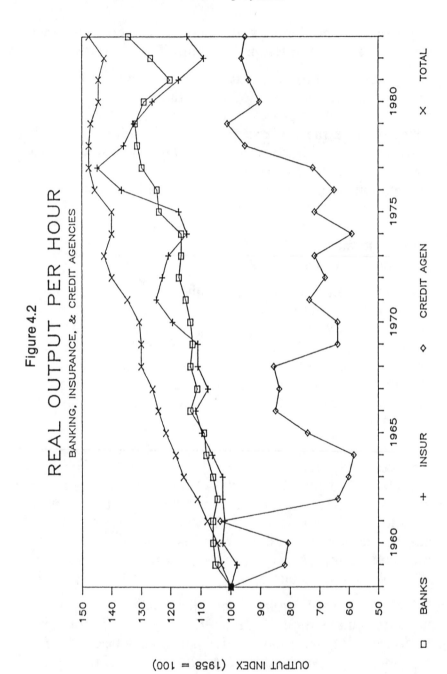

Figure 4.2

REAL OUTPUT PER HOUR

BANKING, INSURANCE, & CREDIT AGENCIES

puts used by BLS in developing their occupational employment projections, which are discussed in the next chapter. It is therefore possible that the BLS productivity data may also provide some insight into their projections.

Conceptually the BLS measure of output by industry in the input-output series is consistent with the national income and product account measures, where output is defined as value added, i.e., gross output less the material costs of the firm. But there are many well-known problems of measuring output and productivity in the service sector, a detailed discussion of which is well beyond the scope of this work.[13] Suffice it to say that the BLS office responsible for the official U.S. government estimates of productivity[14] does not publish estimates for detailed sectors within finance and insurance, except for commercial banking. Furthermore, the productivity estimates for commercial banking attempt to measure direct banking transactions rather than some measure of value added on sales (Brand and Duke, 1982). The reluctance of the BLS to publish official estimates for the sectors within finance and insurance implies that the estimates contained in this monograph may be subject to considerable error.

Nevertheless, the surprise from figure 4.2 is that there is no discernible productivity trend that can be attributed to office automation. The productivity gains in banking, insurance, and credit agencies, security and commodity brokers, have all tended to lag the average for the total private nonfarm economy. In fact, productivity for credit agencies, security and commodity brokers was very slightly lower in 1983 than in 1958, and productivity deteriorated absolutely in insurance after 1977. Since 1981, banking productivity has improved relative to all private nonfarm productivity, but it hardly looks like a revolution, especially given that banking productivity declined from 1979 to 1981.

It should be emphasized once again that these productivity measures are industrywide estimates for *all* employment rather than the specific productivity gains that can be attributed to office automation or to clerical workers. However, these industries are dominated by clerical jobs and it is generally believed that these sectors are the leaders in office automation. Thus it is surprising that no significant productivity gains are apparent. One possible explanation for the lack of productivity gains within these sectors is that perhaps these industries have not been investing in office automation in the way it is popularly believed.

As mentioned earlier, the investment data do not report office automation expenditures separately, but the aggregate data should reveal if there are any new trends in investment in these sectors. Data are available for investment spending in finance and insurance, but without any industrial detail below that level. Figure 4.3 reports in index number form new investment spending by finance and insurance firms in real terms, while figure 4.4 relates that new investment spending to the total number of employees in the sector.[15] Once again, the totals for private nonfarm employment are also shown to provide a reference point for the analysis.

In contrast to the lack of any "take-off" evident in the productivity data for finance and insurance, the investment data in figures 4.3 and 4.4 clearly indicate much higher than average increases in investment in finance and insurance after 1966-67. In fact, investment virtually exploded, even accounting for the significant employment gains in finance and insurance over that time period. Investment per employee in finance and insurance grew a little more than five times the average for all private nonfarm employment after 1966-67.[16]

There is no doubt that the finance and insurance industry is investing heavily in new capital equipment. However, it is

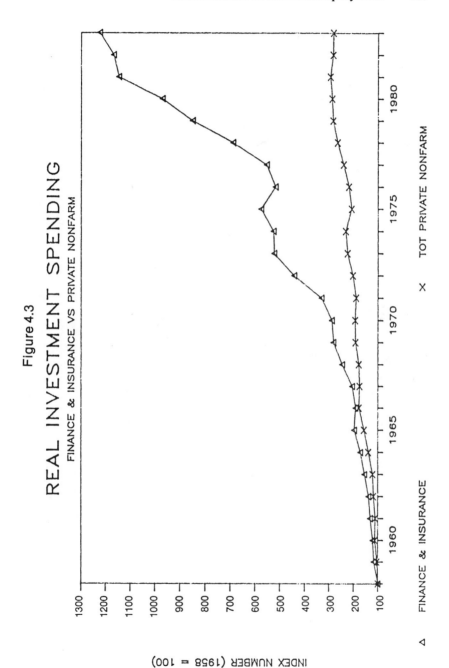

Figure 4.3

REAL INVESTMENT SPENDING
FINANCE & INSURANCE VS PRIVATE NONFARM

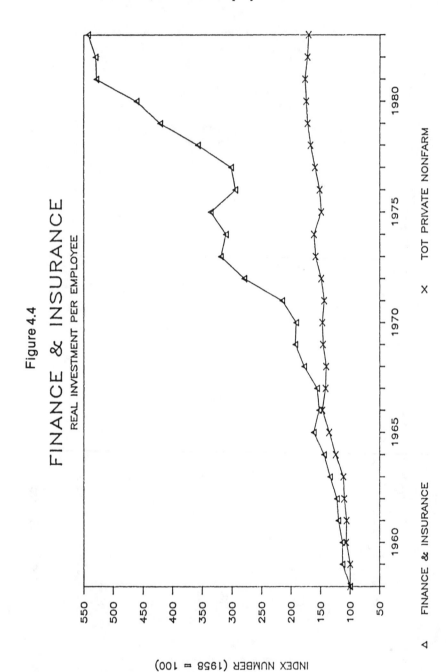

Figure 4.4

FINANCE & INSURANCE
REAL INVESTMENT PER EMPLOYEE

△   FINANCE & INSURANCE   ✕   TOT PRIVATE NONFARM

less certain that finance and insurance is really investing in office automation. Again, the truth is that we do not know how much of investment in this sector can be identified as "office automation spending." What can be concluded is that the dramatic growth in investment in finance and insurance has not resulted in measurable labor productivity gains to date.

Another explanation for the apparent lack of productivity gains in finance and insurance is that the aggregate industry output data may be seriously flawed. This possibility cannot be ruled out given the many problems inherent in estimating productivity in these sectors. It should be noted, however, that the separate transactions-based productivity index for commercial banking developed by BLS also indicates that productivity gains for this sector have been slightly below that for all private nonfarm employment (Brand and Duke, 1983:19). Furthermore, the results reported here are consistent with those obtained by Kendrick and Grossman (1980) and Kendrick (1983). All that can be fairly concluded is that there is nothing in the aggregate industry data to support the contention that office automation has produced significant overall productivity gains in finance and insurance.

There are a number of other possible explanations for the lack of demonstrable productivity gains in the finance and insurance industry. Perhaps the analysis is too aggregated; if office automation has only been adopted by the leading firms (insufficient diffusion), one cannot expect to find productivity gains throughout the industry. It is possible that there has not been sufficient office automation investment to make an impact on total industry investment by 1983. Thus the investment that is analyzed here may involve investment support for other trends in the industry (like the spread of branch banking) that mask the impact of office automation.

Or perhaps the productivity picture would have been even worse without the gains of office automation in these sectors.

Looking beyond finance and insurance to include all industries, it must be admitted that there is surprisingly little quantitative data to support the contention that office automation has raised labor productivity dramatically. Various trade journals and popular business magazines have reported stories about successful installations of office automation equipment, but these reports appear to be relatively unsystematic and self-serving.[17]

There are also some rather optimistic projections about the likely future productivity gains from office automation. Two of these forecasts will be reviewed in the next chapter. In fact, it is these forecasts which are quoted most often in support of the position that office automation will significantly impact on the employment of office workers. However, it will be seen later that one of these forecasts relies at least in part on the trade journal data which is so dubious, while the other study utilizes an engineering approach which may assess technological capability rather than actual operational results.

Formal case studies of the economic impacts of office automation are generally lacking, but there is fragmentary information available which at least casts some doubt on the most wildly optimistic productivity claims of advocates of office automation. First, a number of recently published books (Bailey, 1985; Diebold, 1985; and Katzan, 1982) were designed to be guides to managers interested in improving productivity through office automation. The surprise is that these books contain so few references to the actual experiences of firms or to the productivity gains which managers can reasonably hope to achieve with office automation. For instance, Katzan includes an entire chapter on word processing, but provides no hint about the likely productivity gains. For whatever the reasons, these guides to office automation written for managers are almost totally devoid of specifications of the potential productivity gains from office automation.

Second, Paul Strassman, an executive and office automation specialist with Xerox, has recently assessed (1985) the technology which he has been associated with for over 20 years. Although Strassman is optimistic about the potential productivity gains from computers and information technology generally, he eschews the current focus on hardware, saying that it is less relevant than the people using that hardware. In fact, he suggests (1985:151-152) that the growth rates of the early 1980s and the euphoria about this technology are unsustainable unless they produce demonstrable investment returns. Strassman does not find much evidence of such returns currently:

> The preliminary findings of my research raises doubts about the assumptions which managements in the businesses I have sampled so far must have made when they increased their computer-technology budgets in pursuit of improved productivity (1985:159).

Strassman thinks the payoff will come when management focuses on strategic goals and the people who will accomplish those goals rather than on the methods for achieving them.

Third, it is very interesting to note that International Data Corporation (IDC), one of the information industry's largest market research and consulting firms, has repeatedly stressed that the labor productivity gains from office automation fall far short of justifying the purchase of the equipment. According to IDC (1982, 1983, 1984), the direct labor savings attributable to an office automation project over a five-year period usually amounts to no more than one-half the cost of implementation of the system. Further, IDC states that this rule of thumb does not include the training costs of implementing office automation. On the other hand, it does not include any improvements in the *quality* of the output of offices either. IDC concludes that it is the quality improvements which justify the adoption of office automation.

Perhaps the most eloquent statement of the thesis that the adoption of information technology, which includes office automation, does not lead to dramatic productivity gains has been written by John Leslie King and Kenneth L. Kraemer (1981), who are researchers at the University of Southern California and the University of Arizona respectively. They contend that while the cost of hardware is falling, the total cost of electronic computing is rising rapidly (1981:101). Furthermore, many of the nonhardware costs tend to be hidden from normal accounting procedures used to justify implementation. So these costs do not necessarily affect the implementation decision itself, although they would adversely impact the firm's actual operating results.

King and Kraemer (1981:102) find that ". . .software procurement, software maintenance, and data management and computing management, are all becoming increasingly expensive." New positions and even departments are springing up in firms to evaluate software, perform system maintenance, coordinate among different users, etc. It is not unusual for firms to find that "off-the-shelf" software is unsatisfactory for their computing needs, necessitating significant investment in software programming. As electronic computing becomes more widespread in firms through the adoption of personal computers, King and Kraemer (1981:101) think that it will become increasingly difficult for management to track these costs. Users at all levels dedicate some portion of their time to routine maintenance tasks.

Some may even develop a personal interest in the technology which diverts them from other work.

According to King and Kraemer (1981:101), management seldom knows the ongoing costs of training, normal system maintenance, or unplanned downtime that are in fact incurred because of the firm's utilization of information technologies. They cite (1981:103) a variety of other studies and fragmentary data which appear to indicate that the annual costs for system maintenance run at least 20 percent of the cost of the development of the system itself and may even be much higher. They think the costs due to breakdowns may be particularly significant in highly integrated systems. According to King and Kraemer (1981:107),

> . . .when systems become integrated and units become more interdependent in a real-time sense, problems in one system or unit can literally stop progress in others simply by disruption of the *process* of interaction. As integration increases, interdependency increases. Together, these two phenomena result in increased costs.

It was just these kinds of changes in manufacturing process technology that led to the extreme reliability requirements that can impede the introduction of new technology. King and Kraemer's arguments should not be dismissed lightly.

Finally, it should be mentioned that even some computer vendors are not emphasizing cost savings *per se* in their attempts to sell office automation. Wang Laboratories (1985) makes available to potential customers a booklet about cost justification. It stresses the complexity of the cost justification process for office automation. One of the premises of the booklet (1985:3) is that information technology systems are fundamentally ". . .different from other kinds of capital equipment investments and should be treated differently with regard to cost justification." The booklet includes six examples of firms which have successfully cost-justified their systems. The emphasis in all cases is on improvements in quality rather than direct cost savings.

Although there appear to be no documented case studies of the economic impacts of office automation,[18] there is scattered evidence that at least casts some doubt on the most optimistic expectations for office automation. In general, these sources indicate that the costs of installation and continued operation of office automation systems are higher than most people think. If true, these additional costs would obviously translate into reduced productivity gains from office automation. But there are still other reasons why office automation may not have a significant impact on productivity.

First, one of the most obvious reasons that office automation may not have created measurable industrywide productivity gains is that the diffusion of the technology may not have proceeded nearly as far as implied by the popular media. According to a national random survey by Honeywell, Inc. (1983), of 1,264 general office secretaries employed in information-intensive establishments with 100 or more employees, office automation equipment was not yet in widespread use in many offices. Fewer than one-half of the secretaries reported having access to an electronic memory typewriter/word processor/personal computer in the general office area in which they work, less than one-fourth possessed any of this equipment at their individual workstation (1983:III-5). Given these results, it should not be surprising that almost none of the secretaries reported having direct access to electronic mail, computerized scheduling or computerized filing, while about 15 percent said that such equipment was located somewhere in the office area (1983:III-5).

These results are surprising in part because the sampling frame included only establishments with 100 or more employees, i.e., predominantly larger establishments, in information-intensive industries,[19] exactly where one would expect to find office automation in place. It should also be mentioned that there was a significant positive correlation in the survey between establishment size and the likelihood of having office automation equipment. Thus, this report lends some credence to the notion that very few small firms are using office automation equipment currently.

The second reason that office automation may not be having an impact on productivity is that investment in electronic office technology may not be synonymous with actually "automating the office." First, some portion of the purchases of office automation equipment is actually replacement investment, part of the normal capital requirement in that industry necessary to maintain productivity at today's levels. In other words, all capital equipment wears out and requires replacement, but ordinary replacement investment, even if it is microprocessor based, is really capital for capital substitution rather than office automation, or capital for labor substitution.

Second, office automation equipment may represent the deepening of capital supporting office workers rather than capital actually replacing labor. Competitive market pressures may be forcing some firms to adopt electronic office technology to insure their own survival. Apart from the question of whether electronic office technology saves labor time directly, there is no doubt that it permits more adequate analytical support for decisionmaking, more timely answers to customer inquiries, more rapid tracking of firm sales data allowing better inventory control, etc. It is simply not clear how or if such gains in quality translate directly into productivity.

Third, it appears that the adoption of office automation may eventually transform the product being produced rather than simply the process which is used to produce that product. Innovative products and services are being designed because electronic office technology is available to deliver those services. This new production and delivery of services creates jobs.

For example, the market for cash management accounts now easily exceeds $100 billion dollars annually. These accounts are used to maximize the interest yield from a customer's idle funds in checking, savings, credit cards, securities, and other similar accounts by transferring such monies to a money market account. The customer then receives one monthly statement summarizing the activities in the account. Merrill Lynch introduced these accounts in 1978. The point is that the electronically-based capital equipment which allowed the development of cash management accounts is generally the same hardware that is used in office automation, yet the development of cash management accounts creates jobs.

Another example of the evolution of products is the computerized reservation systems now is use by most airlines. How much have these systems contributed to the growth of air traffic? Would frequent flyer plans be possible without these systems? Would travel agents be as numerous if they were not tied into one of the general reservations systems? Would airlines fly as many passengers? Computerization may eliminate jobs through automation but it also begins to change some features of the products and services being produced, thereby creating jobs.

The problem is that it is impossible to look into the future and foresee the entirely new products and services that will eventually become commonplace. Along the way there will also be failures, products that are either not accepted by customers or which prove to be technically infeasible. But surely no one would disagree that major technological changes such as the railroads, autos and electricity, to name only a few, transformed the marketplace in ways that were not anticipated at first. Even though it may not be possible to identify the new products and goods that will be produced *because* new office technologies are available, it will occur nevertheless.

The third reason that office automation may not produce the anticipated productivity gains is the phenomena of added work. Anyone who is acquainted with word processors knows that it is irresistible to make one last revision when the marginal cost is so low. Those who have utilized electronic spreadsheet software know that it results in a whole new world of opportunities for tabular and graphical analyses. The problem is that since the output of offices cannot be measured simply and unequivocally, it is extremely difficult to know how much the new technologies have added to the effectiveness of the firm.

The expansion of existing work due to the capabilities of the technology cannot be dismissed as simply the failure of management to properly control the technology. What manager is satisfied with the information which he or she has available for decisionmaking? The installation of personal computers taps hidden computing needs that executives always had but that there was not the manpower or the time available to do on the firm's mainframe computer. The diffusion of the newer and cheaper microelectronic-based computer systems beyond the formally designated computer centers eliminates this roadblock. Suffice it to say that even the best managers and the best-managed offices take advantage of the lower marginal cost of computing by utilizing it in new and different ways.

The fourth reason that office automation may not be producing the promised productivity gains is that there may be technical constraints inherent in the current technology which reduce its effectiveness. For example, there are severe hardware and software compatibility problems across different computer systems. Complaints from firms abound concerning the current limitations of electronic mail. It is undoubtedly true that many firms discover the hard way that it doesn't work in the real world quite the way it did in the sales demonstration. This is a characteristic of new technology. It is not totally predictable until someone has found all the bugs and resolved all the problems.

When direct computer to computer communications systems are installed, say in the form of a local area network (LAN), it is still at present a relatively primitive system. It may not be possible to use the LAN to access the large data bases on the firm's mainframe computer. It may not be possible to transmit a graph via the network. While it may be possible to access a user who is not on the local area network, the procedure may be too tedious and cumbersome to be truly useful in the transmission of serious business messages. In short, the allowable traffic on the local area network may be very structured and severely limited by the available hardware and software. The office with instantaneous access to any data base around the world and total communications flexibility still lies somewhat in the future.

Many writers have compared this stage in the evolution of computers to that of autos in the 1920s. Automotive technology had already been firmly established by that time. What was needed, however, were the highways which would make it possible to effectively utilize the technological capability which already existed. According to this analogy, computers now need "pathways" to effectively communicate across dissimilar hardware and software systems before it is possible to realize their full potential.

In summary, this review of the technological influences on clerical employment has been realtively unsatisfying. There are no general time series data about office automation spending by industry or about the application of devices to the work done by particular occupations. The analysis of real output per hour of labor input in finance and insurance did not provide any evidence that office automation is producing significant productivity gains in that sector, despite the fact that real investment spending in finance and insurance has skyrocketed since the late 1960s.

There appear to be many possible explanations for the apparent lack of productivity gains from office automation to date. The data may be flawed. The diffusion of office automation may not have proceeded as far as many have thought. The equipment may be technically limited, more expensive and less productive than many think. It is also possible that much of what we term office automation is not being purchased as labor-saving process technology at all. There may be a deepening of capital occurring as products and services become more information-intensive.

Finally, it may well be that the major impact of office automation is not on the *quantity* of work at all. Rather the new office technologies may be manifest in the *quality* of work and in the hidden increases in output that are not measured by conventional techniques. The employment implications of office automation for clerical workers hinge on this issue. What is clear is that these questions have not yet been resolved.

Decomposition of Occupational Employment Changes

In earlier chapters the focus was on the overall trends in occupational employment, whereas in this chapter it has been on those factors which might explain occupational employment, namely (1) general economic conditions, (2) changes in the sectoral composition of the economy, and (3) the relative importance of the occupations within those sectors. What is needed is an analytical device to summarize the effects of these influences on occupational employment. Otherwise, it is all too easy to become lost in a morass of details.

The analytical tool which will be used to summarize changes in occupation-industry employment is a mathematical decomposition of occupational employment changes into the components due to overall economic growth, differences in the rates of growth of industries, and changes in the staffing ratios within industries. This tool is applied to the occupational employment changes which have occurred from 1972 to 1982, using the one-digit industries and occupations from the CPS data. It will also be used in the next chapter in analyzing the BLS occupational projections. A formal description of the decomposition can be found in the technical appendix to this chapter. The reader may also wish to refer back to tables 4.3 and 4.4 which introduced the concept of staffing ratios and the industry-occupation employment matrix.

Conceptual Description of Decomposition

Total employment by occupation is obtained by summing the employment in each occupation across all industries. The trend in occupational employment can be thought of as arising from three factors. First, the overall health of the economy, as indicated by total employment, exerts a strong influence on occupational employment. Without sufficient aggregate demand, employment in most occupations will surely fall. The second influence on occupational employment is the relative importance of the different industries in the total economy. Earlier in this chapter it was demonstrated that there are very wide differences in the proportions of clerical employment in different industries. Thus, if fast growth occurs only in those sectors with few clerical workers, overall clerical employment growth might still be slow. Finally, the third influence on occupational employment trends is the set of staffing ratios that characterize the different industries. Furthermore, changes in those occupational staffing ratios themselves can contribute to occupational employment trends.

It is really the simultaneous interaction of all three factors which determines employment trends in any particular occupation. But it is possible to artificially separate or decompose the change in occupational employment from one time period to another into components due to overall economic growth, differences in the rates of growth of industries, and changes in the staffing ratios within industries. The application of this mathematical method is limited, of course, by the availability of consistent data by industry and occupation. In the discussion that follows, the most recent time period for which data are available will be referred to as the current time period, while some earlier point is denoted as the base period.

The effects of changes in staffing ratios on occupational employment can be determined by comparing current employment by occupation to simulated employment levels in those occupations obtained by holding the staffing ratios constant at their base period values but using current industry employment as the multiplier. In other words, the simulated employment by occupation uses the "correct" industry employment levels—the actual current employment in those industries—but the "wrong" staffing ratios—those that existed in the base period. Thus the differences between current employment by occupation and the simulated employment levels indicate the extent to which changes in occupational employment can be attributed solely to staffing ratio changes.

As explained earlier, staffing ratios may change for many reasons, but one of those reasons is technological change. In fact, changing staffing ratios are probably the most visible manifestation of the *specific* effects of technological change on occupational employment. For example, the staffing ratios for computer-related occupations have risen in many industries over time due to the dramatic increases in the use of computers. On the other hand, the staffing ratios for stenographers have been falling over a long period of time due to the adoption of dictation machines, a technological change which reduces the need for stenographers.

If the net effect of office automation is truly the displacement of clerical jobs, then over time clerical staffing ratios will fall. Thus, the decomposition methodology provides another opportunity to assess the technological influence of office automation on clerical jobs. This attempt is sorely needed since the analysis in the previous section proved to be inconclusive about the productivity gains from office automation.

However, it should be emphasized that staffing ratios may change for other reasons, such as organizational change, job title change with no change in job content, or others. In particular it should be understood that any time an individual occupational staffing ratio changes, all of the remaining staffing ratios in that industry will change as well. This occurs because the sum of the staffing ratios in an industry must equal one (recall that staffing ratios are obtained by dividing each occupation's employment in that industry by total employment in the industry). Thus, if a particular industry were very successful in automating production worker jobs, perhaps by using robots, then the *relative* importance of other jobs such as clericals, professionals, etc. would increase. This demonstrates that changes in staffing ratios should not be considered in isolation; other changes may be taking place as well.

The effect of differential rates of industry growth on occupational employment can be examined by comparing the simulated employment levels which are obtained by holding the staffing ratios constant to yet another simulation which holds *both* staffing ratios and industry mix constant at their base period values, but uses total employment from the current period. In other words, this new simulation of occupational employment adds a second "error"—it uses the "wrong" industry mix as well as the "wrong" staffing ratios—but the "correct" total employment from the current period. The comparison of these two simulations isolates the occupational employment changes resulting from the concentration of particular occupations in industries growing at different rates. For example, clerical workers are particularly concentrated in finance and public administration. So clerical jobs will grow faster than the average for all jobs if these industries grow faster than the average for all industries (even without any changes in staffing ratios).

The remaining change in occupational employment can be attributed to overall growth in the economy. This effect is found by comparing the simulated employment levels which hold both staffing ratios and industry mix constant at base period levels to actual current employment in those occupations. If there were no changes in staffing ratios or the relative employment levels of industries, the importance of each occupation as a proportion of total employment would remain the same. In this case, differences between the simulated occupational employment levels and those of the base period are due entirely to total employment growth. This aspect of occupational employment change is referred to hereafter as constant employment shares since it assumes no change in either staffing ratios or the relative importance of industries.

It can be shown mathematically that the decomposition of occupational employment growth into changes due to

(1) constant employment shares (economic growth), (2) differential rates of industry growth, and (3) staffing ratio changes accounts for all of the change in occupational employment. But it is not an explanation of cause and effect; many complex economic and noneconomic factors lie hidden behind the numbers. It should also be mentioned that the results can be influenced by the level of aggregation and by the choice of the base period. Suffice it to say that the approach described in this section is used throughout this paper because it appears to approximate what BLS itself must do in adjusting historical staffing ratios for their projections. This matter is discussed further when the BLS projections are evaluated in chapter 5.

Occupational Decomposition, CPS Data

The three-way decomposition of occupational employment growth discussed in the previous section is applied to historical data for 1972 to 1982 from the Current Population Survey (CPS).[20] Although the major occupational and industrial groupings at the one-digit level are actually very heterogeneous, those industries and occupations are used in this analysis because the CPS sample is far too small to provide *both* industrial and occupational detail below that level. The time period for the analysis is 1972-1982 because that is the only recent time span for which consistent data are available. However, since 1982 was a recession year, there may be some distortions in the data. In sum, there are legitimate questions about the appropriateness of the time period and the level of aggregation used in this analysis. The expectation is that the one-digit CPS data will provide an overall perspective on trends in U.S. occupational employment growth that is not possible otherwise.

The results of the decomposition for the major occupational groupings are presented in table 4.7 and summarized in figure 4.5. Since this same approach will be used several times in this paper, the data for clerical workers in the table will be discussed carefully to insure a full understanding of the decomposition.

From 1972 to 1982 the number of clerical jobs increased by just over 4 million for a 28.8 percent gain over 1972 employment levels. During that same time span total employment increased by 21.1 percent. So clerical jobs grew faster than the average for all jobs, which also means that clerical jobs were becoming relatively more important in the national economy. This fact was demonstrated in chapter 1.

Turning to the occupational decomposition, it is possible to examine the factors which contributed to that clerical job growth. The bulk of all new clerical jobs, a little over three million, were added as a consequence of the overall growth of the economy, identified as constant employment shares in the table. Another 625,000 clerical jobs were added because clerical workers were more prevalent in industries that were growing faster than the average for all industries. This factor is labeled differential rates of industry growth in the table. Finally, 466,000 clerical jobs were added due to increasing staffing ratios for clerical jobs; that amounts to 3.3 percent of the 1972 employment level for clerical workers. This does not mean that staffing ratios in all industries were increasing for clerical occupations, but rather that the net effect across all industries was positive at this level of aggregation and for this time period.

Table 4.7 demonstrates very rapid growth in the professional and technical occupations and in the management and administrative field, more than double the average growth for all jobs. It is also very interesting to note that a significant proportion of the growth in these fields can be attributed to increasing staffing ratios for those jobs. In contrast, the impacts of changing staffing ratios for such oc-

Table 4.7
U.S. Occupational Employment Growth, 1972–1982

| | Employment changes | | | | Decomposition of employment changes, 1972–1982 | | | | | |
| | 1972 employment (000s) | 1982 employment (000s) | Change in employment 1972–1982 (000s) | Change in employment 1972–1982 (percent) | Absolute changes | | | Percent of 1972 occupational employment | | |
Occupation					Constant employment shares (000s)	Differential rates of industry growth (000s)	Staffing ratios (000s)	Constant employment shares	Differential rates of industry growth	Staffing ratios
Professional, technical	11,536	16,952	5,416	46.9	2,439	922	2,055	21.1	8.0	17.8
Managers, administrators	8,082	11,494	3,412	42.2	1,709	246	1,457	21.1	3.0	18.0
Sales workers	5,383	6,580	1,197	22.2	1,138	281	-222	21.1	5.2	-4.1
Clerical workers	14,326	18,446	4,120	28.8	3,029	625	466	21.1	4.4	3.3
Craft and kindred workers	10,867	12,271	1,404	12.9	2,298	-790	-104	21.1	-7.3	-1.0
Operatives	13,612	12,807	-805	-5.9	2,878	-1,457	-2,226	21.1	-10.7	-16.4
Laborers, non-farm	4,241	4,517	276	6.5	897	-203	-418	21.1	-4.8	-9.9
Service	11,024	13,736	2,712	24.6	2,331	1,102	-721	21.1	10.0	-6.5
Total	82,155	99,528	17,373	21.1						

SOURCE: Calculations by the authors based upon data from the *Current Population Survey*.

NOTE: Some occupational detail is omitted. Totals and percentages may not add exactly due to omission of some occupational detail and rounding error. The decomposition was accomplished using 1-digit SIC code industries.

Figure 4.5

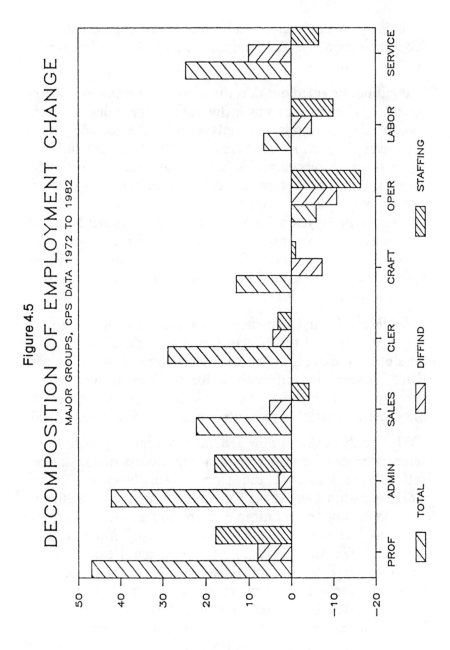

DECOMPOSITION OF EMPLOYMENT CHANGE

MAJOR GROUPS, CPS DATA 1972 TO 1982

cupations as craft and kindred workers, operatives, and laborers were all negative, undoubtedly influenced in part by the recession.

It cannot be ruled out that the reported increase in staffing ratios for clerical jobs was influenced to some degree by the level of aggregation in the analysis or by the declining staffing ratios for jobs that are traditionally more susceptible to layoffs during recessions. What can be said is that neither changing staffing ratios nor differential rates of industry growth were major contributors to clerical employment growth in the 10 years from 1972 to 1982, although both factors were modestly positive during the period. Both contributed to an overall occupational employment growth rate for clericals that was about one-third higher than the average growth rate for all jobs.

Since total employment growth for each occupation is merely the sum of the effects across all industries, it is also possible to look at the details of the decomposition for a particular occupation in each industry. The results of the decomposition of the growth in clerical jobs for each of the one-digit industries is presented in table 4.8 and figure 4.6.

This analysis shows how general economic expansion, differential rates of industry growth, and occupational staffing ratios have impacted the employment level of clerical workers within each of the listed industries. To take durable manufacturing as an example, there was an actual increase of 161,000 clerical workers (or 11.9 percent) in the industry between 1972 and 1982. Due to the general expansion of employment with economic growth, under the assumption of constant employment shares, clerical employment would have increased by 286,000 in this industry for this period. Furthermore, the positive figure for staffing ratio indicates that the more intensive utilization of clerical workers in durable manufacturing over the decade would have added

Table 4.8
U.S. Clerical Employment Growth by Industry, 1972–1982

| | Employment changes | | | | Decomposition of clerical employment changes, 1972–1982 | | | | | |
| | | | | | Absolute changes | | | Percent of 1972 employment | | |
Occupation	1972 employment (000s)	1982 employment (000s)	Change in employment 1972–1982 (000s)	Change in employment 1972–1982 (percent)	Constant employment shares (000s)	Differential rates of industry growth (000s)	Staffing ratios (000s)	Constant employment shares	Differential rates of industry growth	Staffing ratios
Agriculture.........	48	83	35	72.9	10	-11	36	21.1	-22.9	75.0
Mining	59	128	69	116.9	12	29	28	21.1	49.1	47.5
Construction	362	451	89	24.6	77	-44	56	21.1	-12.1	15.5
Durables..........	1,352	1,513	161	11.9	286	-244	119	21.1	-18.0	8.8
Nondurables	1,040	1,074	34	3.3	220	-222	36	21.1	-21.3	3.5
Utilities..........	1,307	1,463	156	11.9	276	-23	-97	21.1	-1.8	-7.4
Wholesale trade....	684	844	160	23.4	145	86	-71	21.1	12.6	-10.4
Retail trade........	2,099	2,840	741	35.3	444	45	252	21.1	2.1	12.0
Finance...........	2,007	2,750	743	37.0	424	457	-138	21.1	22.8	-6.9
Services..........	3,691	5,473	1,782	48.3	781	605	396	21.1	16.4	10.7
Public administration	1,678	1,827	149	8.9	355	-53	-153	21.1	-3.2	-9.1
Total...........	14,326	18,446	4,120	28.8	3,029	625	466	21.1	4.4	3.2

SOURCE: Calculations by the authors based upon data from the *Current Population Survey*.
NOTE: Totals and percentages may not add exactly due to rounding.

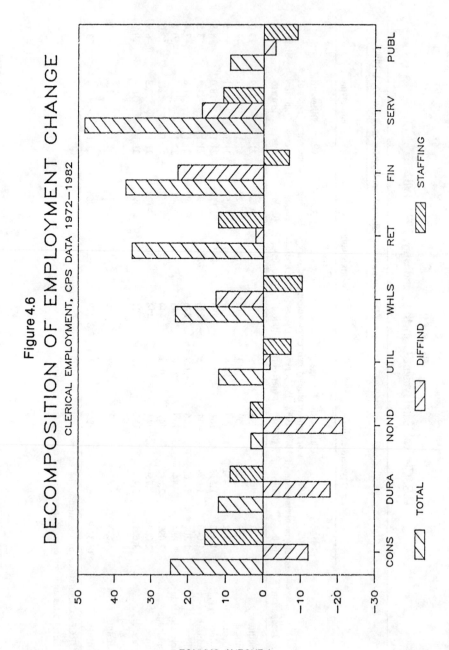

Figure 4.6

DECOMPOSITION OF EMPLOYMENT CHANGE

CLERICAL EMPLOYMENT, CPS DATA 1972–1982

another 119,000 clerical jobs. However, the slow rate of growth of durable manufacturing employment meant that 244,000 fewer clerical jobs were created than would have been created if durable manufacturing employment had expanded at the same rate as all employment.

What is particularly striking in this second set of tables is that staffing ratios for clerical jobs were *falling* in a number of sectors. Most interesting are the results for the finance sector, probably the biggest user of office automation to date. The finance sector has been a rapidly growing sector as indicated by the 37 percent overall growth rate of clerical jobs in that sector versus the 28.8 percent growth rate for all clerical jobs. Thus, the effects of falling staffing ratios, which alone would have reduced jobs in this sector by 6.9 percent from 1972 employment levels, were more than made up by the fast growth of the industry itself. However, if the industry had not expanded so rapidly, there might have been actual reductions in employment of clerical workers in the finance sector.

Staffing ratios for clerical jobs have also been falling in three other important industries—utilities, wholesale trade, and public administration. The decline in public administration is difficult to explain. No one maintains that government has been in the forefront in adopting office automation. On the other hand, the postal service has automated a great many clerical jobs in the mail sorting operation. It is also true that government was one of the slowest growing sectors during this time period. So it is possible that government administrators, when faced with tight budgets and rising demands for services, economized more on clerical jobs than other positions. It is not yet possible to provide an adequate explanation of the fall in staffing ratios for public administration or the other industries. Clearly, more study of these trends is called for.

In summary, the occupational decomposition using the CPS data indicates that clerical jobs have at a minimum maintained their relative importance in the economy from 1972 to 1982. In fact, both the effects of differential rates of industry growth and change in staffing ratios were moderately positive. Thus, clerical jobs were actually slightly more important at the end of the period than at the beginning of the period. This confirms the results in chapter 1 on the overview of clerical employment. However, 1982 was a recession year so these results should be interpreted with caution. It is also true that some of the major employers of clerical workers demonstrated negative staffing ratio trends over this period. Finance, generally acknowledged to be the biggest user of office automation today, experienced declining staffing ratios for clericals during this time period. Similar trends were observed for clerical employment in utilities, wholesale trade, and public administration. So it is possible that office automation is negatively impacting clerical jobs in selected sectors.

Conclusions

The decomposition methodology of the last section of this chapter is an attempt to summarize the three important influences on clerical employment growth which were discussed earlier in this chapter. Since it appears to be impossible to directly link office automation to the productivity gains of clerical workers, it might be said that this approach looks at the changes in staffing patterns across industries as an indicator of the net impact of technology and other factors on clerical employment over the time period being examined.

The decomposition also has the added advantage that it puts into proper perspective the important roles that economic growth and the changing composition of industries play in determining clerical employment. According to this analysis, clerical job growth is heavily determined by overall economic growth. This conclusion should not be surprising, but many people find it all too easy to discover other reasons which purportedly explain employment changes. In fact, not only is economic growth by far the most important factor in determining clerical employment, but it appears that the correlation may be growing stronger. If the last recession is a precursor of the future, clerical jobs are becoming more like other jobs in their sensitivity to general economic conditions.

It is well known that the changing composition of industries has tended to favor clerical jobs. But the peak in the influence of industry mix on clerical employment probably occurred during the late 1950s and 1960s. During the 1970s, industry mix continued to positively influence clerical employment but only moderately so. It is also true that some sectors which are heavy employers of clericals have recently begun to experience much slower growth or even absolute declines in total employment. This is particularly apparent for hospitals and state and local government, the latter of which is the largest single employer of clericals. So, even though other sectors, notably services, will likely continue to grow rapidly, there is reason to think that industry mix will play a less positive role in the future employment outlook for clerical workers than it has in the past.

The net effect of changing staffing ratios on clerical employment has also been moderately positive in the last decade or so. Economywide, there appears to be little evidence that office automation has negatively impacted clerical jobs in the past. However, it does appear that staffing ratios for clerical workers are declining slightly in some sectors, especially finance. So, it is at least possible that office automation is raising the productivity of clerical workers and thereby contributing to the falling staffing ratios in those sectors.

It is puzzling that the aggregate productivity data for finance and insurance showed below average productivity growth for the sector as a whole, yet the decomposition analysis showed declining staffing ratios for clerical jobs within finance and insurance. Since clerical jobs are so important to this sector, it is logical to think that falling staffing ratios for these jobs might also be associated with realized productivity gains. But it should be recalled that the aggregate productivity data may be seriously flawed, the loss of jobs in this sector due to falling staffing ratios was relatively modest, and there could have been offsetting employment gains elsewhere in the sector. If nothing else, this review has demonstrated that there are many unanswered questions about employment trends for clericals in some sectors such as finance and insurance. Further study of these trends is critical to a better understanding of the ultimate employment impacts of office automation.

The examination of the historical evidence on clerical jobs has been a sobering experience. Clerical employment has grown rapidly in the last 40 years or so. But many factors appear to confirm that the growth of clerical jobs has slowed in the last decade. Based upon the review in this chapter, it is difficult to see how anyone could expect much more than average growth for clerical jobs in the future.

NOTES

1. The brief discussion in this section draws on the concepts embodied in the national economic accounting system of the U.S. For an introduction to that system, see Young and Tice (1985) and Carson and Jaszi (1981).

2. Edwin Mansfield has spent much of his professional life analyzing the economics of technological change. For a brief nontechnical introduction to this subject, see Mansfield (1971).

3. For a nontechnical introduction to productivity analysis and its relation to employment and income, see Kendrick (1977).

4. Since the beginnings of the Industrial Revolution, there have been periodic "automation scares." It is difficult to determine if robotics, office automation, and other closely related emerging technologies today constitute another such crisis. The concern about automation in the late 1950s-early 1960s was so great that it led to the creation of a national commission to study technology, automation, and economic progress. The commission concluded that sluggish demand was the problem rather than automation. For an abridged version of the voluminous reports and studies conducted by the commission, see Bowen and Mangum (1966).

5. For analytical purposes only and ease of exposition, GNP is being treated here as if it were a composite good.

6. The year 1982 is chosen because it is the most recent year in the CPS data base for which the historical estimates are consistent.

7. The authors kindly thank George I. Treyz, University of Massachusetts, and President, Regional Economic Models, Inc., for constructing the BLS input-output industry series and for aggregating the OES industry-occupation data.

8. It should also be noted that the specificity of industry definition varies. Thus the ranking also reflects a variety of aggregation levels in the industries themselves. In general, more detailed data are available about manufacturing industries than nonmanufacturing industries.

9. Economists have developed multifactor productivity measures, usually denoted as "total factor productivity." Denison (1962, 1974, 1979) pioneered the "growth accounting" approach in which he attempts to isolate the contribution of a variety of causal factors such as education, organization, and research to productivity growth. Kendrick (1973,

1980, 1983) has built industry indexes and recently the BLS (Mark and Waldorf 1983) has released their first measures of multifactor productivity.

10. One alternative possibility, of course, is that the productivity gains across all occupations are homogeneous, which means staffing ratios would remain constant. It is also theoretically possible for productivity gains to be greater for other occupations, implying rising staffing ratios for clericals. These matters are discussed further in the last section of this chapter.

11. The household-based data from the CPS appear to contradict this statement since it showed (table 4.3) that 44 percent of employees in finance are clericals. This broad sector in the CPS data actually includes real estate as well as finance and insurance, but the similarly defined sector in the establishment-based OES survey indicates that 53.4 percent of employees are clericals. Recalling the discussion from chapter 1, this anomaly in the data is most likely an example of respondents in the self-reported household survey (the CPS) exaggerating their job titles and responsibilities, thereby artificially decreasing employment in the lower level specialties such as clericals.

12. For definitions of the constant dollar output and employment measures, see Bulletin 2018, *Time Series Data for Input-Output Industries: Output, Price and Employment* (March 1979). The actual data utilized in this paper are from an unpublished update (April 1985) to the tables in the aforementioned document.

13. Specific units of outputs are much less identifiable in services than in the goods-producing sectors. There may also be significant changes in the types and nature of services provided. See Mark (1982) and Fuchs (1969) for a discussion of the many problems in measuring productivity in service industries.

14. The Office of Productivity and Technology is responsible for the U.S. Government's productivity measurement program. They currently publish about 129 separate industry productivity indexes. See Bureau of Labor Statistics (1985).

15. The investment data are from the national income and product accounts. See Seskin and Sullivan (1985).

16. The trend in investment per employee is important because it indicates whether something new appears to be happening in that sector, but it is by no means the full story. Historically, absolute investment per

employee in finance and insurance has tended to be much less than the average for all nonfarm private industries. That situation reversed itself in the 1970s.

17. An article which appeared recently in the *Harvard Business Review* (Salerno 1985) makes this very point. Vendors have promoted their products excessively, yet there is little hard evidence to support their claims.

18. Salerno (1985) and Strassman (1985) have reached similar conclusions. There is, however, considerable literature about the sociological impacts of office automation. For a review and introduction to this literature, see Attewell and Rule (1984). From the economist's perspective, these studies are lacking in a systematic treatment of output, capital input, prices of outputs and inputs, and other economic variables.

19. The report does not specify the definition of information-intensive industries.

20. It should be mentioned that the other obvious candidate for such a decomposition, the Census of Population data, cannot be used. As discussed in chapter 1, it is a major task to redefine census occupations so that they are consistent over time. It is impossible to do it for occupations within industries without a special dual classification study.

TECHNICAL APPENDIX

OCCUPATIONAL DECOMPOSITION

1. Let E_{ij}^t = employment

    where

    t = time

    $i = 1, 2, 3 \ldots$ m occupations

    $j = 1, 2, 3 \ldots$ n industries

    Then, suppressing the time superscripts until they become necessary,

    E_{ij} = matrix of employment by occupation and industry

    $$E_i = \sum_j^n E_{ij}$$

    $$E_j = \sum_i^m E_{ij}$$

    Thus E_i is a vector of occupational employment, the row sums of E_{ij}, and E_j is a vector of industry employment, the column sums of E_{ij}.

    If measured perfectly, then total employment E_T is given by

    $$E_T = \sum_i^m E_i = \sum_j^n E_j$$

2. Let $e_{ij} = \dfrac{E_i}{E_j}$

    and $s_j = \dfrac{E_i}{E_T}$

    Thus e_{ij} is a matrix of occupational proportions by industry or the staffing ratios of those industries. Each cell represents the relative importance of the ith occupation in the jth industry.

    It is also possible to think of occupational employment by industry then as the product of the staffing ratios, the industry shares, and total employment, i.e.,

    $$E_{ij} = e_{ij} \cdot s_j \cdot E_T = \frac{E_{ij}}{E_j} \cdot \frac{E_j}{E_T} \cdot E_T = E_{ij}$$

197

and the total occupational employment vector as

$$E_i = E_T \cdot \sum_{j}^{n} (e_{ij} \cdot s_j)$$

In other words, occupational employment in a single occupation in any given year can be thought of as being influenced by 3 separate elements:

(1) Total employment (E_T)

(2) the relative importance of that occupation in each industry (e_{ij})

(3) and the relative importance of the industries in the total economy (s_j)

3. It is possible to mathematically decompose occupational change from one time period to another. As an example, consider the time period 1972-1982. The actual occupational change is obviously

$$(E_T^{82} \cdot \sum_{j}^{n} (e_{ij}^{82} \cdot s_j^{82}) - E_T^{72} \cdot \sum_{j}^{n} (e_{ij}^{72} \cdot s_j^{72}))$$

or

$$(E_i^{82} - E_i^{72})$$

Although it is easier notationally to use E_i^t rather than $E_T^t \cdot \sum_{j} (e_{ij}^t \cdot s_j^t)$, the latter illustrates the decomposition much better.

a. *Occupation change due to changing staffing ratios*

One component of the occupational change is that which occurs because of changing staffing ratios across industries. It can be estimated by

$$(E_T^{82} \cdot \sum_{j}^{n} (e_{ij}^{82} \cdot s_j^{82}) - E_T^{82} \cdot \sum_{j}^{n} (e_{ij}^{72} \cdot s_j^{82}))$$

where $E_T^{82} \cdot \sum_{j}^{n} (e_{ij}^{72} \cdot s_j^{82})$ is the occupational employment that would exist in 1982 given the mix of industries that actually exist in 1982 (s_j^{82}) and 1982's total employment *but* using 1972 staffing ratios. Thus, this latter expression is a simulated 1982 employment assuming fixed staffing ratios at the 1972 levels.

198

b. Occupational change due to differential rates of industry growth

The second component of occupational change is that which occurs because of differential rates of industry growth. It can be estimated by

$$(E_T^{82} \cdot \sum_j^n (e_{ij}^{72} \cdot s_j^{82}) - E_T^{82} \cdot \sum_j^n (e_{ij}^{72} \cdot s_j^{72}))$$

The first component is obviously 1982's simulated employment using 1972 staffing ratios, while the second component, $E_T^{82} \cdot \sum_j^n (e_{ij}^{72} \cdot s_j^{72})$, is that employment which would exist in 1982 if *both* staffing ratios and industry shares were fixed at their 1972 levels but 1982's actual total employment. Thus, this second expression is also a simulated 1982 employment, and the difference isolates the effect of differential rates of growth of industries.

c. Occupational change due to total employment change

The third component of occupational change is that due to overall employment growth. It can be estimated by

$$(E_T^{82} \cdot \sum_j^n (e_{ij}^{72} \cdot s_j^{72}) - E_T^{72} \cdot \sum_j^n (e_{ij}^{72} \cdot s_j^{72}))$$

The first component is 1982's simulated employment with staffing ratios and industry shares fixed at the 1972 level, while the second component is 1972's actual employment by occupation. This difference is the occupational employment change which would occur if there were no changes in the relative importance of industries or occupations, i.e., if all occupations would maintain constant employment shares.

4. The sum of the changes in 3a, 3b, and 3c is the total change in employment by occupation. Letting

$$\widetilde{E}_i^{82} = E_T^{82} \cdot \sum_j^n (e_{ij}^{72} \cdot s_j^{82})$$

$$\widetilde{\widetilde{E}}_i^{82} = E_T^{82} \cdot \sum_j^n (e_{ij}^{72} \cdot s_j^{72})$$

then the total change in employment by occupation is:

$$E_i^{82} - E_i^{72} = (E_i^{82} - \widetilde{E}_i^{82}) + (\widetilde{E}_i^{82} - \widetilde{\widetilde{E}}_i^{82}) + (\widetilde{\widetilde{E}}_i^{82} - E_i^{72})$$

5

Forecasts of the Clerical Employment Implications of Technological Change

This monograph heretofore has dealt exclusively with historical data. The purpose of this chapter is to review the existing forecasts for clerical jobs. The Bureau of Labor Statistics (BLS) occupational projections are the major effort of the U.S. government to anticipate the needs for specific occupations. As will be seen shortly, the BLS methodology is based on a modeling framework that accounts for many economic variables. The resulting occupational projections are not necessarily superior to others, but they do have the advantage of being produced in a comprehensive and reasonably consistent manner.

Other forecasts that are less comprehensive than the BLS efforts but potentially useful are also reviewed. First, Wassily Leontief and Faye Duchin (1984) of New York University have produced an analysis of the impacts of automation on employment, 1963-2000. The research is limited to certain specified computer technologies and does not consider other productivity-enhancing technologies or any other source of productivity growth. Second, the work of Matthew P. Drennan (1983) of Columbia University is examined. He focuses on clerical jobs in six office industries, primarily within the finance sector. Finally, the recent work of J. David Roessner (1984), Georgia Institute of Technology, is reviewed. Like

201

Drennan, he examines clerical jobs within the finance sector, but he focuses on only two industries, banking and insurance.

BLS Occupational Employment Projections

In order to understand the BLS occupational projections it is necessary first to review the data base on which those projections are based—the Occupational Employment Statistics (OES) progam. Then the BLS projections methodology will be described. Finally, the most recent projections of BLS are examined.

OES Data Base

The OES data base evolved in the 1970s as a cooperative effort of the Bureau of Labor Statistics and the state employment security agencies to make career guidance information available to educators, guidance personnel, human resource planners, students, and other interested parties.[1] OES is unique in that it is based on a survey of employers. All three-digit SIC industries are grouped into one of three primary areas for data collection. Each of the three primary areas is sampled on a rotating schedule every three years.[2] Thus, for instance, the individual three-digit manufacturing industries were sampled in 1977, 1980, and 1983. Every two years the BLS pulls all of this data together into a national occupational-industrial matrix; the last one was for 1982.

The OES system includes tabulations of nearly 1,700 occupations. The emphasis is on ease of administration, so the occupational classification system reflects employer usage of job titles. This means that there is actually less detail available than is implied by the 1,700 occupational titles in the OES system. A large number of the 1,700 job titles are actually quite specific to a particular industry or sector. According to the most recent OES data, there are almost 1,000 OES occupations with less than 5,000 employees nationwide.

The occupational definitions used by the BLS were developed prior to those in the Standard Occupational Classifiction (SOC) system of the U.S. Department of Commerce, but they are based upon the *Dictionary of Occupational Titles* (Employment and Training Administration 1977), hereafter referred to as the DOT. BLS, like other federal agencies, is trying to make its definitions consistent with the SOC. The next round of occupational projections from BLS will be based upon the SOC. This should make them roughly consistent with 1980 census data, although it will not eliminate the well-known differences between household- and employer-based data. Currently the OES data are not consistent with any other source of occupational information.

The OES data base provides the most detailed information available about occupational employment in the United States. However, it is oriented to job titles and does not really provide any significant skill level information. The DOT, which does provide this type of information, lists over 12,000 specific occupations. While the DOT covers an impressive array of occupations, it includes no information at all on employment levels for those occupations. It was developed as an occupational guidance tool for use in the employment service offices to match unemployed workers with possible occupational opportunities.[3] The emphasis is on the requirements for entry to the occupation, not the number of people employed in the occupation.

In practice there are severe tradeoffs between the specificity of the occupational categories, the skill levels referenced in those occupations, and the cost to collect the data. As the number of occupational categories increases, the definitions for those occupations will become narrower and more ade-

quately convey skill levels. Clearly, the occupational
category of professional and scientific workers is less informative about skill requirements than that of chemical
engineers. At the same time, it should be obvious that costs
may increase dramatically as the detail of occupational information increases. It also adds to the reporting burden on
firms or households where the data are collected.[4]

BLS Occupational Projections Methodology

The OES system is used primarily as a data base for BLS
employment projections by occupation. The 1995 occupational employment projections for manufacturing utilize the
OES survey results from 1980 and industry employment
figures for 1982 as a baseline. It is helpful to examine the
OES forecasting system in more detail for the insight it offers into the complexity of making occupational projections.

The OES forecasting system is actually a group of separate
projections which are linked to each other for consistency.
Aggregate economywide economic activity is forecast first.
This includes labor force projections by age, race and sex,
and aggregate output decomposed into its major components, among other variables. Due to BLS budget constraints and the large amount of staff time necessary to
maintain an aggregate econometric model, the most recent
aggregate forecasts were made using the existing model at
Chase Econometrics, Inc. BLS produced the forecasts using
their own assumptions but accepting the economic interrela-
tions implicit in the Chase model.

The second step in the OES forecasting system is to
develop industry output projections that are consistent with
the aggregate output projections of step one. The 156-sector
input-output model, prepared by the Bureau of Economic
Analysis, U.S. Department of Commerce, is used as a base
for these projections. Given a set of industry demand

figures, an input-output model can calculate the total industrial production required to meet those demands. The BLS input-output system utilizes "bridge tables" to update the historical input-output coefficients and to allow for anticipated shifts in demand for inputs and/or outputs over the period of the projection.

Once the industry output projections are determined, then productivity levels are forecast to arrive at total industry employment requirements. The productivity gains are estimated separately for each industry utilizing an econometric equation. Worker-hours are estimated as a function of the industry's output, capacity utilization, relative price of labor, and (as a proxy for technology) the output/capital ratio. The implication of the technology proxy is that more capital per unit of output implies the need for less worker-hours. Finally, the estimates of total worker-hours are combined with other estimates of average annual hours per person to arrive at the industry employment levels.

The last step in the OES projections system is to forecast occupational employment within these industry total employment levels. The basis for these projections is the occupational staffing patterns from the latest OES surveys. The individual occupational coefficients are adjusted on a judgmental basis to account for the changes in occupational demand anticipated as a result of technological change, changes in industry structure, or other reasons. For example, computer-related occupations will likely become relatively more important in many industries as computers are more widely applied in those industries. So the coefficients for these occupations are increased correspondingly. These revised staffing coefficients are then applied to the previously forecast level of industry total employment. The sum of the employment across all industries for a given OES occupation then becomes the new occupational employment projection of BLS.

Several features of the OES system should be noted, particularly those that relate to technological change. Technological change actually enters the system in at least three places. First, the industry output projections should account for anticipated changes in demand induced by technological change. Second, the estimated productivity gains forecast for each industry should be influenced by technological change. Finally, the staffing patterns themselves are altered directly to account for technological change. In other words, technological change will have specific effects on some occupations, it will have an overall impact on the productivity of workers, and it will affect the demand for goods and services generally.

It is worthy of note that this system involves a considerable amount of judgment, especially in anticipating the effects of technological change. There are no simple equations that predict changes in staffing ratios within an industry. In fact, the BLS staff has found that trends in industry employment levels can be predicted more accurately than the changes in occupational employment (Kutscher 1982:8; and Office of Economic Growth and Employment Projections, 1981). This is due in large part to the difficulty of projecting specific occupational impacts of technological change.

One of the primary motivations in developing the occupational decomposition as an analytical tool in chapter 4 is its usefulness in evaluating the BLS occupational projections. Note that the last step in the BLS methodology is to change the staffing ratios in the industry occupation matrix to account for technological change and other factors. In other words, BLS takes the best industrial demand and productivity forecast that it can muster and converts that into projections of total employment by industry. Then it considers changing the staffing ratios from their historical levels.

Thus, by using the historical staffing ratios from the base period of the BLS projections, the occupational decomposition will measure the extent to which BLS *expects* staffing ratios to change over the course of the projection. Since BLS does not currently publish information on why or how much it has changed staffing ratios, this analysis should prove very helpful in understanding their projections.

The current base period for the BLS projections is 1982, while the year of projection is 1995. The industry-occupation matrix contains 378 industries, but those industries are aggregated to 105 industries in this analysis. These 105 industries are the lowest common denominator between the 156 industrial sectors of the BLS input-output model and the 378 industries of the BLS/OES industry-occupation matrix. Since the BLS makes available *annual* projections for its industry employment series, it is thereby possible to compare the historical industry employment trends developed here to the BLS projections for those industries.

However, it should be pointed out that the BLS input-output industry employment series is not strictly comparable to the BLS/OES industry employment estimates.[5] There are differences in their treatment of government, agriculture, and the self-employed, among others. The important point for this paper is that the 378 OES industries were first aggregated to 105 OES industries. Thus the occupational decomposition of the BLS occupational projections is always accomplished with industry employment data from OES itself. The BLS input-output industry data is reserved exclusively to examine trends in industry employment. Since the BLS input-output industry data feed into the OES system, it should be clear that the employment trends from those data are an important determinant of the occupational projections as well.

BLS Industry Employment Projections

In chapter 4 the historical employment trends for the 10 BLS input-output industries which account for the largest number of clerical jobs were reviewed. Those 10 industries employed about two-thirds of all clerical workers in 1982. Thus the fortunes of these industries will have a major impact on the employment of clerical workers in the years ahead. In this section the BLS projections of employment for these industries are reviewed. It provides an opportunity to evaluate the industry forecasts independent of their occupational content. Since the occupational decomposition summarizes the effects of differences in the rates of growth of all industries, the focus here is limited to the 10 industries responsible for the most clerical jobs.

The combined employment trends for the top 10 industries in terms of clerical employment are presented in figure 5.1, while the employment trends for each of those 10 industries follows in table 5.1. The figure depicts the historical growth trends, 1967-1982, as well as the projected growth trends, 1983-1995. Remember, the most recent BLS occupational projections used 1982 as the base year, so BLS did not have the benefit of the industry employment data from 1983 and 1984 presented in chapter 4 of this monograph when making their forecast. The data are reported in index number form to emphasize the relative growth of the industries. The total employment trend for all 105 industries is also presented to facilitate comparison of the growth of each industry to the overall growth of employment.

In the past, the industries with the most clerical jobs have been much faster growing than the average for all industries.[6] But the magnitude of that positive differential was reduced sharply in the last decade and BLS does not expect it to reappear by 1995. If these projections are correct, the 10 industries which account for about two-thirds of all

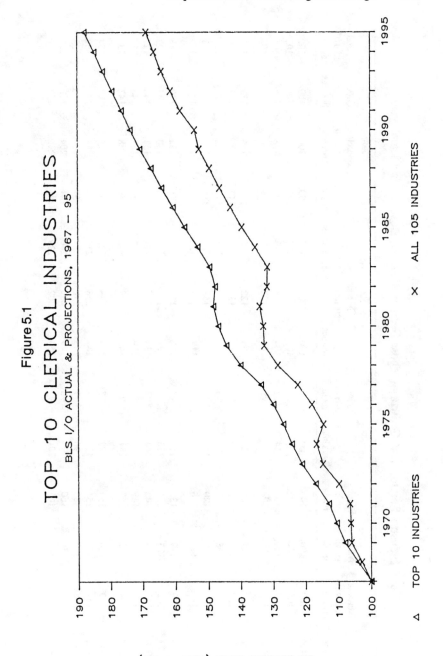

Figure 5.1

TOP 10 CLERICAL INDUSTRIES

BLS I/O ACTUAL & PROJECTIONS, 1967 – 95

Table 5.1
Total Industry Employment Growth of Those Sectors with the Most Clerical Employees

Year	State & local government	Misc. retail trade	Whole- sale trade	Banking	Federal govern- ment	Insurance	Misc. business services	Hospitals	Social services/ museums	Credit agencies/ commodity brokers	Total top 10 industries	Total all 105 industries
1967	100	100	100	100	100	100	100	100	100	100	100	100
1968	105	104	102	106	101	103	107	106	105	109	104	103
1969	109	108	106	114	102	104	118	113	103	118	108	106
1970	113	110	108	121	99	108	122	118	103	116	111	106
1971	117	112	109	124	98	108	122	126	110	116	113	107
1972	122	115	112	129	97	110	131	137	114	122	117	110
1973	127	118	117	136	96	113	145	143	114	126	121	115
1974	131	119	120	144	98	117	153	151	116	127	124	117
1975	137	115	126	147	98	119	157	158	125	128	127	115
1976	139	119	130	151	98	121	168	164	128	132	130	118
1977	142	123	135	156	97	127	183	170	130	140	134	122
1978	148	128	142	164	97	133	204	177	134	151	140	129
1979	151	130	149	173	98	139	225	183	137	161	144	133
1980	154	129	150	181	99	143	239	192	139	168	147	133
1981	153	130	153	188	97	145	253	203	139	179	148	134
1982	151	129	151	191	97	147	256	210	139	184	148	132
1983	148	130	155	190	97	145	278	227	137	204	150	132
1984	150	136	160	194	96	149	286	230	141	204	153	136
1985	152	141	163	201	97	154	302	239	145	212	157	140

Year												
1986	153	145	166	207	96	158	319	248	149	220	161	143
1987	155	149	169	211	96	162	333	256	152	225	164	146
1988	158	152	171	216	96	166	344	262	155	230	167	150
1989	161	156	172	221	97	171	355	269	158	236	171	153
1990	164	159	172	225	98	174	368	276	160	243	174	154
1991	167	164	174	228	99	177	366	276	162	240	176	158
1992	168	168	178	234	99	180	374	281	164	143	179	161
1993	169	170	181	238	99	183	389	288	165	249	182	164
1994	171	172	184	241	99	184	410	297	166	258	185	166
1995	172	172	185	244	99	184	445	312	166	274	188	169

SOURCE: Calculations by the authors based upon data from BLS.

clerical jobs will grow at roughly the same rate as all jobs over the period of the projection.

It is natural for the combined growth trend of all 10 industries to mask some important differences among the industries. The figures for the individual industries in table 5.1 reveal that the laggards in terms of industry growth are state and local government and the federal government. Employment by the federal government is not expected to increase at all, while state and local government are expected to reverse the declines suffered in the 1980-82 recession and grow once again, albeit significantly more slowly than average. Apparently BLS is convinced that the demands for a smaller and more efficient government will continue in the coming years. The data on employment in state and local government in 1983-84 are supportive of the BLS outlook.

The fastest growing industries among the top 10 employers of clerical workers according to the BLS projections are credit agencies and commodity brokers, hospitals, miscellaneous business services, and banking. Of these, one of the more surprising projections is the growth anticipated for banking, which outgrows the overall economy throughout the period of the projection. Considerable attention has been focused on banking employment in the last couple of years, and it does appear that the industry is experiencing significant structural change due to deregulation, among other factors. The closing of branch or satellite banks, especially in such states as California, and employment declines in a few of the largest banks in the nation, have contributed to speculation that the growth of banking employment may slow. There is also the question of the impacts of office automation equipment such as automatic teller machines. In contrast, deregulation has also increased the number of financial services banks provide, so it is possible to argue that banking employment will continue to grow.

If one were to judge the quality of the BLS industry projections strictly on their ability to anticipate the trends which actually occurred during 1983-84, only two years into the projection period, then unquestionably BLS's greatest failure was in missing the turnaround which actually occurred in hospital employment. As demonstrated in chapter 4, employment in hospitals grew slowly in 1983 and actually declined in 1984. By 1984 hospital employment was 1 percent below the employment levels which prevailed in 1982, the base year for the BLS projection. But the BLS projections had forecast a 10 percent growth in employment in hospitals from 1982-84.

This example demonstrates some of the problems in employment forecasting. Employment in hospitals increased every year from 1958 to 1983, more than tripling throughout that period. The concern about cost containment in this sector is not new, but it appears that only in the last few years has the federal government taken policy actions that might reduce the growth of those costs. These actions have also encouraged insurance firms and hospitals to follow suit with their own programs. The health care industry today is also generally becoming more competitive. The bottom line is that it is extremely difficult to foresee these turnarounds, yet easy to explain them after they have occurred. BLS will undoubtedly take advantage of the new information about this sector in the next round of projections.

Decomposition of Major Occupational Groups, *BLS Occupational Employment Projections*

The decomposition of the BLS occupational employment projections at the major group level are presented in table 5.2 and summarized graphically in figure 5.2. As discussed earlier, the 378 OES industries were first aggregated to 105 industries before accomplishing the decomposition. It

Table 5.2
BLS Projected Occupational Employment Growth, 1982-1995

| | Employment changes | | | | Decomposition of employment changes, 1982-1995 | | | | | |
| | | | | | Absolute changes | | | Percent of 1982 occupational employment | | |
Occupation	1982 employment (000s)	1995 employment (000s)	Change in employment 1982-1995 (000s)	Change in employment 1982-1995 (percent)	Constant employment shares (000s)	Differential rates of industry growth (000s)	Staffing ratios (000s)	Constant employment shares	Differential rates of industry growth	Staffing ratios
Professional, technical	15,071	20,177	5,106	33.9	4,228	-99	977	28.1	-0.7	6.5
Managers, officials .	7,696	10,659	2,963	38.5	2,159	162	642	28.1	2.1	8.3
Sales workers	5,906	7,704	1,798	30.4	1,657	141	0	28.1	2.4	0.0
Clerical workers	18,717	23,673	4,957	26.5	5,251	295	-588	28.1	1.6	-3.1
Craft and related workers ..	10,133	13,223	3,089	30.5	2,843	36	211	28.1	0.4	2.1
Operatives	12,504	14,896	2,392	19.1	3,508	-566	-550	28.1	-4.5	-4.4
Laborers, nonfarm .	5,572	6,794	1,222	21.9	1,563	-203	-139	28.1	-3.6	-2.5
Service workers	15,318	19,727	4,408	28.8	4,297	580	-469	28.1	3.8	-3.1
Total	91,950	117,745	25,795	28.1						

SOURCE: Calculations by the authors based upon data tape from the 1982-1995 OES/BLS occupational employment projections.

NOTE: Some occupational detail is omitted. Totals and percentages may not add exactly due to omission of some occupational detail and rounding error. The 378 OES industries were first aggregated to 105 industries before accomplishing the decomposition. The OES data tape includes wage and salary employment only.

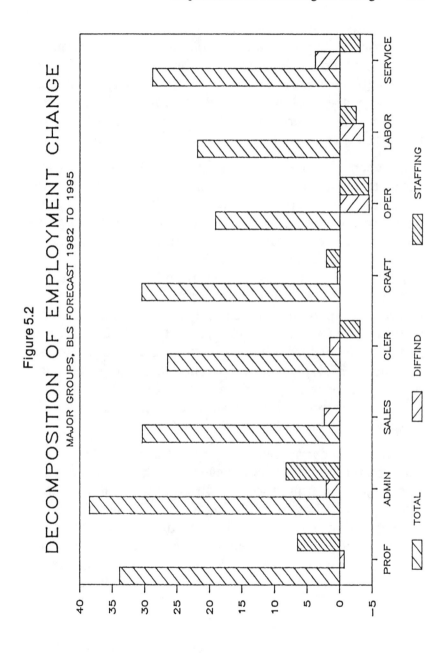

Figure 5.2

DECOMPOSITION OF EMPLOYMENT CHANGE

MAJOR GROUPS, BLS FORECAST 1982 TO 1995

should also be mentioned that the OES data tape used for these calculations is not strictly comparable to the summary data from the projections published in *Monthly Labor Review* (Silvestri 1983). Among other differences, the OES data tape does not include the self-employed. Thus, the results presented here may not be exactly the same as those found in other sources.

In general is it clear that BLS anticipates strong occupational employment growth for most occupations over the course of the projection.[7] In fact, at this level of aggregation, only three of the eight occupational groups are slower growing than the average for all occupations, namely operatives, laborers, and clerical workers. However, the range of the growth rates for the occupations around the average growth rate of all jobs is relatively narrow, from 19.1 percent to 38.5 percent. Compare that to the range from the CPS data, 1972 to 1982 of –5.9 percent to 46.9 percent, or 1972 to 1979 (to avoid the distortions in the data due to the recession) of 8.5 percent to 35.4 percent. Apparently BLS anticipates less relative change in the importance of occupations over the 13 years of their projection than actually occurred during the seven years from 1972 to 1979.

Given these overall results, it is not surprising that the occupational decomposition indicates that the relative impacts of changing staffing ratios and differential rates of industry growth are modest for all occupations. The surprise in the decomposition is that the impact of staffing ratios on forecast clerical employment is actually *negative*. In fact, this is the only turnaround projected by BLS from the existing trends in the historical data. It is an indication that BLS expects office automation and other factors to retard the growth of clerical jobs in the future.

It is possible to compare the historical CPS data with the projections of BLS at the major occupational group level, but one of the difficulties with such a comparison is that the time spans covered are of such unequal length. Figures 5.3 and 5.4 attempt to remedy this problem by stating the staffing ratio changes and the effects of differential rates of industry growth for the major occupational groups in terms of average annual rates of change. The comparisons are done over two historical time periods, 1972-1979 and 1972-1982 to ameliorate distortions in the data due to the recession. It should be noted that the unemployment rate in 1979 was just under 6 percent, virtually the same unemployment rate built into the BLS projections. Overall this approach facilitates a more direct comparison of the BLS projections with the historical data using a consistent unit of measurement.

The results depicted in figures 5.3 and 5.4 indicate unequivocally that BLS anticipates far less impact in the years ahead from staffing ratio changes and differential rates of industry growth than have occurred in the last decade. For most of the major occupational groups, the average annual rate of change during the projection period tends to be *less than one-half* the average annual rate of change during either of the historical periods, 1972-1979 or 1972-1982. Again, the most important exception is probably the turnaround in the effects of staffing ratios on clerical employment. Of course, the impacts of changing staffing ratios on clerical employment have been modest historically as well. The analysis in chapter 4 demonstrated this. Nonetheless, it is interesting that staffing ratio changes for clerical workers are predicted to shift from slightly positive historically to slightly negative during the projection period.

Undoubtedly some observers will find the BLS projections counter-intuitive. The presumption by some today is that change is occurring faster now than ever before, so it is ludicrous to think that staffing ratios and/or differential rates of industry growth will be less in the years ahead than

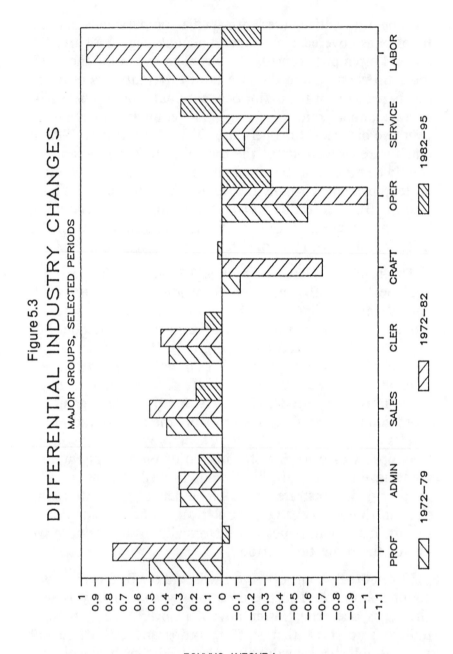

Figure 5.3
DIFFERENTIAL INDUSTRY CHANGES
MAJOR GROUPS, SELECTED PERIODS

Figure 5.4

STAFFING RATIO CHANGES
MAJOR GROUPS, SELECTED PERIODS

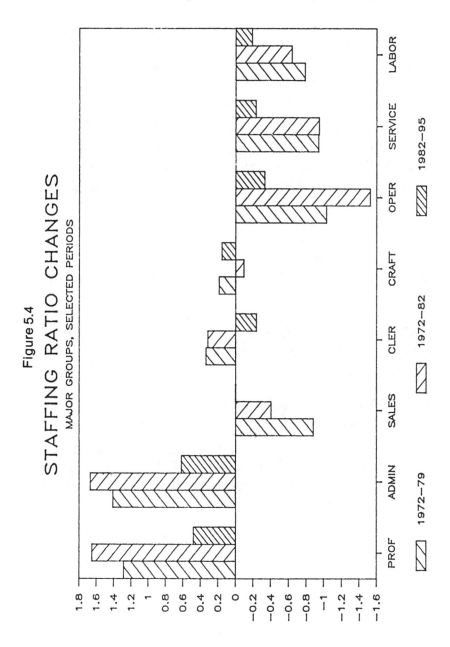

in the recent past. But this is not obvious. Would the BLS projections be superior if all past trends were extrapolated to the future? Which of the major occupational groups will be faster or slower growing than anticipated by BLS? What is the basis for those expectations?

One of the ways to minimize errors in forecasting is to project modest changes, with the goal of at least capturing the correct direction of the trends, if not the exact magnitude of those trends. According to BLS, staffing ratios are changed only when there is substantial evidence to indicate that they will change. It may also be true that to some extent BLS "leans against the wind" because they have found historically that technological change and other major projected disruptions have had far less impact on occupational structure than most experts expected. In this sense the BLS strategy is conservative. This is entirely appropriate if the goal is to provide guidance to those making decisions about investment in human resources that will have very long payback periods.

Decomposition of Detailed Occupations, BLS Occupational Employment Projections

As mentioned earlier, there are about 1,700 occupations in the occupation-industry matrix of the BLS, but only those occupations with 5,000 or more employees are reported on the OES tape which was used in this analysis of the occupational decomposition. That reduces the number of occupations to 765. Of those, there are 104 occupations that fall within the major occupational group of clerical workers. The BLS projected occupational employment growth for all 104 of these occupations is reported in table 5.3. The decomposition of the projected occupational employment growth into the portions due to overall employment expansion, differential industry growth, and staffing ratio changes is also reported in the table.

Since there is such a large amount of detail in table 5.3, the estimates are also reported in two additional tables. Table 5.4 presents the detailed clerical occupations ranked by the level of employment in 1982 in those occupations, while table 5.5 reports the same results ranked by the staffing ratio changes within the clerical occupations (from positive to negative). This approach highlights those clerical occupations with the largest employment and facilitates the discussion of the staffing ratio changes anticipated by BLS.

Before proceeding to a discussion of the results for the specific occupations, it should be understood that the OES data are not directly comparable to the Census or CPS data discussed earlier. First, there is a significant increase in the number of clerical occupations in moving from the Census and CPS classification systems to the OES system.[8] Second, the historical OES data are employer-based rather than household-based. So, even under ideal circumstances, there might be discrepancies in the employment data because of differences between employer classification of workers and the perception of the worker of his own classification. Third, the OES system was developed prior to the SOC, so there is no way currently to bridge the gap between the systems. Hunt and Hunt (1985) discuss these problems further in another paper.

The message of this analysis is that the detailed clerical occupations differ widely in terms of their projected growth rates and staffing ratio changes. The range in the overall forecast growth rate of the detailed clerical occupations is from a plus 76.1 percent to minus 20.0 percent.[9] The range in the staffing ratio changes is from plus 38.4 percent to minus 55.6 percent. The diversity in these results indicates that BLS *is attempting* to capture a variety of influences on the level of occupational demand. It is clearly erroneous to think that BLS is unwilling to alter staffing ratios from their historical

Table 5.3
BLS Projected Occupational Employment Growth, 1982-1995
All Clerical Occupations

| Occupation | Employment changes | | | | Decomposition of employment changes, 1982-1995 | | | | | |
| | | | | | Absolute changes | | | Percent of 1982 occupational employment | | |
	1982 employment (000s)	1995 employment (000s)	Change in employment 1982-1995 (000s)	Change in employment 1982-1995 (percent)	Constant employment shares (000s)	Differential rates of industry growth (000s)	Staffing ratios (000s)	Constant employment shares	Differential rates of industry growth	Staffing ratios
Clerical workers	18,716.6	23,673.5	4,956.9	26.5	5,250.6	294.8	(588.4)	28.1	1.6	-3.1
Adjustment clerks	33.8	47.4	13.6	40.1	9.5	0.3	3.8	28.1	0.9	11.2
Admissions evaluators	10.5	12.1	1.6	15.4	2.9	(1.8)	0.5	28.1	-17.3	4.7
Bank tellers	538.8	693.0	154.2	28.6	151.1	24.1	(21.0)	28.1	4.5	-3.9
New accounts tellers	67.3	79.9	12.6	18.8	18.9	4.1	(10.3)	28.1	6.0	-15.3
Tellers	471.5	613.1	141.6	30.0	132.3	20.1	(10.7)	28.1	4.3	-2.3
Bookkeepers & accounting clerks	1,613.5	1,892.5	279.1	17.3	452.6	46.7	(220.2)	28.1	2.9	-13.6
Accounting clerks	728.7	850.0	121.3	16.7	204.4	6.2	(89.3)	28.1	0.9	-12.3
Bookkeepers, hand	884.8	1,042.5	157.7	17.8	248.2	40.4	(130.9)	28.1	4.6	-14.8
Brokerage clerks	16.5	20.3	3.8	23.0	4.6	3.1	(3.9)	28.1	18.5	-23.5
Car rental clerks	16.2	21.6	5.4	33.3	4.6	2.5	(1.6)	28.1	15.1	-9.9
Cashiers	1,532.4	2,270.5	738.1	48.2	429.9	56.6	251.6	28.1	3.7	16.4
Checking clerks	18.0	22.7	4.7	26.2	5.0	0.5	(0.8)	28.1	2.7	-4.5
Circulation clerks	9.5	11.8	2.3	23.8	2.7	(0.8)	0.4	28.1	-8.4	4.2
Claims adjusters	65.4	97.6	32.1	49.1	18.4	(4.0)	17.8	28.1	-6.2	27.3
Claims clerks	63.0	89.8	26.8	42.5	17.7	(4.2)	13.3	28.1	-6.7	21.1
Claims examiner, insurance	47.3	62.1	14.9	31.5	13.3	(0.9)	2.6	28.1	-2.0	5.4
Clerical supervisors	466.1	627.4	161.3	34.6	130.7	13.4	17.2	28.1	2.9	3.7
Coin machine operators and currency sorters	5.0	6.0	0.9	18.2	1.4	.0	(0.5)	28.1	0.4	-10.3

Collectors, bill & account	90.9	130.9	40.0	44.0	25.5	16.5	(2.0)	28.1	18.1	-2.2
Court clerks	27.3	29.4	2.2	7.9	7.7	(4.7)	(0.8)	28.1	-17.3	-2.9
Credit authorizers	20.2	30.5	10.3	51.2	5.7	0.6	4.0	28.1	3.1	20.0
Credit clerks, banking and insurance	49.6	76.4	26.8	54.0	13.9	5.5	7.4	28.1	11.1	14.9
Credit reporters	15.3	20.5	5.2	34.4	4.3	4.7	(3.7)	28.1	30.8	-24.5
Customer service representatives	88.9	123.8	34.8	39.2	25.0	3.4	6.5	28.1	3.8	7.3
Customer service reps, print. and publish.	8.4	10.3	1.9	22.2	2.4	(0.5)	(.0)	28.1	-5.4	-0.5
Desk clerks, bowling floor	15.4	17.8	2.4	15.4	4.3	1.1	(3.0)	28.1	7.0	-19.7
Desk clerks, ex. bowling floor	85.3	104.3	19.0	22.3	23.9	5.0	(9.9)	28.1	5.8	-11.6
Dispatchers, police, fire and ambulance	47.8	53.4	5.5	11.6	13.4	(7.9)	(.0)	28.1	-16.5	.0
Dispatchers, vehicle serv. or work	86.9	109.7	22.8	26.3	24.4	0.1	(1.7)	28.1	0.2	-2.0
Eligibility workers, welfare	31.5	32.1	0.6	2.0	8.8	(5.4)	(2.8)	28.1	-17.1	-9.0
File clerks	293.0	319.5	26.5	9.1	82.2	21.3	(77.0)	28.1	7.3	-26.3
General clerks, office	2,342.0	3,037.4	695.5	29.7	657.0	20.6	17.8	28.1	0.9	0.8
In-file operators	5.0	6.9	1.9	38.8	1.4	2.8	(2.2)	28.1	55.6	-44.9
Insurance checkers	14.9	22.4	7.4	49.8	4.2	(0.3)	3.5	28.1	-2.0	23.7
Insurance clerks, except medical	10.6	14.6	4.0	37.6	3.0	0.6	0.4	28.1	5.7	3.9
Insurance clerks, medical	85.7	139.1	53.4	62.2	24.1	15.9	13.4	28.1	18.5	15.7
Library assistants	80.2	94.6	14.4	18.0	22.5	(10.8)	2.7	28.1	-13.4	3.4
License clerks	5.7	5.5	(0.2)	-4.0	1.6	(1.0)	(0.8)	28.1	-17.3	-14.7
Loan closers	45.3	64.0	18.8	41.5	12.7	4.2	1.9	28.1	9.2	4.2
Mail carriers & postal clerks	540.6	474.4	(66.2)	-12.2	151.7	(108.1)	(109.7)	28.1	-20.0	-20.3
Postal mail carriers	234.1	222.7	(11.4)	-4.9	65.7	(46.8)	(30.3)	28.1	-20.0	-12.9
Postal service clerks	306.5	251.8	(54.8)	-17.9	86.0	(61.3)	(79.5)	28.1	-20.0	-25.9
Mail clerks	98.7	129.7	31.0	31.4	27.7	1.2	2.2	28.1	1.2	2.2
Messengers	49.7	65.4	15.8	31.8	13.9	4.6	(2.7)	28.1	9.2	-5.5
Meter readers, utilities	30.5	37.9	7.3	24.0	8.6	(1.5)	0.3	28.1	-4.9	0.9
Mortgage closing clerks	15.3	22.6	7.2	47.2	4.3	1.7	1.3	28.1	10.8	8.4
Office machine operators	933.6	1,194.6	260.9	27.9	261.9	73.7	(74.7)	28.1	7.9	-8.0
Bookkeeping & billing operators	226.1	289.9	63.8	28.2	63.4	3.7	(3.4)	28.1	1.7	-1.5
Bookkeeping, billing machine operators	171.5	221.7	50.2	29.3	48.1	3.4	(1.3)	28.1	2.0	-0.8

Table 5.3 (cont.)

| Occupation | Employment changes | | | | Decomposition of employment changes, 1982-1995 | | | | | |
| | | | | | Absolute changes | | | Percent of 1982 occupational employment | | |
	1982 employment (000s)	1995 employment (000s)	Change in employment 1982-1995 (000s)	Change in employment 1982-1995 (percent)	Constant employment shares (000s)	Differential rates of industry growth (000s)	Staffing ratios (000s)	Constant employment shares	Differential rates of industry growth	Staffing ratios
Proof machine operators	47.4	59.4	11.9	25.2	13.3	0.3	(1.6)	28.1	0.6	-3.4
Transit clerks	7.3	8.9	1.6	22.6	2.0	0.1	(0.5)	28.1	0.9	-6.4
Computer operating personnel	578.7	735.9	157.2	27.2	162.3	57.3	(62.5)	28.1	9.9	-10.8
Computer operators	210.0	369.7	159.7	76.1	58.9	20.1	80.7	28.1	9.6	38.4
Data entry operators	318.7	284.6	(34.1)	-10.7	89.4	30.6	(154.1)	28.1	9.6	-48.4
Peripheral EDP equipment operators	47.7	78.6	30.8	64.6	13.4	6.6	10.9	28.1	13.7	22.8
Duplicating machine operators	36.1	42.3	6.2	17.1	10.1	3.8	(7.8)	28.1	10.6	-21.5
All other office machine oprs	89.0	121.8	32.8	36.8	25.0	8.8	(1.0)	28.1	9.9	-1.1
Order clerks	257.0	325.4	68.4	26.6	72.1	(3.0)	(0.7)	28.1	-1.2	-0.3
Payroll & timekeeping clerks	201.2	268.8	67.6	33.6	56.4	6.6	4.5	28.1	3.3	2.2
Personnel clerks	102.3	131.0	28.7	28.0	28.7	(3.3)	3.3	28.1	-3.3	3.2
Policy change clerks	27.6	30.5	2.9	10.5	7.7	(0.6)	(4.3)	28.1	-2.0	-15.6
Procurement clerks	46.9	59.0	12.2	25.9	13.2	(1.9)	(0.9)	28.1	-4.1	2.0
Production clerks	199.8	260.0	60.2	30.1	56.0	1.9	2.2	28.1	1.0	1.1
Proofreaders	16.2	20.6	4.3	26.8	4.5	(0.4)	0.2	28.1	-2.6	1.3
Protective signal operators	6.9	11.7	4.8	69.4	1.9	3.8	(1.0)	28.1	55.6	-14.3
Purchase & sales clerks, security	5.2	4.9	(0.3)	-5.5	1.5	1.0	(2.7)	28.1	18.5	-52.0
Rate clerks, freight	10.2	12.5	2.3	22.6	2.9	(0.7)	0.2	28.1	-7.2	1.8
Raters	52.6	69.0	16.4	31.1	14.8	(1.1)	2.7	28.1	-2.0	5.0
Real estate clerks	16.6	23.5	6.9	41.8	4.7	1.0	1.2	28.1	6.2	7.5
Receptionists	381.1	569.7	188.6	49.5	106.9	54.2	27.5	28.1	14.2	7.2
Reservation agents and transport. tick. clerks	107.5	109.6	2.1	1.9	30.2	(8.5)	(19.5)	28.1	-7.9	-18.2
Reservation agents	52.9	54.9	2.0	3.7	14.8	(3.0)	(9.9)	28.1	-5.7	-18.6

Ticket Agents	49.3	48.9	(0.4)	-0.7	13.8	(5.2)	(8.9)	28.1	-10.6	-18.2
Travel counselors, auto club	5.4	5.9	0.5	9.1	1.5	(0.3)	(0.8)	28.1	-5.1	-13.9
Safe deposit clerks	13.9	18.1	4.2	30.5	3.9	0.3	.0	28.1	2.4	.0
Secretaries and stenographers	2,634.8	3,337.3	702.5	26.7	739.1	97.3	(133.9)	28.1	3.7	-5.1
Secretaries	2,298.7	2,988.5	689.8	30.0	644.8	98.3	(53.3)	28.1	4.3	-2.3
Stenographers	265.6	244.9	(20.7)	-7.8	74.5	(7.8)	(87.4)	28.1	-2.9	-32.9
Typists	974.9	1,128.8	153.9	15.8	273.5	2.0	(121.6)	28.1	0.2	-12.5
Service clerks	23.6	34.9	11.3	48.1	6.6	0.8	4.0	28.1	3.2	16.9
Shipping and receiving clerks	364.3	430.4	66.1	18.2	102.2	(7.4)	(28.7)	28.1	-2.0	-7.9
Shipping packers	339.0	402.1	63.1	18.6	95.1	(15.2)	(16.8)	28.1	-4.5	-5.0
Sorting clerks, banking	7.4	9.3	1.9	25.5	2.1	0.1	(0.3)	28.1	1.5	-4.1
Statement clerks	33.6	44.2	10.7	31.7	9.4	0.8	0.4	28.1	2.3	1.3
Statistical clerks	96.1	110.8	14.7	15.3	27.0	5.7	(18.0)	28.1	5.9	-18.7
Stock clerks, stockroom and warehouse	827.3	983.5	156.3	18.9	232.1	0.9	(76.7)	28.1	0.1	-9.3
Survey workers	51.4	76.1	24.8	48.2	14.4	21.7	(11.4)	28.1	42.3	-22.1
Switchboard oper./receptionists	203.8	281.6	77.9	38.2	57.2	18.5	2.2	28.1	9.1	1.1
Teachers' aides	462.7	593.1	130.3	28.2	129.8	(69.4)	70.0	28.1	-15.0	15.1
Telephone ad takers, newspapers	10.4	14.5	4.2	40.5	2.9	(0.9)	2.2	28.1	-8.8	21.2
Telegraph operators	4.4	6.4	2.0	46.1	1.2	0.3	0.5	28.1	7.5	10.6
Telephone operators	315.8	341.4	25.5	8.1	88.6	36.6	(99.7)	28.1	11.6	-31.6
Switchboard operators	169.6	211.3	41.7	24.6	47.6	25.7	(31.6)	28.1	15.1	-18.6
Central office operators	108.7	86.9	(21.8)	-20.0	30.5	8.1	(60.4)	28.1	7.5	-55.6
Directory assistance operators	37.5	43.1	5.6	14.9	10.5	2.8	(7.7)	28.1	7.5	-20.6
Title searchers	5.1	7.1	2.0	38.5	1.4	0.4	0.2	28.1	7.4	3.1
Town clerks	26.0	29.1	3.1	11.7	7.3	(4.5)	0.3	28.1	-17.3	1.0
Traffic agents	17.8	22.3	4.5	25.1	5.0	(0.6)	0.1	28.1	-3.3	0.4
Traffic clerks	7.1	10.5	3.3	47.0	2.0	2.5	(1.2)	28.1	35.8	-16.9
Transportation agents	20.6	28.1	7.5	36.3	5.8	(0.1)	1.8	28.1	-0.6	8.9
Weighers	24.3	28.7	4.3	17.8	6.8	(2.6)	0.1	28.1	-10.5	0.3
Welfare investigators	11.8	12.3	0.5	4.0	3.3	(2.0)	(0.8)	28.1	-17.1	-7.0
Worksheet clerks	10.6	15.3	4.7	44.1	3.0	(0.2)	1.9	28.1	-2.0	18.1
All other clerical workers	1,220.5	1,542.0	321.6	26.3	342.4	(14.0)	(6.8)	28.1	-1.1	-0.6

SOURCE: Calculations by the authors based upon data tape from the 1982-1995 OES/BLS occupational employment projections.

NOTE: Some occupational detail is omitted. Totals and percentages may not add exactly due to omission of some occupational detail and rounding error. The 378 OES industries were first aggregated to 105 industries before accomplishing the decomposition. The OES data tape includes wage and salary employment only.

Table 5.4
BLS Projected Occupational Employment Growth, 1982-1995
Detailed Clerical Occupations Ranked by Level of Employment in 1982

| | Employment changes | | | | Decomposition of employment changes, 1982-1995 | | | | | |
| | | | | | Absolute changes | | | Percent of 1982 occupational employment | | |
Occupation	1982 employment (000s)	1995 employment (000s)	Change in employment 1982-1995 (000s)	Change in employment 1982-1995 (percent)	Constant employment shares (000s)	Differential rates of industry growth (000s)	Staffing ratios (000s)	Constant employment shares	Differential rates of industry growth	Staffing ratios
Clerical workers	18,716.6	23,673.5	4,956.9	26.5	5,250.6	294.8	(588.4)	28.1	1.6	-3.1
General clerks, office	2,342.0	3,037.4	695.5	29.7	657.0	20.6	17.8	28.1	0.9	0.8
Secretaries	2,298.7	2,988.5	689.8	30.0	644.8	98.3	(53.3)	28.1	4.3	-2.3
Cashiers	1,532.4	2,270.5	738.1	48.2	429.9	56.6	251.6	28.1	3.7	16.4
All other clerical workers	1,220.5	1,542.0	321.6	26.3	342.4	(14.0)	(6.8)	28.1	-1.1	-0.6
Typists	974.9	1,128.8	153.9	15.8	273.5	2.0	(121.6)	28.1	0.2	-12.5
Bookkeepers, hand	884.8	1,042.5	157.7	17.8	248.2	40.4	(130.9)	28.1	4.6	-14.8
Stock clerks, stockroom and warehouse	827.3	983.5	156.3	18.9	232.1	0.9	(76.7)	28.1	0.1	-9.3
Accounting clerks	728.7	850.0	121.3	16.7	204.4	6.2	(89.3)	28.1	0.9	-12.3
Tellers	471.5	613.1	141.6	30.0	132.3	20.1	(10.7)	28.1	4.3	-2.3
Clerical supervisors	466.1	627.4	161.3	34.6	130.7	13.4	17.2	28.1	2.9	3.7
Teachers' aides	462.7	593.1	130.3	28.2	129.8	(69.4)	70.0	28.1	-15.0	15.1
Receptionists	381.1	569.7	188.6	49.5	106.9	54.2	27.5	28.1	14.2	7.2
Shipping and receiving clerks	364.3	430.4	66.1	18.2	102.2	(7.4)	(28.7)	28.1	-2.0	-7.9
Shipping packers	339.0	402.1	63.1	18.6	95.1	(15.2)	(16.8)	28.1	-4.5	-5.0
Data entry operators	318.7	284.6	(34.1)	-10.7	89.4	30.6	(154.1)	28.1	9.6	-48.4
Postal service clerks	306.5	251.8	(54.8)	-17.9	86.0	(61.3)	(79.5)	28.1	-20.0	-25.9
File clerks	293.0	319.5	26.5	9.1	82.2	21.3	(77.0)	28.1	7.3	-26.3
Stenographers	265.6	244.9	(20.7)	-7.8	74.5	(7.8)	(87.4)	28.1	-2.9	-32.9
Order clerks	257.0	325.4	68.4	26.6	72.1	(3.0)	(0.7)	28.1	-1.2	-0.3

Postal mail carriers	234.1	222.7	(11.4)	-4.9	65.7	(46.8)	(30.3)	28.1	-20.0	-12.9
Computer operators	210.0	369.7	159.7	76.1	58.9	20.1	80.7	28.1	9.6	38.4
Switchboard operators/recepts.	203.8	281.6	77.9	38.2	57.2	18.5	2.2	28.1	9.1	1.1
Payroll and timekeeping clerks	201.2	268.8	67.6	33.6	56.4	6.6	4.5	28.1	3.3	2.2
Production clerks	199.8	260.0	60.2	30.1	56.0	1.9	2.2	28.1	1.0	1.1
Bookkeeping, billing machine operators	171.5	221.7	50.2	29.3	48.1	3.4	(1.3)	28.1	2.0	-0.8
Switchboard operators	169.6	211.3	41.7	24.6	47.6	25.7	(31.6)	28.1	15.1	-18.6
Central office operators	108.7	86.9	(21.8)	-20.0	30.5	8.1	(60.4)	28.1	7.5	-55.6
Personnel clerks	102.3	131.0	28.7	28.0	28.7	(3.3)	3.3	28.1	-3.3	3.2
Mail clerks	98.7	129.7	31.0	31.4	27.7	1.2	2.2	28.1	1.2	2.2
Statistical clerks	96.1	110.8	14.7	15.3	27.0	5.7	(18.0)	28.1	5.9	-18.7
Collectors, bill and account	90.9	130.9	40.0	44.0	25.5	16.5	(2.0)	28.1	18.1	-2.2
All other office machine operators	89.0	121.8	32.8	36.8	25.0	8.8	(1.0)	28.1	9.9	-1.1
Customer service representatives	88.9	123.8	34.8	39.2	25.0	3.4	6.5	28.1	3.8	7.3
Dispatchers, vehicle serv. or work	86.9	109.7	22.8	26.3	24.4	0.1	(1.7)	28.1	0.2	-2.0
Insurance clerks, medical	85.7	139.1	53.4	62.2	24.1	15.9	13.4	28.1	18.5	15.7
Desk clerks, ex. bowling floor	85.3	104.3	19.0	22.3	23.9	5.0	(9.9)	28.1	5.8	-11.6
Library assistants	80.2	94.6	14.4	18.0	22.5	(10.8)	2.7	28.1	-13.4	3.4
New accounts tellers	67.3	79.9	12.6	18.8	18.9	4.1	(10.3)	28.1	6.0	-15.3
Claims adjusters	65.4	97.6	32.1	49.1	18.4	(4.0)	17.8	28.1	-6.2	27.3
Claims clerks	63.0	89.8	26.8	42.5	17.7	(4.2)	13.3	28.1	-6.7	21.1
Reservation agents	52.9	54.9	2.0	3.7	14.8	(3.0)	(9.9)	28.1	-5.7	-18.6
Raters	52.6	69.0	16.4	31.1	14.8	(1.1)	2.7	28.1	-2.0	5.0
Survey workers	51.4	76.1	24.8	48.2	14.4	21.7	(11.4)	28.1	42.3	-22.1
Messengers	49.7	65.4	15.8	31.8	13.9	4.6	(2.7)	28.1	9.2	-5.5
Credit clerks, banking & ins.	49.6	76.4	26.8	54.0	13.9	5.5	7.4	28.1	11.1	14.9
Ticket agents	49.3	48.9	(0.4)	-0.7	13.8	(5.2)	(8.9)	28.1	-10.6	-18.2
Dispatchers, police, fire and ambulance	47.8	53.4	5.5	11.6	13.4	(7.9)	(.0)	28.1	-16.5	.0
Peripheral EDP equip. operators	47.7	78.6	30.8	64.6	13.4	6.6	10.9	28.1	13.7	22.8
Proof machine operators	47.4	59.4	11.9	25.2	13.3	0.3	(1.6)	28.1	0.6	-3.4
Claims examiner, insurance	47.3	62.1	14.9	31.5	13.3	(0.9)	2.6	28.1	-2.0	5.4
Procurement clerks	46.9	59.0	12.2	25.9	13.2	(1.9)	0.9	28.1	-4.1	2.0
Loan closers	45.3	64.0	18.8	41.5	12.7	4.2	1.9	28.1	9.2	4.2
Directory assistance operators	37.5	43.1	5.6	14.9	10.5	2.8	(7.7)	28.1	7.5	-20.6
Duplicating machine operators	36.1	42.3	6.2	17.1	10.1	3.8	(7.8)	28.1	10.6	-21.5

Table 5.4 (cont.)

| Occupation | Employment changes | | | | Decomposition of employment changes, 1982-1995 | | | | | |
| | | | | | Absolute changes | | | Percent of 1982 occupational employment | | |
	1982 employment (000s)	1995 employment (000s)	Change in employment 1982-1995 (000s)	Change in employment 1982-1995 (percent)	Constant employment shares (000s)	Differential rates of industry growth (000s)	Staffing ratios (000s)	Constant employment shares	Differential rates of industry growth	Staffing ratios
Adjustment clerks	33.8	47.4	13.6	40.1	9.5	0.3	3.8	28.1	0.9	11.2
Statement clerks	33.6	44.2	10.7	31.7	9.4	0.8	0.4	28.1	2.3	1.3
Eligibility workers, welfare	31.5	32.1	0.6	2.0	8.8	(5.4)	(2.8)	28.1	-17.1	-9.0
Meter readers, utilities	30.5	37.9	7.3	24.0	8.6	(1.5)	0.3	28.1	-4.9	0.9
Policy change clerks	27.6	30.5	2.9	10.5	7.7	(0.6)	(4.3)	28.1	-2.0	-15.6
Court clerks	27.3	29.4	2.2	7.9	7.7	(4.7)	(0.8)	28.1	-17.3	-2.9
Town clerks	26.0	29.1	3.1	11.7	7.3	(4.5)	0.3	28.1	-17.3	1.0
Weighers	24.3	28.7	4.3	17.8	6.8	(2.6)	0.1	28.1	-10.5	0.3
Service clerks	23.6	34.9	11.3	48.1	6.6	0.8	4.0	28.1	3.2	16.9
Transportation agents	20.6	28.1	7.5	36.3	5.8	(0.1)	1.8	28.1	-0.6	8.9
Credit authorizers	20.2	30.5	10.3	51.2	5.7	0.6	4.0	28.1	3.1	20.0
Checking clerks	18.0	22.7	4.7	26.2	5.0	0.5	(0.8)	28.1	2.7	-4.5
Traffic agents	17.8	22.3	4.5	25.1	5.0	(0.6)	0.1	28.1	-3.3	0.4
Real estate clerks	16.6	23.5	6.9	41.8	4.7	1.0	1.2	28.1	6.2	7.5
Brokerage clerks	16.5	20.3	3.8	23.0	4.6	3.1	(3.9)	28.1	18.5	-23.5
Car rental clerks	16.2	21.6	5.4	33.3	4.6	2.5	(1.6)	28.1	15.1	-9.9
Proofreaders	16.2	20.6	4.3	26.8	4.5	(0.4)	0.2	28.1	-2.6	1.3
Desk clerks, bowling floor	15.4	17.8	2.4	15.4	4.3	1.1	(3.0)	28.1	7.0	-19.7
Mortgage closing clerks	15.3	22.6	7.2	47.2	4.3	1.7	1.3	28.1	10.8	8.4
Credit reporters	15.3	20.5	5.2	34.4	4.3	4.7	(3.7)	28.1	30.8	-24.5
Insurance checkers	14.9	22.4	7.4	49.8	4.2	(0.3)	3.5	28.1	-2.0	23.7
Safe deposit clerks	13.9	18.1	4.2	30.5	3.9	0.3	.0	28.1	2.4	.0
Welfare investigators	11.8	12.3	0.5	4.0	3.3	(2.0)	(0.8)	28.1	-17.1	-7.0

Worksheet clerks	10.6	15.3	4.7	44.1	3.0	(0.2)	1.9	28.1	-2.0	18.1
Insurance clerks, except medical	10.6	14.6	4.0	37.6	3.0	0.6	0.4	28.1	5.7	3.9
Admissions evaluators	10.5	12.1	1.6	15.4	2.9	(1.8)	0.5	28.1	-17.3	4.7
Telephone ad takers, newspapers	10.4	14.5	4.2	40.5	2.9	(0.9)	2.2	28.1	-8.8	21.2
Rate clerks, freight	10.2	12.5	2.3	22.6	2.9	(0.7)	0.2	28.1	-7.2	1.8
Circulation clerks	9.5	11.8	2.3	23.8	2.7	(0.8)	0.4	28.1	-8.4	4.2
Customer service reps., print. and publish.	8.4	10.3	1.9	22.2	2.4	(0.5)	(.0)	28.1	-5.4	-0.5
Sorting clerks, banking	7.4	9.3	1.9	25.5	2.1	0.1	(0.3)	28.1	1.5	-4.1
Transit clerks	7.3	8.9	1.6	22.6	2.0	0.1	(0.5)	28.1	0.9	-6.4
Traffic clerks	7.1	10.5	3.3	47.0	2.0	2.5	(1.2)	28.1	35.8	-16.9
Protective signal operators	6.9	11.7	4.8	69.4	1.9	3.8	(1.0)	28.1	55.6	-14.3
License clerks	5.7	5.5	(0.2)	-4.0	1.6	(1.0)	(0.8)	28.1	-17.3	-14.7
Travel counselors, auto club	5.4	5.9	0.5	9.1	1.5	(0.3)	(0.8)	28.1	-5.1	-13.9
Purchase & sales clerks, security	5.2	4.9	(0.3)	-5.5	1.5	1.0	(2.7)	28.1	18.5	-52.0
Title searchers	5.1	7.1	2.0	38.5	1.4	0.4	0.2	28.1	7.4	3.1
Coin machine operators and currency sorters	5.0	6.0	0.9	18.2	1.4	.0	(0.5)	28.1	0.4	-10.3
In-file operators	5.0	6.9	1.9	38.8	1.4	2.8	(2.2)	28.1	55.6	-44.9
Telegraph operators	4.4	6.4	2.0	46.1	1.2	0.3	0.5	28.1	7.5	10.6

SOURCE: Calculations by the authors based upon data tape from the 1982-1995 OES/BLS occupational employment projections.

NOTE: Some occupational detail is omitted. Totals and percentages may not add exactly due to omission of some occupational detail and rounding error. The 378 OES industries were first aggregated to 105 industries before accomplishing the decomposition. The OES data tape includes wage and salary employment only.

Table 5.5
BLS Projected Occupational Employment Growth, 1982-1995
Detailed Clerical Occupations Ranked by Staffing Ratio Changes

| Occupation | Employment changes | | | | Decomposition of employment changes, 1982-1995 | | | | | |
| | | | | | Absolute changes | | | Percent of 1982 occupational employment | | |
	1982 employment (000s)	1995 employment (000s)	Change in employment 1982-1995 (000s)	Change in employment 1982-1995 (percent)	Constant employment shares (000s)	Differential rates of industry growth (000s)	Staffing ratios (000s)	Constant employment shares	Differential rates of industry growth	Staffing ratios
Clerical workers	18,716.6	23,673.5	4,956.9	26.5	5,250.6	294.8	(588.4)	28.1	1.6	-3.1
Computer operators	210.0	369.7	159.7	76.1	58.9	20.1	80.7	28.1	9.6	38.4
Claims adjusters	65.4	97.6	32.1	49.1	18.4	(4.0)	17.8	28.1	-6.2	27.3
Insurance checkers	14.9	22.4	7.4	49.8	4.2	(0.3)	3.5	28.1	-2.0	23.7
Peripheral EDP equip. operators	47.7	78.6	30.8	64.6	13.4	6.6	10.9	28.1	13.7	22.8
Telephone ad takers, newspapers	10.4	14.5	4.2	40.5	2.9	(0.9)	2.2	28.1	-8.8	21.2
Claims clerks	63.0	89.8	26.8	42.5	17.7	(4.2)	13.3	28.1	-6.7	21.1
Credit authorizers	20.2	30.5	10.3	51.2	5.7	0.6	4.0	28.1	3.1	20.0
Worksheet clerks	10.6	15.3	4.7	44.1	3.0	(0.2)	1.9	28.1	-2.0	18.1
Service clerks	23.6	34.9	11.3	48.1	6.6	0.8	4.0	28.1	3.2	16.9
Cashiers	1,532.4	2,270.5	738.1	48.2	429.9	56.6	251.6	28.1	3.7	16.4
Insurance clerks, medical	85.7	139.1	53.4	62.2	24.1	15.9	13.4	28.1	18.5	15.7
Teachers' aides	462.7	593.1	130.3	28.2	129.8	(69.4)	70.0	28.1	-15.0	15.1
Credit clerks, banking and ins.	49.6	76.4	26.8	54.0	13.9	5.5	7.4	28.1	11.1	14.9
Adjustment clerks	33.8	47.4	13.6	40.1	9.5	0.3	3.8	28.1	0.9	11.2
Telegraph operators	4.4	6.4	2.0	46.1	1.2	0.3	0.5	28.1	7.5	10.6
Transportation agents	20.6	28.1	7.5	36.3	5.8	(0.1)	1.8	28.1	-0.6	8.9
Mortgage closing clerks	15.3	22.6	7.2	47.2	4.3	1.7	1.3	28.1	10.8	8.4
Real estate clerks	16.6	23.5	6.9	41.8	4.7	1.0	1.2	28.1	6.2	7.5
Customer service representatives	88.9	123.8	34.8	39.2	25.0	3.4	6.5	28.1	3.8	7.3
Receptionists	381.1	569.7	188.6	49.5	106.9	54.2	27.5	28.1	14.2	7.2
Claims examiner, insurance	47.3	62.1	14.9	31.5	13.3	(0.9)	2.6	28.1	-2.0	5.4

Raters	52.6	69.0	16.4	31.1	14.8	(1.1)	2.7	28.1	-2.0	5.0
Admissions evaluators	10.5	12.1	1.6	15.4	2.9	(1.8)	0.5	28.1	-17.3	4.7
Loan closers	45.3	64.0	18.8	41.5	12.7	4.2	1.9	28.1	9.2	4.2
Circulation clerks	9.5	11.8	2.3	23.8	2.7	(0.8)	0.4	28.1	-8.4	4.2
Insurance clerks, except medical	10.6	14.6	4.0	37.6	3.0	0.6	0.4	28.1	5.7	3.9
Clerical supervisors	466.1	627.4	161.3	34.6	130.7	13.4	17.2	28.1	2.9	3.7
Library assistants	80.2	94.6	14.4	18.0	22.5	(10.8)	2.7	28.1	-13.4	3.4
Personnel clerks	102.3	131.0	28.7	28.0	28.7	(3.3)	3.3	28.1	-3.3	3.2
Title searchers	5.1	7.1	2.0	38.5	1.4	0.4	0.2	28.1	7.4	3.1
Payroll & timekeeping clerks	201.2	268.8	67.6	33.6	56.4	6.6	4.5	28.1	3.3	2.2
Mail clerks	98.7	129.7	31.0	31.4	27.7	1.2	2.2	28.1	1.2	2.2
Procurement clerks	46.9	59.0	12.2	25.9	13.2	(1.9)	0.9	28.1	-4.1	2.0
Rate clerks, freight	10.2	12.5	2.3	22.6	2.9	(0.7)	0.2	28.1	-7.2	1.8
Statement clerks	33.6	44.2	10.7	31.7	9.4	0.8	0.4	28.1	2.3	1.3
Proofreaders	16.2	20.6	4.3	26.8	4.5	(0.4)	0.2	28.1	-2.6	1.3
Production clerks	199.8	260.0	60.2	30.1	56.0	1.9	2.2	28.1	1.0	1.1
Switchboard oper./receptionists	203.8	281.6	77.9	38.2	57.2	18.5	2.2	28.1	9.1	1.1
Town clerks	26.0	29.1	3.1	11.7	7.3	(4.5)	0.3	28.1	-17.3	1.0
Meter readers, utilities	30.5	37.9	7.3	24.0	8.6	(1.5)	0.3	28.1	-4.9	0.9
General clerks, office	2,342.0	3,037.4	695.5	29.7	657.0	20.6	17.8	28.1	0.9	0.8
Traffic agents	17.8	22.3	4.5	25.1	5.0	(0.6)	0.1	28.1	-3.3	0.4
Weighers	24.3	28.7	4.3	17.8	6.8	(2.6)	0.1	28.1	-10.5	0.3
Safe deposit clerks	13.9	18.1	4.2	30.5	3.9	0.3	.0	28.1	2.4	.0
Dispatchers, police, fire and ambulance	47.8	53.4	5.5	11.6	13.4	(7.9)	(.0)	28.1	-16.5	.0
Order clerks	257.0	325.4	68.4	26.6	72.1	(3.0)	(0.7)	28.1	-1.2	-0.3
Customer service reps., print, and publish	8.4	10.3	1.9	22.2	2.4	(0.5)	(.0)	28.1	-5.4	-0.5
All other clerical workers	1,220.5	1,542.0	321.6	26.3	342.4	(14.0)	(6.8)	28.1	-1.1	-0.6
Bookkeeping, billing machine operators	171.5	221.7	50.2	29.3	48.1	3.4	(1.3)	28.1	2.0	-0.8
All other office machine operators	89.0	121.8	32.8	36.8	25.0	8.8	(1.0)	28.1	9.9	-1.1
Dispatchers, vehicle serv. or work	86.9	109.7	22.8	26.3	24.4	0.1	(1.7)	28.1	0.2	-2.0
Collectors, bill and account	90.9	130.9	40.0	44.0	25.5	16.5	(2.0)	28.1	18.1	-2.2
Tellers	471.5	613.1	141.6	30.0	132.3	20.1	(10.7)	28.1	4.3	-2.3
Secretaries	2,298.7	2,988.5	689.8	30.0	644.8	98.3	(53.3)	28.1	4.3	-2.3
Court clerks	27.3	29.4	2.2	7.9	7.7	(4.7)	(0.8)	28.1	-17.3	-2.9
Proof machine operators	47.4	59.4	11.9	25.2	13.3	0.3	(1.6)	28.1	0.6	-3.4

Table 5.5 (cont.)

| Occupation | Employment changes | | | | Decomposition of employment changes, 1982-1995 | | | | | |
| | 1982 employment (000s) | 1995 employment (000s) | Change in employment 1982-1995 (000s) | Change in employment 1982-1995 (percent) | Absolute changes | | | Percent of 1982 occupational employment | | |
					Constant employment shares (000s)	Differential rates of industry growth (000s)	Staffing ratios (000s)	Constant employment shares	Differential rates of industry growth	Staffing ratios
Sorting clerks, banking	7.4	9.3	1.9	25.5	2.1	0.1	(0.3)	28.1	1.5	-4.1
Checking clerks	18.0	22.7	4.7	26.2	5.0	0.5	(0.8)	28.1	2.7	-4.5
Shipping packers	339.0	402.1	63.1	18.6	95.1	(15.2)	(16.8)	28.1	-4.5	-5.0
Messengers	49.7	65.4	15.8	31.8	13.9	4.6	(2.7)	28.1	9.2	-5.5
Transit clerks	7.3	8.9	1.6	22.6	2.0	0.1	(0.5)	28.1	0.9	-6.4
Welfare investigators clerks	11.8	12.3	0.5	4.0	3.3	(2.0)	(0.8)	28.1	-17.1	-7.0
Shipping & receiving clerks	364.3	430.4	66.1	18.2	102.2	(7.4)	(28.7)	28.1	-2.0	-7.9
Eligibility workers, welfare	31.5	32.1	0.6	2.0	8.8	(5.4)	(2.8)	28.1	-17.1	-9.0
Stock clerks, stockroom and warehouse	827.3	983.5	156.3	18.9	232.1	0.9	(76.7)	28.1	0.1	-9.3
Car rental clerks	16.2	21.6	5.4	33.3	4.6	2.5	(1.6)	28.1	15.1	-9.9
Coin machine operators and currency sorters	5.0	6.0	0.9	18.2	1.4	.0	(0.5)	28.1	0.4	-10.3
Desk clerks, ex. bowling floor	85.3	104.3	19.0	22.3	23.9	5.0	(9.9)	28.1	5.8	-11.6
Accounting clerks	728.7	850.0	121.3	16.7	204.4	6.2	(89.3)	28.1	0.9	-12.3
Typists	974.9	1,128.8	153.9	15.8	273.5	2.0	(121.6)	28.1	0.2	-12.5
Postal mail carriers	234.1	222.7	(11.4)	-4.9	65.7	(46.8)	(30.3)	28.1	-20.0	-12.9
Travel counselors, auto club	5.4	5.9	0.5	9.1	1.5	(0.3)	(0.8)	28.1	-5.1	-13.9
Protective signal operators	6.9	11.7	4.8	69.4	1.9	3.8	(1.0)	28.1	55.6	-14.3
License clerks	5.7	5.5	(0.2)	-4.0	1.6	(1.0)	(0.8)	28.1	-17.3	-14.7
Bookkeepers, hand	884.8	1,042.5	157.7	17.8	248.2	40.4	(130.9)	28.1	4.6	-14.8
New accounts tellers	67.3	79.9	12.6	18.8	18.9	4.1	(10.3)	28.1	6.0	-15.3
Policy change clerks	27.6	30.5	2.9	10.5	7.7	(0.6)	(4.3)	28.1	-2.0	-15.6
Traffic clerks	7.1	10.5	3.3	47.0	2.0	2.5	(1.2)	28.1	35.8	-16.9

Ticket agents	49.3	48.9	(0.4)	-0.7	13.8	(5.2)	(8.9)	28.1	-10.6	-18.2
Switchboard operators	169.6	211.3	41.7	24.6	47.6	25.7	(31.6)	28.1	15.1	-18.6
Reservation agents	52.9	54.9	2.0	3.7	14.8	(3.0)	(9.9)	28.1	-5.7	-18.6
Statistical clerks	96.1	110.8	14.7	15.3	27.0	5.7	(18.0)	28.1	5.9	-18.7
Desk clerks, bowling floor	15.4	17.8	2.4	15.4	4.3	1.1	(3.0)	28.1	7.0	-19.7
Directory assistance operators	37.5	43.1	5.6	14.9	10.5	2.8	(7.7)	28.1	7.5	-20.6
Duplicating machine operators	36.1	42.3	6.2	17.1	10.1	3.8	(7.8)	28.1	10.6	-21.5
Survey workers	51.4	76.1	24.8	48.2	14.4	21.7	(11.4)	28.1	42.3	-22.1
Brokerage clerks	16.5	20.3	3.8	23.0	4.6	3.1	(3.9)	28.1	18.5	-23.5
Credit reporters	15.3	20.5	5.2	34.4	4.3	4.7	(3.7)	28.1	30.8	-24.5
Postal service clerks	306.5	251.8	(54.8)	-17.9	86.0	(61.3)	(79.5)	28.1	-20.0	-25.9
File clerks	293.0	309.5	26.5	9.1	82.2	21.3	(77.0)	28.1	7.3	-26.3
Stenographers	265.6	244.9	(20.7)	-7.8	74.5	(7.8)	(87.4)	28.1	-2.9	-32.9
In-file operators	5.0	6.9	1.9	38.8	1.4	2.8	(2.2)	28.1	55.6	-44.9
Data entry operators	318.7	284.6	(34.1)	-10.7	89.4	30.6	(154.1)	28.1	9.6	-48.4
Purchase & sales clerks, security	5.2	4.9	(0.3)	-5.5	1.5	1.0	(2.7)	28.1	18.5	-52.0
Central office operators	108.7	86.9	(21.8)	-20.0	30.5	8.1	(60.4)	28.1	7.5	-55.6

SOURCE: Calculations by the authors based upon data tape from the 1982-1995 OES/BLS occupational employment projections.

NOTE: Some occupational detail is omitted. Totals and percentages may not add exactly due to omission of some occupational detail and rounding error. The 378 OES industries were first aggregated to 105 industries before accomplishing the decomposition. The OES data tape includes wage and salary employment only.

levels. It is hoped that BLS will be more open in the future about explaining the judgments which were made in adjusting staffing ratios, however.

The analysis of specific occupations is difficult because of the sheer number of those occupations. The discussion here is limited to the largest, the fastest growing, and the declining occupations. The three largest occupations are general office clerks, secretaries, and cashiers. The staffing ratios for cashiers is expected to increase significantly, contributing to the overall 48.2 percent growth forecast for that occupation. Apparently BLS does not expect point-of-sales automation devices will impact the employment of cashiers in the foreseeable future.

The effects of staffing ratio changes for secretaries are expected to be slightly negative. Looking at the effects of staffing ratios alone, the occupational decomposition indicates a projected decline in employment from 1982 levels of 2.3 percent, but the effects of differential rates of industry growth more than make up for this loss. The net result is that secretaries are expected to grow slightly faster than all occupations. This is entirely consistent with the historical data in chapter 3. It seems that BLS does not expect office automation to have a significant negative impact on the employment of secretaries over the course of the projections, since the staffing ratio change is actually less negative than the average for all clerical workers.

The fastest growing clerical jobs are expected to be computer operators, claims adjusters, insurance checkers, peripheral EDP equipment operators, telephone ad takers, claims clerks, and credit authorizers. All are expected to have staffing ratio impacts equivalent to increases in employment levels of 20 percent or more. Besides the obvious technological impacts of computers on this list, it may be important to note that many of these occupations require the worker to interact in some way with the customer being served. That may provide a clue as to why BLS thinks secretaries will not decline in importance, or perhaps why cashiers are the 10th fastest growing occupation. Again a world of both high-tech and high-touch is anticipated.

Obviously, various electronic office technologies threaten to replace the human element—through utilization of automatic bank tellers or automatic checkout devices in retail trade or even computerized ad takers at newspapers. It is extremely difficult, however, to know when and if customers will be willing or able to accept such devices. The fact that such devices *can* be developed does not guarantee that they *will* be used, or that they will prove to be profitable once they are used. At least through 1995, BLS apparently thinks that the human link will be an important source of occupational employment growth for clerical workers.

Turning to the clerical occupations which are declining the most in terms of their staffing ratios, the single greatest decline is projected for central office telephone operators. Next in order come (security purchase and sales) clerks, data entry operators, in-file operators, stenographers, file clerks, and postal service clerks. All are projected to have staffing ratio impacts equivalent to reductions in employment of 25 percent or more. Most of these occupations have been declining historically as well, as demonstrated in chapters 2 and 3, so there are not really many surprises. BLS thinks that the decline in the relative importance of file clerks will continue in the years ahead, thus continuing the trend established in the 1970s. But this occupation is still expected to grow slowly on an absolute basis. It is worth reiterating that it is easier to provide a technological explanation for the declining occupations than for many of the growing occupations.

It is also clear that many of the declining occupations are "back office" jobs that do not require direct contact with the customer. It is not known whether BLS thinks these jobs are simply easier to automate or whether it represents a judgment about the willingness of firms and/or their customers to sever the human links in conducting transactions.

Summary

BLS projections of U.S. occupational employment growth are made once every two years using a reasonably consistent economic methodology. The analysis of the major occupational groups indicated that BLS appears to be conservative in their projections, in that the relative changes anticipated for the next 13 years are much less than those which actually occurred in the last 10 years. This approach may represent the accumulated experience from past BLS projections, i.e., the most widely anticipated changes sometimes failed to materialize, while completely unexpected changes did occur. It may also be true that the two-year projection cycle of BLS encourages them to take a "show me" approach, since modifications can always be incorporated in the next round of projections. The BLS goal may be to capture the direction of change rather than the exact magnitude of change.

BLS anticipates that clerical job growth will be slightly below the average growth of all jobs through 1995. The staffing ratio effect is slightly negative in the BLS projections, whereas the historical data show that staffing ratios have tended to increase somewhat, at least from 1972-82. The analysis of the detailed clerical occupations showed that the anticipated staffing ratio changes are substantial and vary widely across clerical occupations. It is hoped that in the future BLS will provide information about the judgments which must have been made, at least implicitly, to justify these staffing ratio changes. It will be seen in the remaining sections of this chapter that other researchers have explicitly accounted for staffing ratio changes.

Other Occupational Employment Projections

Leontief-Duchin Study

Wassily Leontief and Faye Duchin of the Institute for Economic Analysis (IEA) at New York University have attempted to isolate the impact of computer-based technologies on employment by industry and occupation in *The Impacts of Automation on Employment, 1963-2000* (1984). They utilize a comprehensive input-output framework with four separate but interrelated matrices. The model is dynamic in that investment is a function of output changes in the individual producing sectors. The Leontief-Duchin study begins with the various BEA input/output tables and the census-based employment data by occupation. The key forecasting task is to alter the individual technical coefficients to account for the new computer-based automation.

The technological assessment is limited to computer-based technologies; specifically robots, computers, CNC machine tools, electronic office equipment, electronic education devices, and the industries which will use the aforementioned equipment. The technological forecasting is open in that the assumptions are clearly stated and based primarily upon the expert judgment of the researchers. The overall model is driven by the same final demand forecast used by the Bureau of Labor Statistics in the OES occupational projection effort, except for allowing greater investment in computer-based technologies where the authors deem appropriate.

It is important to emphasize at the outset that one of the assumptions in the Leontief-Duchin study is that no technical change outside computer-based technologies is allowed to affect future employment levels. This leads to dramatic gains in projected employment for occupations that are largely unaffected by these technologies such as

farmers, bakers, truckers, etc. While this assumption isolates
the pure impact of computers in a modeling sense, the
Leontief-Duchin approach seriously limits the usefulness of
the occupational employment projections. Since it is assumed that final demand grows as projected by BLS, obviously
the growth of output in nonautomated sectors requires
massive infusions of labor to produce that output.

One of the most dramatic illustrations of the impact on
this assumption occurs for IEA occupational group #53,
Farmers and Farm Workers. According to the Leontief-
Duchin presentation, one might be led to expect that the long
secular decline in job opportunities for farm workers has
ended, as shown in figure 5.5. In fact, the study makes it appear that this will be a significant growth occupation in the
future. Of course, no one really predicts such a result. It occurs because of the assumptions in the Leontief-Duchin
model.

Specifically, in the case of agricultural workers, the expansion of final demand for foodstuffs combined with no (or
minimal) increases in labor productivity leads to substantial
increases in the demand for farm workers. Labor productivity gains for farm workers are nil because most farm work is
presumably not amenable to the utilization of computer-
based technologies, the only source of productivity growth
allowed for in the Leontief-Duchin framework. Clearly, this
is purely an artifact of the model and should not be regarded
as a projected occupational trend. In fact, most analysts
believe that the phenomenal increases in productivity in
agricultural production will continue, so that future food
supplies will be generated without substantial increases in
human resource inputs. To repeat, Leontief and Duchin
assume *no* productivity increases in the economic system
other than those induced by computer-based technologies.

Figure 5.5

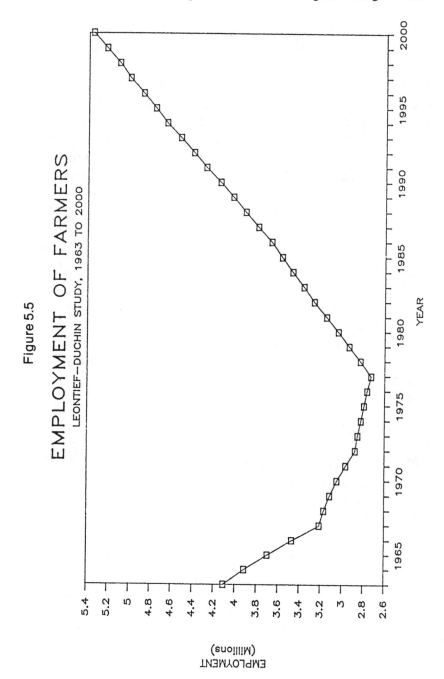

EMPLOYMENT OF FARMERS

LEONTIEF–DUCHIN STUDY, 1963 TO 2000

The Leontief-Duchin employment projections utilize four different scenarios which differ in their technological assumptions. Scenario S1 is the baseline scenario; it assumes no further automation or any other technological change after 1980. Scenarios S2 and S3 are identical to S1 through 1980 but S3 assumes more rapid adoption of computer-based technologies than S2 thereafter. Since the BLS estimates of demand drive the model, scenario S1, with no productivity gains, generates employment estimates that are far beyond reasonable projections of the labor force available. It turns out that both S2 and S3 do also (i.e., there are more jobs anticipated than people to fill those jobs) although S3 is closer to realistic projections of the labor force than S2. The fourth and final scenario in the Leontief-Duchin study, S4, adjusts the level of demand for labor downward (using the composition of demand from S3) until it is just consistent with the labor supply which will likely be available to produce that output (i.e., full employment). The employment estimates from S4 are used throughout this paper in reviewing the Leontief-Duchin study.

The Leontief-Duchin projections for employment in the major occupational groups are presented in table 5.6. The time period selected is for 1982-1995 to facilitate comparison with the BLS projections. However, it should be noted that this is actually several years into the Leontief-Duchin projections, while 1982 is the base year for BLS. The occupational decomposition in the table is limited to the constant employment shares and all other structural change, thus combining the effects of staffing ratios and differential rates of industry growth. However, this is not likely to be a serious problem since Leontief and Duchin use the final demand forecast of BLS, for which it has already been shown that the impacts of differences in the rates of growth of industries is relatively modest. The real differences between the BLS and the Leontief-Duchin projections arise from the assumed changes

Table 5.6
Leontief-Duchin Projected Occupational Growth, 1982-1995
Major Occupational Groups

| Occupation | Employment changes | | | | Decomposition of clerical employment changes, 1982-1995 | | | |
| | | | | | Absolute changes | | Percent of 1982 employment | |
	1982 employment (000s)	1995 employment (000s)	Change in employment 1982-1995 (000s)	Change in employment 1982-1995 (percent)	Constant employment shares (000s)	Other structural change* (000s)	Constant employment shares	Other structural change*
Professionals . . .	16,292	25,858	9,566	58.7	5,538	4,028	34.0	24.7
Managers	11,218	12,484	1,266	11.3	3,813	(2,548)	34.0	-22.7
Sales	6,861	9,328	2,466	36.0	2,332	134	34.0	2.0
Clerical	18,032	17,786	(246)	-1.4	6,129	(6,375)	34.0	-35.4
Craftsmen	15,314	21,554	6,240	40.7	5,206	1,034	34.0	6.7
Operatives	17,852	23,945	6,093	34.1	6,069	24	34.0	0.1
Service	12,909	20,023	7,114	55.1	4,388	2,725	34.0	21.1
Laborers	5,535	8,015	2,480	44.8	1,882	598	34.0	10.8
Farmers	3,270	4,761	1,491	45.6	1,112	379	34.0	11.6
Total	107,284	143,753	36,469	34.0				

SOURCE: Calculations by the authors based upon data kindly provided by Faye Duchin.

NOTE: Totals and percentages may not add exactly due to omission of some occupational detail and rounding error.

*Other structural change includes the combined effects of changes in staffing ratios and differential rates of industry growth.

in the staffing ratios as well as the assumption of no productivity growth other than that connected with computer-based technologies.

An examination of the employment projections for the major occupational groups in table 5.6 clearly illustrates the impacts of assuming no general productivity gains. The employment growth rate for farmers is nearly 46 percent, about one-third higher than the growth of all jobs. Professionals and service workers also show fantastic increases. This latter result may appear less unreasonable since it is part of conventional wisdom that service sector jobs have been the major growth sector for the last 20 years or more. However, the estimates in the Leontief-Duchin study result from the same assumptions as in the case of the farm workers.

What is most significant from the standpoint of this study is that Leontief and Duchin project an *absolute decline* in the employment of clerical workers as well as very slow growth in managers. Regardless of the problems in interpreting the projections that emanate from this model, if Leontief and Duchin are at all correct, it could not only mean displacement for large numbers of clerical workers but also portend difficulties for those workers seeking higher level positions in the office.

The Leontief-Duchin study disaggregates total clerical jobs into five specific clerical occupations, namely secretaries, office machine operators, bank tellers, phone operators, and cashiers, plus a sixth category for all other clericals. The projections for these jobs are shown in table 5.7 using the same format as shown for the major occupational groups. Secretaries, office machine operators, and bank tellers are all expected to experience absolute declines in employment. Phone operators are expected to remain constant. Only cashiers are growing faster than the average for

Table 5.7
Leontief-Duchin Projection Occupational Growth, 1982-1995
Detailed Clerical Occupations

| Occupation | Employment changes | | | | Decomposition of clerical employment changes, 1982-1995 | | | |
| | | | | | Absolute changes | | Percent of 1982 employment | |
	1982 employment (000s)	1995 employment (000s)	Change in employment 1982-1995 (000s)	Change in employment 1982-1995 (percent)	Constant employment shares (000s)	Other structural change* (000s)	Constant employment shares	Other structural change*
Clerical	18,032	17,786	(246)	-1.4	6,129	(6,375)	34.0	-35.4
Secretaries	4,951	4,592	(359)	-7.2	1,683	(2,042)	34.0	-41.2
Office machine oper. .	811	224	(587)	-72.4	276	(863)	34.0	-106.4
Bank tellers	494	404	(90)	-18.2	168	(258)	34.0	-52.1
Phone operators	355	356	1	0.3	121	(119)	34.0	-33.7
Cashiers	1,568	2,186	618	39.4	533	85	34.0	5.4
Other clerical . . .	9,853	10,024	171	1.7	3,349	(3,178)	34.0	-32.3
Total employment . .	107,284	143,753	36,469	34.0				

SOURCE: Calculations by the authors based upon data kindly provided by Faye Duchin.

NOTE: Totals and percentages may not add exactly due to omission of some occupational detail and rounding error.

*Other structural change includes the combined effects of changes in staffing ratios and differential rates of industry growth.

all occupations. The inference is that Leontief and Duchin think that cashiers will be relatively unaffected by computer technology, while the other clerical occupations will experience significant displacement.

Unlike the BLS model, Leontief and Duchin openly state their assumptions about technological change and the subsequent impact on the staffing ratios of the occupations. Therefore, it is possible to evaluate those assumptions independently of the overall reasonableness of the projections. Given the much slower than average growth for most of the clerical field, the staffing ratios for those jobs must be expected to fall rapidly. Thus, the selected analysis of some of those assumptions is critical for this study.

The technological assumptions for secretaries and typists will be examined in detail to illustrate the approach of Leontief and Duchin. According to Leontief and Duchin (1984:5.21), the direct impact of office automation on particular occupations is based on the findings of case studies wherever possible. In general, they find that word processing equipment "produces remarkable gains in productivity when it is properly selected and used" (1984:5.29). They reference an article in *Administrative Management* (no author, 1978:70-71) which concludes that word processing can increase output from 500 to 1,000 percent. They also suggest that several other studies support labor savings of up to 50 percent—Murphree (1981) in a Wall Street legal firm and Downing (1980). Finally, they cite Karan (1982) as concluding that word processing equipment in one research organization reduced labor requirements by 20 percent.

None of these studies constitute a formal case study of the quantitative economic impacts of word processing, but the purpose of this discussion is not so much to question the findings of the references cited but rather to illustrate how Leontief and Duchin used these estimates to alter the staffing ratios for typists and secretaries. Leontief and Duchin assume that 100 percent of a typist's time will be affected by word processing and that word processing technology will produce labor savings of 80 percent. That amounts to a whopping 500 percent gain in productivity for typists who use word processing equipment. The surprise is that Leontief and Duchin adopt the most optimistic projection of productivity gains for word processing equipment, those in *Administrative Management,* without any discussion of why the other studies which show less spectacular gains are any less reasonable.

Furthermore, Leontief and Duchin assume that word processing equipment produces only a temporary increase in the amount of work that originators will request, which can be eliminated through a properly managed installation. Thus, word processing creates no "new" work, such as more revisions or more perfect copies. All the assumed productivity gain adds "directly or indirectly to the total output of the firm" (1984:5.30). But, as explained in chapter 4, the capabilities of the microprocessor are ideally suited to redrafts, more form letters, updated statistical reports, etc. Word processing is not adopted simply to save labor time, i.e., to accomplish the same old work with fewer workers, but because there is additional work that needs to be done. Thus the production in the firm becomes more intensive in information content, a trend which has been ongoing for many years.

The technological capability of word processing to save the time that a secretary or typist would have spent doing the same work on a typewriter is only one of the links in estimating the expected changes in staffing ratios. A separate question is that of how many such workers will have word processors, in other words the diffusion of the technology. A 500 percent gain in labor productivity by a small percentage of the workers will have little impact at the aggregate level.

Leontief and Duchin assume that the 500 percent gain in labor productivity from using word processing affects 100 percent of the tasks of typists and that 70 percent of all typists will have word processing by 1990 (1984:5.31-32). The assumptions are the same for secretaries except that only 24 percent of them type full time, while the remainder type 20 percent of the time. It should be mentioned that there are separate assumptions about the adoption of integrated office systems that link various devices together. These networks will also decrease overall requirements for secretaries.

In the Leontief-Duchin study, the diffusion rates for word processing equipment are not influenced by industrial sector or by size of firm, i.e., the technology is assumed to diffuse steadily with the same impacts regardless of industry or size of firm. In reality these assumptions may not be accurate. For example, certain sectors, such as insurance and banking, are already significant users of electronic office technology. Thus some proportion of secretaries and typists may already be using this equipment (before the base period of the research study). Obviously they cannot benefit a second time from its introduction.

Along a similar vein, it is likely that the work in particular sectors is more amenable to electronic office technology. Examples may be law offices, where some types of legal briefs are repetitive except for a few sections and where a high premium is assigned to the correctness of language used in each brief. In these sectors, just as in banking and insurance, the new office technologies may be more productive and hence spread rapidly. On the other hand, the situation may be more clouded in other sectors, where the work tends to be more unique and less repetitive. It seems logical that the productivity gains will vary widely depending on the precise nature of the output of the office.

Finally, it is also possible that the size of firm is a crucial variable in determining the impacts of electronic office technology. The most obvious example is the one-secretary office where the labor savings may free the secretary to do other tasks but the firm has no intention of eliminating this job. Thus the hypothetical productivity gains, even if they are realized, do not reduce the actual number of secretaries in such an environment. Ideally these positions would be excluded from the calculations developed by Leontief and Duchin.[10]

Although Leontief and Duchin do not specifically account for size of firm and industry, it could be argued that their estimates represent average gains over a very long period of time. However, it seems clear that the productivity gains anticipated by Leontief and Duchin are only possible for tasks that are very repetitive and which therefore require little individual attention. The notion advanced by Leontief and Duchin that word processing equipment will create zero net new work is untenable. While word processing equipment may lower labor requirements absolutely, surely some of that static gain (based on the old work regime) will be dissipated through the creation of new work. It is also impossible to believe that the average static productivity gain from word processing will be as large as assumed by Leontief and Duchin.

In general, the Leontief-Duchin model produces three different types of projected occupational impacts. The first type (direct impacts) results from stated assumptions about the spread of computer-based technologies and the hypothesized labor displacement potential of those technologies. The second type (indirect impacts) results from the workings of the input-output model itself. It represents the secondary impacts from the changes in investment and labor demand associated with the direct impacts. The third type (unintentional impacts) represents the forced growth occupational demand in areas not substantially affected by computer-based technologies.

To make the projections of the occupational impact of computer-based technologies most useful for policy decisions, the projections should be compared to an alternative state of the world that represents a *realistic* baseline. Even a simple linear extrapolation of historical employment trends by sector or occupation would provide a more realistic baseline than the counterfactual assumption of no productivity gains except those due to computer-based technologies.

While the Leontief-Duchin configuration may be useful as a modeling device, it obscures the true policy implications of the model. In fact, the results may be seriously misleading to policymakers. For policy purposes it is more important to focus on the marginal changes that will result from a specific treatment rather than to focus on the aggregate change from an alternative state of the world that could never happen.

It is also important that the global scope of the results presented in the Leontief-Duchin study not conceal the fact that the actual assumptions about the spread of computer-based technologies and the labor displacing impacts are *judgmental*. This is not meant as a criticism of the Leontief-Duchin effort, but the elegance of the final presentation can mislead the unwary into the mistaken impression that the model is responsible for the predictions. In fact, the model is *simply a tool* to project the implications of the stated assumptions about the technology. Some of the assumptions about the spread of computer-based technologies are reasonable and some are not. It is natural that people will differ in these judgments; what is important is that it be clear that it is the assumptions that drive the model, not vice versa.

In addition, it seems clear that the changes they studied are not the only changes that will take place, nor are they necessarily the most important ones. The model does not address substitution among different inputs based upon price changes, or changes in final demand induced by price effects resulting from use of the new technologies. Nor does it include scale economies and agglomeration economies, both of which may be influenced directly by technological change. This latter point may be particularly important since some experts expect computer-based technologies to transform the traditional manufacturing environment.

There is also an important question about the degree of substitution among different kinds of capital goods. It is not necesssarily true that because an industry adopts some form of automation it will achieve better than average gains in productivity. The reason is that it may at the same time reduce its investment in other productivity-enhancing areas. In other words, the new investment may simply be the current manifestation of labor-saving technology that will help these firms to achieve productivity gains at the historic average. Resolution of this issue is of major importance in assessing the effects of computer-based technologies.

The Leontief-Duchin study represents a significant advance in modeling that holds considerable promise for studying the employment implications of technological change. It moves the field one step closer to a general equilibrium model that could incorporate all direct and indirect influences on employment that emanate from technological change or other structural change in the economy. However, the true contribution of the Leontief-Duchin model to understanding future occupational trends cannot yet be determined. The model needs a more realistic baseline scenario, including trend values of productivity increase by sector, to determine the marginal employment impacts of computer-based technology.

Drennan Study

Matthew P. Drennan (1983) has explored the impacts of office automation on clerical employment in six industries in *Implications of Computer and Communications Technology for Less Skilled Service Employment Opportunities.* The industries examined were banking, credit agencies, securities, insurance, business services, and miscellaneous services. The analysis of clerical employment uses the job classification system from the 1970 Census of Population.

The Drennan study is both quantitative and qualitative. The quantitative portion of the study utilizes a variety of data sources, while the qualitative portion is based on the author's interviews with a selected number of producers and users of office automation. The review here is limited to the projections methodology used by Drennan and the important judgments and assumptions which appear to drive those projections.

The Drennan projections methodology utilizes simple extrapolation to forecast industry-occupation employment to 1990. First, industry employment in the six industries from 1983 onward is assumed to grow at the historical average rate experienced from 1969-1979 based on data from the national income and product accounts. The notion is that following the 1980-1982 recessionary period these industries will return to prerecessionary growth patterns. In addition, Drennan also includes an alternative 1990 forecast which assumes a productivity growth rate that is .5 percentage point higher per year in each industry than the historical average for those industries.

Once the estimates for 1990 industry employment are obtained, then employment by occupation in those industries is estimated by assuming that the change in occupational staffing patterns from 1970 to 1978 will continue to 1990, what

Drennan (1983:88) calls "more of the same." The occupational staffing patterns were obtained from the *National Industry-Occupation Employment Matrix, 1970, 1978, and Projected 1990* (Bureau of Labor Statistics 1981). In brief, the occupational employment estimates for these six industries are derived from past changes in occupational staffing patterns and past industry growth trends.

It should be mentioned that the 1978 BLS industry-occupation matrix was CPS-based, the last such matrix developed before BLS switched to the OES survey. This is significant for two reasons. First, the CPS is household-based whereas the newer OES survey is establishment-based. BLS thinks the occupational staffing patterns developed from the establishment survey are much more reliable than those self-reported by households. Second, the small size of the CPS sample, about 60,000 households, contributes to the variability of the detailed occupational estimates. Moreover, the CPS sample is far too small to provide detailed industry by occupation estimates, so the 1978 CPS-based matrix was itself statistically estimated from the 1970 Census of Population industry by occupation matrix. The procedure used the 1978 industry and occupation employment control totals from the CPS and adjusted the 1970 staffing ratios to be consistent with those totals. The adjustments were based on historical census trends and an analysis of factors that might influence those trends such as product mix changes or changes in production methods. The important point is that there may be much more error in the 1978 matrix than the 1970 matrix since the 1978 matrix is statistically estimated rather than survey-based.

A brief summary of Drennan's overall projections is presented in table 5.8. Since staffing ratios for clerical employment fell in these six industries by nearly 3 percent from 1970 to 1978, the extrapolation indicates a similar

decline from 1978 to 1990. Total employment in these industries grew 70 percent from 1970 to 1978, but it is only expected to grow 44 percent from 1978 to 1990. This slower
growth is presumably due to the interruption of growth in
these industries during the 1980-1982 recession. Since staffing ratios are falling for clerical workers, clerical employment growth is much slower than total employment growth
in these industries. Drennan concludes (1983:90)

> The expectation of markedly slower employment
> growth in clerical jobs in those industries is firmly
> based and is difficult to contest. The chief implica-
> tion for the labor force is the same as it was a
> decade ago: education beyond secondary school is
> the key passport to job security in the 1990s.

There are a number of strengths to Drennan's simple extrapolation technique. Since these industries have been the
leaders in office automation, the assumed scenario is plausible if one thinks the current impacts of office automation
will continue in the future. The important point is that if the
past is any guide to the future for these industries, then
clerical jobs will continue to grow, but much slower than the
average of all jobs in these industries. On the other hand, it is
also easy to dismiss any extrapolation technique as too
simplistic. Demand changes do occur; technological change
tends to be uneven. But, besides these rather obvious questions that can be directed at any extrapolation methodology,
there are a number of other concerns about Drennan's projections.

First, it should be made clear that the alternative 1990 industry employment estimates, which assume an additional .5
percent productivity growth, are not logically related to any
of the other data in the extrapolations. Specifically, it is in-
conceivable that the extra productivity growth (which ranges
from just under 20 percent to in excess of 100 percent de-

pending on the industry) would not lead to price declines which in turn would positively affect industry sales. It is really not meaningful to fix demand and then vary productivity to show that less workers would be needed if the existing workers would only produce more. The arithmetic in these calculations is easy to do, perhaps too easy, but in reality the growth in demand for these service industries has been robust over the last decade or so. The strong implication is that price declines would be accompanied by at least some increase in demand for these services in the future.

Table 5.8
Drennan: Projected Employment by Occupation
in Six Office Industries
(thousands)

Occupation	1970 employment*	1978 employment*	1990 employment	Alternative 1990 employment
Professionals	1,005	1,595	2,611	2,458
Managers	814	1,176	1,755	1,637
Sales	577	770	1,015	950
Clericals	2,325	3,092	4,153	3,867
Other.	705	1,081	1,620	1,611
Total	5,426	7,714	11,156	10,525

*Bureau of Labor Statistics, U.S. Department of Labor, *The National Industry-Occupation Employment Matrix, 1970-1978 and Projected 1990,* Bulletin 2086, April 1981.

Second, the assumption of the continuation of past trends in staffing ratios appears to be contradicted to some extent by Drennan's own qualitative analysis. According to him (1983:69), managers' employment will "experience a marked curtailment of growth" in the years ahead. This slowdown will be due to the diffusion of integrated office systems, where executives will be able to communicate with each other electronically and access data bases and all other software using desktop computers. Although Drennan points to several reasons why these systems will not diffuse as rapidly as perhaps some experts think, it is clear that he includes the alternative 1990 industry projections to incorporate the possibility of faster diffusion. But, even in the alternative scenario, the productivity gains are spread out evenly over all occupations.

In summary, Drennan has forecast clerical jobs to 1990 in six industries. He uses a simple extrapolation technique, after accounting for the lack of growth during the 1980-1982 recession. There may be some problems in the data used for the extrapolations, questions about the alternative employment growth scenario, and some questions about the logical relationship between the qualitative analysis and the quantitative extrapolations. Nonetheless, to the extent that the past decade is a guide to the future for these industries, the projections deserve serious consideration.

Roessner Study

J. David Roessner and his colleagues at Georgia Tech examined the impact of office automation on clerical employment in two industries, banking and insurance, in *Impact of Office Automation on Office Workers* (1984). Roessner stresses the need to extend current employment forecasts such as those by BLS beyond 10 years. He (II, 1984:2) also concludes that there are weaknesses in existing employment forecasts, especially in the way in which jobs are defined and the incorporation of technological change in the projections methodology. The forecast horizon in the Roessner study extends to the year 2000.

The Roessner study focuses on an explicit and systematic technology assessment and forecast and the relationship of that forecast to occupational employment. He describes his method as more of an engineering approach but one that also takes account of economic considerations. (III,

1984:4-5). He stresses the importance of making the process as open and transparent as possible to facilitate its use by others and to encourage improvements in the methodology.

The Roessner study team (10 people) first developed a time-phased technology forecast for office automation in banking and insurance. This initial forecast formed the basis for deriving technical assumptions which were then distributed to officials from these two industries who were asked to participate in a Delphi exercise. The Delphi methodology attempts to develop a consensus forecast from iterative and independent polling of experts in a given field. Roessner (III, 1984:96-97) conducted two rounds of polling of eight experts each in banking and insurance. The insurance representatives were all suggested by the Life Office Management Association, Atlanta, Georgia. It is not reported whether the insurance experts were representative of all segments of the insurance industry or simply life insurers. It should also be mentioned that Delphi studies usually involve more than two rounds of polling and generally sample more than eight experts. It is unknown what impacts the Roessner approach might have had on the final technology assumptions and forecast.

Space limitations prohibit reporting the full technology forecast, or "technology morphology" as Roessner calls it (III, 1984:46-55). However, the emphasis was on the identification of breakthrough technologies that might have a significant impact on clerical employment. According to Roessner's projections, there are two breakthrough technologies on the horizon that will likely impact clerical employment in the 1990s, namely optical scan and voice recognition systems and artificial intelligence (AI). The market for the former devices, which will eliminate the human keying of data and text, will be about $4 billion by 1992, and these systems will be in widespread use by that year. The market for various types of AI systems will lag that of voice recognition; but by 1998 we will have "self-generating" software (II, 1984:8). As will be seen later, these two breakthrough technologies will indeed have a significant impact on Roessner's projections of clerical employment in the 1990s.

The second step in the Roessner methodology was to develop a task characteristic/function matrix for each detailed clerical job using the job classification system of BLS. This was done to overcome the weaknesses of current BLS job descriptions which tend to link the job to existing technologies. For instance, the tasks of typing and data entry might both be classified simply as the input function. The six functions identified by Roessner were: input, processing, output, data base, communications, and monitoring. According to him the advantage of the functional terms is that they are independent of technologies currently in use. The identification of the task/function matrices was essentially judgmental (III, 1984:73). The detailed BLS jobs were then grouped into clerical job clusters by the similarity of their functions. Roessner used secondary sources supplemented by a small number of interviews and survey questionnaires to determine the time clericals spend in each task/function.

The third step of the Roessner methodology was to conduct an industry Delphi forecast to provide estimates of the impacts of office automation on the structure of work. These estimates were not nearly as detailed as the task characteristic/function matrix but were designed to identify in broad terms different organizational structures and employment mixes that might prevail in the future. They provide an input to the next step of the process, which develops the estimated labor savings, plus they provide an independent means of verifying or validating the final employment forecast itself.

The fourth step of the Roessner methodology was to actually estimate the impact of office automation on the clerical job clusters using the functions of those jobs developed earlier. It amounts to producing time phased estimates of labor savings due to the new technology. This was done internally by the study team using a modified Delphi process which Roessner (III, 1984:122) calls "estimate-talk-estimate." The goal of the method was to gain stability in the responses among the study team about the various judgments which had to be made to quantitatively estimate the labor savings for each job cluster.

The fifth step of the Roessner methodology was to generate the employment forecasts for each of the clerical job clusters. These estimates used a base year of 1980 and provided forecasts at five-year intervals to the year 2000. Demand for the output of these industries, what Roessner calls "workload," is a straight line regression extrapolation of value added in banking and insurance plus a special output index in banking which was constructed from various deposit transactions (II, 1984:22).

The final step of the Roessner methodology is to conduct a sensitivity analysis of the results and to validate those results. The primary validation is to return to the industry Delphi forecast which identifies the general job mixes and compare those with the more detailed approach. According to Roessner, the two methods provide remarkably consistent employment estimates (II, 1984:27). For the sake of brevity, only the standard or most likely estimates from the Roessner study are presented in this review.[11]

Among the most important sets of summary estimates in the Roessner study are those that pertain to the labor savings which are most likely to be realized by the installation of office automation in banking and insurance. These estimates are actually the heart of the study; they summarize the interaction of the technology forecast with the task/function matrix which describes the job activities of clerical workers. Recall also that demand is a simple extrapolation of past trends in these industries, so it is truly the labor savings estimates which are novel and which obviously drive the employment projections.

The labor savings or productivity gains attributable to office automation for each of the occupational clusters developed by Roessner are presented in table 5.9. Roessner states these in index number form as the percent of the 1980 base time required. Thus a falling index number indicates that the same amount of work in the specified future year can be accomplished in less time than in the base year, 1980. What is surprising about these labor savings estimates are that they are so similar across the job clusters and even across the two industries. Thus the productivity gains for filing/data entry clerks is almost the same as that for receptionists/telephone operators.

The strong implication is that clerical jobs will not change much in relative importance from 1980 to 2000. This conclusion is illustrated in table 5.10 which shows the importance of each of the clerical job clusters as a percent of total clerical employment in those industries. Roessner (IV, 1984:145) acknowledges that some readers might be surprised at the homogeneity of the results across occupations. But he suggests one interpretation of the findings:

> One possibility is that this surprisingly even, across-the-board projected reduction in clerical time per work function will prove accurate because market forces will act to stimulate new technological development to improve productivity evenly across clerical activities. For instance, while automation of structured input is commencing earlier than automation of unstructured input, that very gap

may accentuate efforts to bring technologies such as voice recognition to market. There appear to be relatively few work functions that are "safe" from a substantial degree of automation.

Again, if Roessner's projections are correct, all clerical jobs will be impacted similarly by office automation, *in the short run as well as the long run.*

Table 5.9
Roessner: Percent of 1980-Base Time Required by
Occupational Cluster, Most Likely Scenario for Banking and Insurance

Occupational cluster	1980	1985	1990	1995	2000
Banking					
Computation/bookkeeping clerks	100.00	92.75	81.73	63.36	42.10
General office clerks	100.00	92.75	81.56	63.36	42.03
Typists/word processor operators	100.00	94.00	83.29	66.25	45.86
Secretary/administrative assistants	100.00	93.62	82.15	65.61	46.01
Filing/data entry clerks	100.00	92.44	80.82	61.42	39.07
Information retrieval/ communications clerks	100.00	92.35	80.33	61.37	40.06
Mail handlers	100.00	92.71	80.76	63.64	42.25
Clerical supervisors	100.00	93.39	82.46	65.75	46.71
Receptionists/telephone operators	100.00	92.23	79.40	60.94	39.30
Computer/office equipment operators	100.00	91.69	80.47	61.58	39.42
Tellers	100.00	92.22	60.92	61.79	38.80
Information maintenance clerks	100.00	92.96	81.45	63.24	41.60
Insurance					
Computation/bookkeeping clerks	100.00	92.52	81.57	62.89	42.00
General office clerks	100.00	92.76	81.37	63.28	42.31
Typists/word processor operators	100.00	94.10	83.42	67.02	47.37
Secretary/administrative assistants	100.00	93.38	82.15	64.93	44.71
Filing/data entry clerks	100.00	92.55	81.21	61.77	40.12
Information retrieval/ communications clerks	100.00	92.66	80.38	61.27	38.96
Mail handlers	100.00	92.61	80.88	63.49	41.51
Clerical supervisors	100.00	93.76	82.81	65.96	46.47
Receptionists/telephone operators	100.00	92.10	79.39	60.34	39.29
Computer/office equipment operators	100.00	92.02	80.99	61.89	39.43

SOURCE: J. David Roessner, *Impact of Office Automation on Office Workers,* Volume IV, *Appendices,* prepared for the Employment and Training Administration, U.S. Department of Labor, April 1984, Appendix P, Runs #1 and #51.

Table 5.10
Roessner: Percent of Clerical Labor by Year,
Most Likely Scenario for Banking and Insurance

Occupational cluster	1980	1985	1990	1995	2000
Banking					
Computation/bookkeeping clerks	5.78	5.79	5.81	5.82	5.91
General office clerks	21.45	21.48	21.51	21.59	21.89
Typists/word processor operators	2.71	2.75	2.78	2.85	3.02
Secretary/administrative assistants	7.67	7.75	7.75	7.99	8.57
Filing/data entry clerks	2.86	2.85	2.84	2.79	2.71
Information retrieval/ communications clerks	2.35	2.34	2.32	2.29	2.29
Mail handlers	2.09	2.09	2.08	2.11	2.14
Clerical supervisors	5.29	5.33	5.36	5.53	6.00
Receptionists/telephone operators	1.59	1.58	1.55	1.54	1.52
Computer/office equipment operators	1.99	1.97	1.97	1.95	1.90
Tellers	37.37	37.20	37.18	36.68	35.20
Information maintenance clerks	.97	.97	.97	.97	.98
Insurance					
Computation/bookkeeping clerks	15.30	15.23	15.27	15.11	14.98
General office clerks	25.99	25.94	25.88	25.82	25.63
Typists/word processor operators	7.89	7.99	8.05	8.30	8.71
Secretary/administrative assistants	9.77	9.82	9.82	9.96	10.18
Filing/data entry clerks	7.36	7.33	7.31	7.14	6.88
Information retrieval/ communications clerks	1.06	1.06	1.04	1.02	.96
Mail handlers	1.85	1.84	1.83	1.84	1.79
Clerical supervisors	5.49	5.54	5.56	5.68	5.95
Receptionists/telephone operators	1.46	1.45	1.42	1.38	1.34
Computer/office equipment operators	2.96	2.93	2.93	2.88	2.72

SOURCE: J. David Roessner, *Impact of Office Automation on Office Workers,* Volume IV, *Appendices,* prepared for the Employment and Training Administration, U.S. Department of Labor, April 1984, Appendix P, Runs #1 and #51.

A summary of Roessner's employment forecast for banking and insurance is presented in table 5.11. The overall demand or workload forecast is presented first; it is the linear extrapolation of demand referred to earlier, stated as the number of workers required assuming no productivity gains (1980 base). That is followed by the presentation of the overall productivity gains for clerical workers, what

Table 5.11
Roessner: Summary Employment Projections
for Banking and Insurance, Most Likely Scenario

Item	1980	1985	1990	1995	2000
Banking					
Clerical workload forecast (employees x 1,000)	1,100	1,326	1,551	1,781	2,001
Percent reduction due to technology	0.0	7.37	18.67	37.05	58.81
Clerical workforce required (employees x 1,000)	1,100	1,228	1,261	1,121	824
Average annual productivity gain for each five-year period	---	1.474	2.260	3.676	4.352
Insurance					
Clerical workload forecast (employees x 1,000)	924	1,024	1,124	1,225	1,324
Percent reduction due to technology	0.0	7.07	18.28	36.30	57.09
Clerical workforce required (employees x 1,000)	924	952	919	780	568
Average annual productivity gain for each five-year period	---	1.414	2.242	3.604	4.158

SOURCE: J. David Roessner, *Impact of Office Automation on Office Workers*, Volume IV, *Appendices*, prepared for the Employment and Training Administration, U.S. Department of Labor, April 1984, Appendix P, Runs #1 and #51.

Roessner calls the percent reduction due to technology. Third, the actual clerical workforce required to accomplish the projected workload, taking account of the productivity gains, is derived, i.e., the employment projections. Finally, for purposes of explanation, the annual average productivity gains for each five years of the projections are presented.

The data in table 5.11 illustrate the major conclusions of the Roessner study. He expects a drastic curtailment of the growth of clerical jobs in banking and insurance, which will accelerate in the 1990s. By the year 2000 there will be fewer clerical workers in banking and insurance than there were in 1980. Although only the results from the most likely scenario are presented in this review, employment declines are projected by Roessner even for the most conservative technological assumptions (III, 1984:149). It should be clear that if demand increases linearly, while the productivity gains from office automation accelerate exponentially over the 20 years of the projection period, the logical result must be decline in clerical employment.

But the truth is that the Roessner projections may not be any more usable by policymakers than those of Leontief-Duchin. Whatever the merits of the Roessner methodology, the results do not appear to describe real world events. This conclusion is demonstrated by table 5.12 which presents the actual BLS staffing ratios for selected clerical occupations for 1970 and 1978 in the banking industry. In so far as possible Roessner's occupational clusters have been related to the BLS system. The match is at least roughly consistent for 8 of the 12 occupational clusters. Actually, the match is not nearly as important as simply noting how dramatic the actual changes in staffing ratios were. From 1970 to 1978 the changes in staffing ratios for the selected clerical occupations presented in table 5.12 ranged from –60 percent to + 115 percent.[12]

Table 5.12
Staffing Ratios for Selected Clerical Positions in Banking
Based Upon the National Industry-Occupation Employment Matrix,
1970 and 1978, Grouped by Roessner's Occupational Clusters

Occupation (Roessner/BLS)	1970	1978	Percent change in staffing ratios 1970-1978
Typists/word processor operators			
Typists	2.94	2.24	−23.8
Secretaries/administrative assistants			
Secretaries	6.93	6.28	−9.4
Filing/data entry clerks			
File clerks	1.27	.96	−24.4
Keypunch operators	1.78	1.27	−28.7
Mail handlers			
Mail handlers	.62	.57	−8.1
Messengers	.63	.46	−27.0
Clerical supervisors			
Clerical supervisors	.73	.80	+9.6
Receptionists/telephone operators			
Receptionists	.60	.56	−6.7
Telephone operators	.45	.18	−60.0
Computer/office equipment operators			
Computer operators	1.26	2.72	+115.9
Duplicating machine operators	.03	.03	0.0
Tellers			
Bank tellers	26.27	30.28	+15.3
Total clerical	64.77	64.50	0.0

SOURCE: Bureau of Labor Statistics, U.S. Department of Labor, *The National Industry-Occupation Employment Matrix, 1970, 1978, and Projected 1990,* Volume I, 1981, p. 289.

Yet Roessner asserts that the relative importance of clerical jobs will not change much in the future. Back-office jobs such as file clerks have been declining in relative importance for a long time, while computer-related positions have been increasing dramatically in relative importance. Absent a complete break with history, clerical occupations are likely to continue to rise and fall at differential rates.

There appear to be three major problem areas in the Roessner study which may have contributed to these counter-intuitive conclusions about the likely relative importance of clerical jobs in banking and insurance in the future. These same problems may also have contributed to Roessner's overall pessimistic outlook for clerical jobs in these two industries. Each problem area is discussed briefly in turn.

First, there is no consideration of a whole host of investment questions or the possibility that the information content of output will increase. As in Drennan's study, it is presumed that the enormous gains in productivity attributable to office automation will not alter the linear increase in demand for the output of banking or insurance. Such an assumption may be acceptable for a sector like agriculture when we already have enough foodstuffs to eat. But it is not appropriate to apply that assumption to services. Again, a more reasonable position is that productivity gains of the magnitude expected by Roessner would lead to price declines which in turn would surely expand the markets for those services.

It should also be mentioned that the changes envisioned by Roessner may not only save labor but may also be the catalyst for the development of entirely new products within banking and insurance. Although it appears to be impossible to identify those new products in advance, banking and insurance have offered innovative services in the past and will likely continue to do so in the future. To the extent that new products and services are developed, they will tend to mitigate any employment declines from office automation.

It is also bothersome that Roessner appears to allow for no slack or slippage of any kind in calculating the productivity gains. Organizations and the technologies used do not fit together perfectly; there tend to be bottlenecks and downtime. Most important of all, it is well known that the potential labor savings of any technology may not actually be realized in fact. It is unknown if Roessner took these factors into account, but on the surface his estimates appear so optimistic that he may not have accounted for them sufficiently.

The second major problem area in the Roessner study is in the task/function matrix. Researchers have been looking for an objective way to define jobs for a long time. Job content tends to be very amorphous, however. That is one of the reasons why the OES system now in place at BLS concentrates on job titles. The definition of jobs, whether by task characteristics, by Roessner's functions, or by any other means, tends to be a moving target which is impossible to hit squarely. The functions identified by Roessner may be so general (input, data processing, etc.) that they do not truly describe job activities in a meaningful way. In short, there is a possibility that Roessner's task/function matrix may have introduced a homogeneity across jobs that does not exist in reality. This problem was then compounded by the aggregation of those occupations into job clusters.

The final problem area in the Roessner study may be in the technology forecast itself. Roessner concludes that it is important to extend these forecasts beyond 10 years, ". . .to anticipate major changes in time for policy machinery to move and related institutions to adjust" (II, 1984:34). However desirable Roessner's goal may be, it probably cannot be achieved.

History is littered with technological forecasts which turned out to be false or at best only partially true, while other radical changes were not foreseen at all. Artificial intelligence is not a new technology; there were high hopes for it in the early 1960s (Winston, 1985:75-78). Many experts also thought that various types of electronic funds transfer would replace paper transactions by the early 1980s. Indeed, a recent study of the financial services sector by the Office of

Technology Assessment (OTA), begins by acknowledging that past technology forecasts for this sector have not been particularly accurate (1984:7). Nonetheless, the OTA study forges ahead to make new forecasts claiming that the dimensions of the technology which will most likely be used in the financial services sector can now be seen more clearly.

Our judgment is that the state of the art in technology forecasting is not sufficiently advanced to permit the kind of long-run analysis performed by Roessner; even 10-year projections of occupational employment stretch current forecasting abilities. Indeed, Roessner's attempt to identify so-called "breakthrough" technologies vividly demonstrates the problems of extending the forecast horizon beyond 10 years. Knowledge becomes so limited that it is easy to imagine greater and greater change. Extending the forecast horizon removes all of the constraints that logically hinder the development and diffusion of new technologies. All the rigors of the marketplace, such as competing products and other investment goals evaporate. Problems that inevitably arise with new technology but are not known until it is implemented, simply do not exist in these long-run projections. Uncooperative consumers who do not wish to use the new technologies are ignored. What remains is the euphoria about what tomorrow's technologies will be able to accomplish.

Stated differently, employment projections beyond 10 years require knowledge about technological breakthroughs, the amount of time it will take to bring the new systems to the marketplace, the rate at which the technology will diffuse or be adopted by firms, the organizational structure and the structure of jobs in those firms, and the specific jobs which will be affected by those new technologies. All this presumes that the products being produced with the new technologies will be deemed desirable by consumers and that it is known which of these goods will be purchased through import markets. Furthermore, all of this knowledge of the future must be precisely time phased to properly estimate the occupational impacts.

Roessner says that new public policy initiatives should not be taken on the basis of only one study. But, his emphasis on breakthrough technologies coupled to his long-run projections horizon raises some fundamental questions about forecasting and its relation to policymaking. Are we willing to commit public funds to correct for problems which have not yet actually arisen? How many tax dollars should be spent retraining clerical workers in banking and insurance because voice recognition and artificial intelligence, among other technologies, many eliminate their jobs in the future? What jobs should these workers be trained for? Do we train people for jobs that don't yet exist, but may exist after the technological breakthroughs occur? How are they to be employed in the meantime? How many problems that *might* develop in the future can a society afford to solve now?

Roessner's long-run employment projections cannot be taken seriously as a practical guide for policymaking. In the short run, the projections appear to contradict the best current evidence available about the uneven impacts of new technologies on occupations. In the long run (beyond 10 years), virtually any technological event is possible, so it is unwise to seriously shape public policy now for events which may or may not occur. There will be "technological surprises" in the years ahead just as there have been in the past. No one (or group) has the immense amount of insight necessary to predict detailed occupational employment in the long run with enough precision to develop a consensus view of what public policy should be today.

Conclusions

In this chapter the major existing forecasts of the impacts of office automation on clerical employment have been reviewed. Although there appear to be great disparities between the forecasts of BLS, Leontief-Duchin, Drennan, and Roessner, there is broad agreement that clerical jobs will not continue their rapid growth of the past few decades.

Except for Roessner, there is also broad agreement that the so-called back-office jobs will continue to be automated first, slowing their growth dramatically. These jobs appear to be more structured and repetitive, therefore more subject to automation. This represents the continuation of a long historical trend that has its roots in the manufacturing sector but will apply to computer and office electronic technology as well. Computer technology is still not ready to tackle the unstructured situations where humans excel, however.

On a more positive note, there will likely continue to be strong growth in relative terms for computer-related clerical positions for the foreseeable future and more or less average growth for clerical positions that directly interface with customers or other coworkers. Many of these latter positions, though not all, are more generalist in nature. Roessner notwithstanding, a variety of skills probably helps to insure that the automation of any one of those skills leaves the job intact. It also implies that a worker can, in effect, purchase job insurance by possessing numerous skills.

The methodologies of these studies are very different, but they share one important characteristic which should not be overlooked. Regardless of the modeling used, it is the technology forecast, its presumed relationship to specific occupations, and the demand outlook that drive any employment impacts. Too often it appears that somehow the model itself produced the results, whereas in reality it is the assumptions which determine the results.

In this regard it is important to applaud the openness of the work of Leontief-Duchin, Drennan, and Roessner. An evaluation of their studies would be virtually impossible without the explicit reporting of their technological assumptions. BLS is currently much less open about their handling of technological change. The mathematical decomposition was used to determine the quantitative change in the staffing ratios in the industry-occupation matrix. These are the most visible signs of the specific occupational impacts of technological change in the BLS system. The results showed that BLS is indeed changing the staffing ratios, but they do not report the basis for the judgments which guide the process.

Doubts have been expressed about the long-run technology forecasts of Leontief-Duchin and Roessner, especially in determining the occupational impacts thereof. It is not necessary to repeat the details of these arguments. Suffice it to say that it is far easier to calculate simple labor-savings estimates based on engineering concepts than to specify and quantify the new jobs which will be created by a growing, dynamic economy. Furthermore, if history is any guide, our abilities to calculate theoretical labor-savings exceed our ability to actually achieve those savings in practice. Bela Gold, an economist who has studied technological change for over 25 years, concludes (1981:91) that even major technological changes have "fallen far short of their expected effects."

Absolute declines in total clerical employment for the foreseeable future are extremely unlikely. Even more significantly, shaping public policy today because of the chance that clerical jobs may decline in the future is sheer folly. The most likely scenario for the future is that clerical jobs will grow, but more slowly than the average for all jobs.

NOTES

1. For an introduction to the OES system, see Bureau of Labor Statistics (1982:135-146).

2. Based on the authors interviews with BLS officials, comparisons across OES surveys accomplished to date are not possible due to the lack of consistency in the data. As the OES survey becomes more firmly established, BLS hopes to be able to make such comparisons.

3. For a comprehensive evaluation of the DOT, see Miller, et al. (1980).

4. See Hunt and Hunt (1985) for a thorough discussion of data problems inherent in studying the employment implications of technological change.

5. The authors kindly thank George I. Treyz, University of Massachusetts, and President, Regional Economic Models, Inc., for constructing the BLS input-output industry series and for aggregating the OES industry-occupation data.

6. Although it was shown in chapter 4 that this was largely because the clerical-intensive industries appeared to be immune from the business cycle.

7. The BLS does not actually forecast occupational employment growth at the major group level, but it is still helpful to analyze the projections at this level of aggregation to provide an overview of the system. It also enables us to compare those projections to the historical CPS data reviewed in chapter 4.

8. There were 42 clerical occupations available for analysis in Census data and 32 in CPS data.

9. There are 104 clerical occupations, including nine summary major groups, but only 95 nonoverlapping detailed occupations. The rankings by level of employment, table 5.4, and staffing ratio changes, table 5.5, report the results only for the 95 detailed occupations.

10. In some instances, such as bank tellers, Leontief and Duchin have accounted for the likelihood that the size of the bank will impact the adoption of automatic teller machines. There is no indication that such an adjustment has been made for secretaries.

11. This brief summary of the Roessner methodology does not do justice to its complexity; there are actually many parts to each of the major steps.

12. During this same period of time, there was essentially no change in the relative importance of all clerical jobs in banking.

____ 6
Conclusions

The objectives of this monograph have been (1) to review the trends in clerical employment over the last 30 years and (2) to assess the existing forecasts for clerical jobs. Of particular concern has been the potential impact of office automation on these jobs. Although it is impossible to develop a new forecast for clerical jobs based on this review, we have tried to be forthright with our own judgments along the way. Now it is time to bring together the various themes of the paper.

The Data Problems

The most obvious conclusion is that the data are insufficient to make a full and final assessment of the impact of office automation on clerical jobs. Time series data are not available on office automation spending by industry. It is not even possible to get adequate time series data on detailed clerical employment by industry. We have tried to openly state the data problems in this paper. Some may think we have gone too far in this. But it is important to remember how easy it is to utilize data which look similar on the surface, and end up drawing inferences which reflect nothing more than differences in measurement. The existing data are so fragmentary and so uneven that conclusions drawn from them may always be tenuous.

We have done our best to insure that the data reported in this paper are reasonably consistent. It is unfortunate that time series data could not be developed for all clerical occupations and that the analysis halts abruptly in 1982 in some cases. Suffice it to say that we endeavored to avoid reporting results which might be misleading, but yet to get as much from existing data sources as possible.

The truth is that consistent time-series data on occupational employment are very difficult to develop. This has become a policy problem in recent years due to the increasing interest in forecasting the jobs of the future. It is difficult to forecast the future without a good understanding of the past. Perhaps the recent adoption of the Standard Occupational Classification (SOC) system will begin to bring some order to tracking occupations over time, but it will be years before we know if the SOC truly produces a net gain.

Another problem encountered in this review is that a number of separate influences developed simultaneously in 1982 which make it extremely difficult to interpret recent occupational employment trends. First, the bottom of the worst recession since World War II occurred in 1982. This distorted the employment figures in a number of ways. Second, at about this same time there appear to be some real changes occurring in the patterns of growth across different industries. This is particularly evident for state and local government and perhaps hospitals. Third, it is possible that office automation had diffused sufficiently to make some real impact by 1982. Finally, among the data problems alluded to earlier, it turns out that 1982 was the last year in which the CPS used the 1970 Census classification system for occupations. Since the SOC-based data from 1983 and 1984 utilize a different occupational measurement structure, even at the major group level, it is extremely difficult to conduct meaningful analysis of occupational employment trends across this time span.

The problem is that the confluence of these events makes it very difficult to determine what the causes of recent trends have been. The employment of secretaries fell slightly in 1981 and 1982. That is very unusual, even during a recession. Did office automation cause the decline? Was it simply that this recession was the worst since World War II? Or did some other factor such as changing utilization of job titles or some technical problem with the data cause the fall? These questions cannot be answered with confidence, but as shown earlier the growth of secretarial employment resumed in 1983 and 1984. This argues that the decline was probably due to the recession. The point is that it may be all too easy to draw false inferences about the last few years since so many trends coincided in time.

Trends in Clerical Employment

Chapters 2 and 3 carefully reviewed the available data on clerical employment trends. The focus in chapter 2 was on the long-term trends in clerical employment from 1950 to 1980 and on the recent trends from 1972 to 1982. In addition, the demographics of clerical workers were examined to determine the way in which clerical job opportunities have impacted the employment results for specific race-sex populations. Chapter 3 took the detailed clerical occupations as the point of departure and reviewed the data presented in chapter 2 from this perspective.

The trends in employment levels were presented for some 42 clerical occupations from the decennial census data over a 30-year period. These data required extensive adjustment for consistency due to the differences between the various occupational classification systems used in Census observations. For the short-term analysis, employment data for a slightly different set of 32 clerical occupations were presented from the Current Population Survey.

In general, the results of these reviews were disappointing. The amazing variety of clerical jobs was depicted, and the diversity in their employment trends clearly emerged from the analysis. But the trends in employment proved to be very difficult to tie conclusively to technological change or any other single cause. The general conclusion was that this aggregate analysis of occupational employment data was not sufficient to reveal the causes behind the trends.

Yet for policy purposes it is critical to put clerical occupational growth into some larger perspective. That was the function of the mathematical decomposition of clerical employment growth in chapter 4. This analysis emphasized the role of economic growth in determining the fortunes of individual occupations. It was also seen that the growth of particular industries (the changing sectoral composition of output) can have an enormous impact on occupational employment. In the long run there is no doubt that the evolution of the service economy has been a favorable influence on clerical employment levels.

The occupational decomposition also showed how changing staffing ratios influence occupational employment. Goods and services have been growing more information-intensive per unit of output over the last decade. This has boosted clerical employment significantly. In addition, by showing how much staffing ratios differ across industries, the analysis reinforced the notion that industry structure cannot be ignored in studying occupational employment.

It is also the changes in staffing ratios that best summarize the direct impacts of technological change on occupational employment. From 1972 to 1982 the net effect on clerical employment of changing staffing ratios was modestly positive for the total economy. But there were a few sectors, notably finance, where the effect was negative. This is taken as possible emerging evidence of the adverse impact of technological change on clerical employment. Even in finance, however, the strong industry mix effect and overall economic growth dwarfed the negative staffing ratio effect by a margin of more than 6 to 1. So employment of clericals continued to rise despite the impact of automation.

The attempt to find empirical evidence on the productivity gains from office automation was also relatively unsatisfying. What is available consists of mostly undocumented claims in trade journal articles which are hard to take seriously. It was shown that the measured productivity gains in finance and insurance did *not* support the thesis that office automation was having a significant impact. Yet investment in this sector has been dramatically higher than the historical average for that sector for the last 15 years, so this lack of measured productivity results remains a puzzle. Our judgment is that there does not appear to be overwhelming empirical evidence of dramatic productivity gains due to office automation at this time. Some possible explanations for these results are offered later.

The Forecasts of Clerical Employment

The review of existing forecasts of employment in clerical occupations in chapter 5 showed that they were unanimous in predicting that staffing ratios for clerical jobs would fall in the years ahead, presumably due to office automation. The fall in staffing ratios anticipated by BLS is modest and will be just about offset by employment growth due to the favorably industry mix of clerical jobs. So the BLS anticipates average growth for clerical jobs. Still, it is significant that the only turnaround from historical trends anticipated by BLS among major occupational groups due to changing staffing ratios is that for clerical workers. Our analysis demonstrated that, at least through 1982, CPS data showed that the staffing ratio for clerical jobs was rising, whereas the BLS forecast (base year 1982) and other forecasts predict that this trend will be reversed in the years ahead.

The other forecasts of clerical employment growth are not nearly as comprehensive as that of the BLS. Leontief and Duchin focus on modeling questions and, to a much lesser extent, the technology assessment. Roessner concentrates on the technology forecast and its relationship to job functions. Roessner develops the job functions in such a way that they are independent of the technologies currently in use. But Roessner's analysis is limited to two industries, banking and insurance. Drennan looks at clerical employment in six industries. His projection methodology utilizes extrapolation of historical trends after accounting for the effects of the 1980-82 recession.

Before presenting our critical analysis, we would like to applaud Leontief and Duchin, Roessner, and Drennan for openly stating the assumptions of their studies. In our opinion, technological forecasts will always be treacherous and require careful judgment. The open statement of those assumptions facilitates dialogue, invites criticism, and thereby contributes to future research. Our comments on these studies are offered in this same spirit. The occupational forecasting program at BLS should be encouraged to follow a similar strategy.

All of these researchers conclude that office automation will have a much greater impact on clerical jobs than the BLS predicts. Roessner is particularly pointed about his concerns regarding the BLS methodology and forecasts, while Drennan's projections appear to be nearer the BLS position. Unfortunately we find the studies of Leontief-Duchin and Roessner to be seriously flawed from the point of view of serving policy needs. This is not an unqualified endorsement of the methodology or projections of BLS or Drennan. But it does mean that we think the Leontief-Duchin and Roessner studies are unduly pessimistic about the outlook for clerical jobs.

There are a variety of reasons that support our contention. First, it is important to note that Leontief and Duchin actually use the BLS aggregate demand forecast in their research, whereas both Drennan and Roessner use simple extrapolation methods to obtain estimates of demand for their studies. What this means is that output is expected to grow as it has in the past, but the impacts of technological change (i.e., office automation) will differ from what they were previously. Thus, the revolution in office techniques will leave the demand side of the marketplace unchanged.

But that is not the way a complex, dynamic market economy operates. If office automation had a dramatic productivity impact and was adopted rapidly, it should change the relative costs of production for those goods and services which are intensive users of office automation. These lower production costs will lead to more competition and lower prices. There is every reason to think that the new, lower prices will generate additional demand, thereby mitigating the direct labor displacing effects of office automation.

This scenario is even more plausible when one realizes that the product markets themselves are not static. So the new electronic office technologies may provide the impetus for the development of entirely new goods and services. Industry interrelationships may change or scale economies may be so significant that they fuel the development of a mass market that heretofore was undreamed of. In our opinion it is inappropriate to fix demand or the growth of demand and then assume a revolutionary change on the supply side of the market. Obviously, such a partial analysis will create false impressions about the employment impacts of office automation.

Second, it appears that none of these other studies accounts for the tendency of output to become more information-intensive over time. Yet this has been occurring for a long time. The production recipes for many different goods and services today require more information processing than they did earlier. This is not simply a function of the changing composition of demand, but relates to the content of a standard unit of output. To the extent that this trend continues in the future, it means that office automation will have less overall impact on clerical employment levels than anticipated by some researchers.

Third, these studies do not account for the fact that the new technologies must be cost effective and reliable before they achieve widespread application. The technologies may appear to the uninitiated to be costless, producing quantum leaps in productivity for the users. Yet there are purchase and installation costs and ongoing costs that must be accounted for. The ongoing costs include system maintenance, software development, employee training, and many others. There is also the cost of unscheduled downtime, which may become even more significant with integrated systems.

Fourth, it should be mentioned once again that office automation is likely to lower the marginal cost of some types of work substantially. Quantity and quality of output may rise sufficiently that labor input increases by more than the impact of the new techniques themselves. One common example is redrafts of documents with word processing. The probability that this will occur may be enhanced by the inability to measure output from offices in the first place. This type of new work or rework is explicitly rejected by Leontief and Duchin, and perhaps implicitly by Roessner.

Finally, Leontief-Duchin and Roessner appear to us to be truly overoptimistic about the new technologies, both in terms of what office automation equipment can do and in the speed of diffusion of that equipment. Leontief and Duchin assume that word processors alone will produce productivity gains for typists and secretaries of 500 percent. This assumption appears to be based upon a trade journal article which is five times more optimistic than the other articles which Leontief and Duchin reference. Roessner, on the other hand, emphasized the potential for two emerging technologies, voice input and artificial intelligence. He assumes that breakthroughs will occur in these technologies in the next few years, that they will be successfully marketed, and that they will dramatically reduce clerical employment in banking and insurance during the 1990s.

Our major complaint with the technological assumptions of both Leontief-Duchin and Roessner is not just that they may be technically wrong, although there is ample reason to question them, but that the level of uncertainty about the technology forecasts is so great that interpretation of the occupational employment implications which are derived from them becomes little more than an academic exercise. We question whether anyone should base policy decisions on a forecast of the capabilities of artificial intelligence, a technology which has been kicking around research labs since the 1950s. Perhaps we will always be overoptimistic about new technologies; it seems to be part of the human condition. But that is no justification to shape public policy based solely on our dreams of the future.

We are unconvinced that technology will evolve as far or as fast as Leontief-Duchin and Roessner predict. But even if it does, the derivative employment impacts foreseen by these researchers are still very far off the mark. The overgeneralization to broad employment impacts based on assumptions about labor productivity at the task or firm level is very dangerous. This is the kind of analysis that leads to the fear that we will experience massive technological unemployment at some point in the future. Various analysts have been predicting such an event at least since the dawn of the industrial age. Somehow the employment apocalypse is always just ahead, yet thankfully we never quite reach it. In any event, when evaluating these studies it is important to remember that the model simply processes the technological assumptions about the economy. It is the technological assumptions that determine the employment impacts in these studies.

Because of the uncertainties about the capabilities of future technologies and their employment impacts, we would encourage a focus on shorter range occupational forecasting. This is exactly opposite to the approach being suggested by Leontief-Duchin and Roessner. Roessner says that public policymakers need a longer time period for planning. But, if technological change is occurring faster today, then it is becoming even less possible to develop long run employment forecasts. Surely it is folly to think that we can peer 15 to 20 years into the future and see the detailed occupational and industrial structure of this nation. We think that the current BLS efforts, which produce about a 10-year planning horizon, tax existing forecasting abilities to the limit.

Rather than try to anticipate the future in great detail and prepare for it in advance, it would be better to make more general preparations for an uncertain future. Thus it makes more sense to increase the training of generic electronics technicians than to try to estimate how many robotics technicians, microprocessor service technicians, or other specific occupations may be required in the future.

The Outlook for Clerical Employment

What has this review shown for the future of clerical jobs? First, we think the pessimists who claim that these jobs will either stop growing absolutely or actually decline are wrong.

The forces of economic growth, the shift toward services, and the current performance limitations of office automation technologies all argue strongly against this scenario.

However, it is clear that the rate of growth of clerical jobs has slowed. Clericals did not prove to be as immune from the last recession as they were in earlier recessions, nor are some of the sectors that are important employers of clericals growing as fast as they once were. Although office automation may not produce a revolution, it should at least contribute to the slowing of employment growth in these occupations in the future. We think that the overall growth of clerical jobs in the future will be average to slightly below average when compared to the growth of total employment.

The common wisdom today is that the back-office jobs will disappear with office automation. There is some truth to this glittering generality; however, there is also an analogy to manufacturing which may be useful. Automation has not caused the total elimination of production workers in manufacturing, but these jobs have not been increasing in absolute terms for the last 40 years either. We think the so-called back-office jobs are more threatened by automation than other positions. They share with production workers a routinization of tasks which tends to support automation. This will not necessarily lead to their demise, but their growth will probably be well below average.

As mentioned earlier in this paper, it is definitely easier to provide a technological explanation for declining occupations than growing occupations. There is an important message here. It is far easier to identify the employment impacts of labor-saving technology than the new jobs which are created by a growing, dynamic economy. Technology is only one aspect of economic growth, whereas the examination of the potential job loss from automation and technological change is much more narrow and focused.

Many people today are ready to add bank tellers to the list of declining occupations. Unfortunately this is one of the occupations for which the time series data are especially poor, but it does appear that the employment growth has slowed in recent years. It also appears that to some extent the future growth prospects for bank tellers are directly tied to the public's acceptance of automatic teller machines. Today these machines are being used mostly for cash withdrawals and cannot be thought of as a substitute for a fully staffed bank. Furthermore, it is difficult to know if and when the public will be willing to break the human link in making banking transactions. As a result, the future for bank tellers is extremely cloudy.

Roessner notwithstanding, we think that the growth of clerical technology jobs will continue to be rapid, particularly the computer-related positions. Office automation is not sufficiently advanced at this point to slow the growth of these jobs. It remains to be seen if that will ever occur. We also think that those clerical positions which require the worker to deal directly with customers will likely experience average growth or better. The office of the future will require both "high-tech" and "high-touch" occupations. Except possibly for bank tellers, there appears to be more emphasis on customer service and the quality of that service rather than less.

Secretaries fall somewhere between the back-office jobs and those positions which involve considerable customer contact. Therefore, secretarial employment growth may slow but these jobs will not decline. It is also true that many of these positions are generalist in nature and less vulnerable to automation. It seems clear that the secretaries of the future will require a greater variety of skills and will utilize much more capital equipment than they do today. We think that the growth of secretarial jobs will be average to below average, but the absolute number of these jobs will definitely increase.

In summary, there is no persuasive evidence today that there will be a significant decline in clerical jobs in the future. The forecasts of declining clerical employment are based on overoptimistic expectations of technological improvements or exaggerated productivity claims on behalf of existing technology. In our opinion, current office technology offers significant improvements in product quality and modest improvements in productivity. There is as yet no empirical evidence of an office productivity revolution that will displace significant numbers of clerical workers.

On the contrary, we think there are many factors which will contribute to the job growth of clericals in the future. Chief among these is the simple fact that clericals are so diffused in the national economy. Moreover, to the extent that clerical jobs are concentrated in particular industries, it has been in sectors growing faster than average. Therefore, even allowing for negative employment impacts from office automation, it is extremely difficult to believe that the growth of this large, diverse, and diffused occupational group could be much below the average growth for all occupations for the next decade.

REFERENCES

Administrative Management
  1978 The Many Cases for WP. *Administrative Management* (April): 70-71.

Andreassen, Arthur J., Norman C. Saunders and Betty W. Su
  1983 Economic Outlook for the 1990's: Three Scenarios for Economic Growth. *Monthly Labor Review* (November): 11-23.

Appelbaum, Eileen
  1984 Technology and the Redesign of Work in the Insurance Industry. Unpublished paper, Temple University.

Attewell, Paul and James Rule
  1984 Computing and Organizations: What We Know and What We Don't Know. *Communications of the ACM* (December): 1184-1192.

Austin, William M. and Lawrence C. Drake, Jr.
  1985 Office Automation. *Occupational Outlook Quarterly* (Spring): 15-19.

Bailey, Andrew D., James H. Gerlach and Andrew B. Whinston,
  1985 *Office Systems Technology and Organizations.* Reston, Virginia: Reston Publishing Company, Inc.

Baldwin, Stephen E.
  1985 *Displaced Workers: Problems, Programs, and Policies.* Washington, DC: National Commission for Employment Policy.

Baran, Barbara
  No   The Technological Transformation of White Collar Work: A
  date Case Study of the Insurance Industry. Berkeley Roundtable on the International Economy.

Bikson, T. K. and B. A. Gutek
  1983 Advanced Office Systems: An Empirical Look at Utilization and Satisfaction. Report No., N-1970-NSF. Santa Monica, CA: Rand Corporation.

Blair, Louis Helion
  1985 Technological Change and Employment in Western Europe. Report No. RR-85-11. Washington, DC: National Commission for Employment Policy.

Blanchard, Francis
1984 Technology, Work and Society: Some Pointers from ILO Research. *International Labour Review* (May-June): 267-285.

Bowen, Howard R. and Garth L. Mangum, editors
1966 *Automation and Economic Progress.* Englewood Cliffs, NJ: Prentice-Hall, Inc.

Brand, Horst and John Duke
1982 Productivity in Banking: Computers Spur the Advance. *Monthly Labor Review* (December): 19-27.

Browne, Lynn E.
1984 Conflicting Views of Technological Progress and the Labor Market. *New England Economic Review* (July/August): 5-16.

Buckingham, Walter
1961 *Automation: Its Impact on Business and People.* New York, NY: Harper and Brothers Publishers.

Bureau of the Census
1982 *1980 Census of Population: Classified Index of Industries and Occupations.* Washington, DC: U.S. Department of Commerce.

Bureau of the Census
1972 *1970 Census of Population, Detailed Characteristics, United States Summary.* Washington, DC: U.S. Department of Commerce.

Bureau of Labor Statistics
1985 *Productivity Measures for Selected Industries, 1954-83.* Bulletin 2224. Washington, DC: U.S. Department of Labor.

Bureau of Labor Statistics
1982 *BLS Handbook of Methods.* Bulletin 2134-1. Washington, DC: U.S. Department of Labor.

Bureau of Labor Statistics
1981 *The National Industry-Occupation Matrix, 1970, 1978, and Projected 1990.* Bulletin 2086. Washington, DC: U.S. Department of Labor.

Bureau of Labor Statistics
1979 *Time Series Data for Input-Output Industries: Output, Price, and Employment.* Washington, DC: U.S. Department of Labor.

Business Week
   1985 The Computer Slump. *Business Week* (June 24): 74-81.

Carey, Max L. and Kevin Kasunic
   1982 Evaluating the 1980 Projections of Occupational Employment.
   Monthly Labor Review. (July): 22-30.

Carson, Carol S. and George Jaszi
   1981 The National Income and Products Accounts of the United
   States: An Overview. *Survey of Current Business* (February):
   22-34.

Computer and Business Equipment Manufacturers Association
   1985 *Computer and Business Equipment Marketing and Forecast
   Data Book.* Hasbrouck Heights, NJ: Hayden Book Company.

Craig, L. C.
   1981 Office Automation at Texas Instruments, Incorporated. Pp.
   202-214 in Mitchell L. Moss, ed., *Telecommunications and Productivity.* Reading, MA: Addison-Wesley Publishing Company.

Denison, Edward F.
   1979 *Accounting for Slower Economic Growth.* Washington, DC:
   Brookings Institution.

Denison, Edward F.
   1974 *Accounting for United States Economic Growth, 1929-1969.*
   Washington, DC: Brookings Institution.

Denison, Edward F.
   1962 *The Sources of Economic Growth in the United States and the
   Alternatives Before Us.* New York, NY: Committee for
   Economic Development.

Diebold, John
   1985 *Managing Information: The Challenge and the Opportunity.*
   New York, NY: AMACOM.

Doody, Alton F. and William R. Davidson
   1967 Next Revolution in Retailing. *Harvard Business Review* (May-
   June): 4-20.

Downing, Hazel
   1980 Word Processors and the Oppression of Women. Pp. 275-288 in
   Tom Forester, ed., *The Microelectronics Revolution.* Cam-
   bridge, MA: MIT Press.

Drennan, Matthew P.
1983 Implications of Computer and Communications Technology for Less Skilled Service Employment Opportunities. Final report prepared for the Employment and Training Administration: U.S. Department of Labor.

Employment and Training Administration
1977 *Dictionary of Occupational Titles.* Washington, DC: U.S. Department of Labor. Fourth Edition.

Fechter, Alan
1974 Forecasting the Impact of Technological Change on Manpower Utilization and Displacement: An Analytic Summary. Report No. 1215-1. Washington, DC: Urban Institute.

Fortune
1985 Fortune Forecast: The Current Quarter Signals Slow Growth. *Fortune* (December 9): 74-75.

Fuchs, Victor R. ed.
1969 *Production and Productivity in the Service Industries.* New York, NY: National Bureau of Economic Research.

Fullerton, Howard N., Jr. and John Tschetter
1983 The 1995 Labor Force: A Second Look. *Monthly Labor Review* (November): 3-10.

Giuliano, Vincent E.
1982 The Mechanization of Office Work. *Scientific American* (September): 149-164.

Gold, Bela
1981 Robotics, Programmable Automation and Increasing Competitiveness. Pp. 91-117 in *Exploratory Workshop on the Social Impacts of Robotics: Summary and Issues.* Office of Technology Assessment, Congress of the United States. Washington, DC: U.S. Government Printing Office.

Goldstein, Harold and Bryna Shore Fraser
1985 Training for Work in the Computer Age: How Workers Who Use Computers Get Their Training. Report No. RR-85-09. Washington, DC: National Commission for Employment Policy.

Gutek, Barbara A. and Tora B. Bikson
    1984 Differential Experiences of Men and Women in Computerized Offices. Unpublished paper, Claremont Graduate School and Rand Corporation.

Gutek, Barbara
    1983 Women's Work in the Office of the Future. Pp. 159-168 in Jan Zimmerman, ed., *The Technological Woman.* New York: Praeger.

Helander, Martin G.
    1985 Emerging Office Automation Systems. *Human Factors* (February): 3-20.

Holmgren. J. E.
    1983 Toward Bell System Applications of Automation Speech Recognition. *The Bell System Technical Journal* (July-August): 1865-1880.

Honeywell, Inc.
    1983 *Office Automation and the Workplace: A National Survey.* Minneapolis, MN: Honeywell, Inc.

Hunt, H. Allan and Timothy L. Hunt
    1983 *Human Resource Implications of Robotics.* Kalamazoo, MI: W. E. Upjohn Institute for Employment Research.

Hunt, Timothy L. and H. Allan Hunt
    1985 An Assessment of Data Sources to Study the Employment Effects of Technological Change. Washington, DC: Panel on Technology and Women's Employment. National Research Council/National Academy of Sciences.

International Data Corporation
    1984 Information Systems for Tomorrow's Office. *Fortune* (October 15): 99-138.

International Data Corporation
    1983 Office Systems for the Eighties: Automation and the Bottom Line. *Fortune* (October 3): 89-162.

International Data Corporation
    1982 Information Systems for Tomorrow's Office. *Fortune* (October 18): 17-81.

292

Jain, Harish C.
1983 Task Force Encourages Diffusion of Microelectronics in Canada. *Monthly Labor Review* (October): 25-29.

James, John A.
1984 Perspectives on Technological Change: Historical Studies of Four Major Innovations. Report No. RR-84-07. Washington, DC: National Commission for Employment Policy.

Johnson, Bonnie M.
1985 Summary of Innovations in Office Systems Implementation. Report No. ISI 8110791. Washington, DC: National Science Foundation.

Johnson, Bonnie M.
1985 Don't Throw Away the Learning. Summary of Report No. ISI 8110791. Washington, DC.

Johnson, Bonnie
1985 Word Processing Jobs: For Those Who Don't Like to Bring the Coffee. Santa Clara, CA: Intel Corporation.

Jonscher, Charles
1983 Information Resources and Economic Productivity. *Information Economics and Policy* (January): 13-35.

Karan, Mary A.
1982 Word Processing: When It Doesn't Work. *Computer World* (March): 16.

Katzan, Harry, Jr.
1982 *Office Automation: A Manager's Guide.* New York, NY: American Management Associations.

Kendrick, John W.
1983 *Interindustry Differences in Productivity Growth.* Washington, DC: American Enterprise Institute.

Kendrick, John W. and Elliot S. Grossman
1980 *Productivity in the United States.* Baltimore, MD: Johns Hopkins University Press.

Kendrick, John W.
1977 *Understanding Productivity.* Baltimore, MD: Johns Hopkins University Press.

Kendrick, John W.
1973 *Postwar Productivity Trends in the United States.* New York, NY: National Bureau of Economic Research.

King, John L. and Kenneth L. Kraemer
1981 Cost as a Social Impact of Information Technology. Pp. 93-129 in Mitchell L. Moss, ed., *Telecommunications and Productivity.* Reading, MA: Addison-Wesley Publishing Company.

Klein, Deborah P.
1984 Occupational Employment Statistics for 1972-82. *Employment and Earnings* (January): 13.

Kramer, Robert L. and W. Putnam Livingston
1967 Cashing In on Checkless Society. *Harvard Business Review* (September-October): 141-149.

Kutscher, Ronald E.
1985 Factors Influencing the Changing Employment Structure of the United States. Paper presented at the Second International Conference of Progretto Milano, Milan, Italy, January 25, 1985.

Kutscher, Ronald E.
1982 New Economic Projections Through 1990, An Overview. Pp. 1-9 in *Economic Projections to 1990.* Washington, DC: U.S. Department of Labor.

Leontief, Wassily and Faye Duchin
1984 *The Impacts of Automation on Employment, 1963-2000.* Final report to National Science Foundation. New York: Institute for Economic Analysis.

Mansfield, Edwin
1971 *Technological Change.* New York, NY: W. W. Norton & Company, Inc.

Mark, Jerome A. and William H. Waldorf
1983 Multifactor Productivity: A New BLS Measure. *Monthly Labor Review* (December): 3-15.

Mark, Jerome A.
1982 Measuring Productivity in Service Industries. *Monthly Labor Review* (June): 3-8.

Mayer, Martin
1983 Here Comes the Smart Card. *Fortune* (August 8): 74-81.

McFadden, Fred R. and James D. Suver
  1983 Costs and Benefits of a Data-Base System. Pp. 249-261 in Lynn
     M. Salerno, ed., *Catching Up With the Computer Revolution.*
     New York: John Wiley and Sons, Inc.

Miller, Ann, Donald J. Treiman, Pamela S. Cain and Patricia A. Roos,
  1980 eds. *Work, Jobs and Occupations: A Critical Review of the*
     'Dictionary of Occupational Titles.' Washington, DC: National
     Academy Press.

Minolta, Inc.
  1983 *The Evolving Role of the Secretary in the Information Age.*
     Ramsey, NJ: Minolta Corporation Business Equipment Divi-
     sion.

Murphree, Mary C.
  1985 Office Technology: The Changing World of the Legal Secretary.
     Forthcoming in Karen Sacks and Dorothy Reny, eds., *Women's*
     Toils and Triumphs at the Workplace. New Brunswick, NJ:
     Rutgers Universtiy Press.

Murphree, Mary
  1981 Rationalization and Satisfaction in Clerical Work: A Case Study
     of Wall Street Legal Secretaries. Ph.D. Dissertation. Columbia
     University.

Office of Economic Growth and Employment Projections
  1981 Comparison of Occupational Employment in the 1978 Census-
     Based and OES Survey-Based Matrices. OES Technical Paper
     Number 1. Washington, DC: Bureau of Labor Statistics.

Office of Economic Growth and Employment Projections
  1981 Projected Occupational Staffing Patterns of Industries. OES
     Technical Paper Number 2. Washington, DC: U.S. Department
     of Labor.

Office of Technology Assessment
  1984 *Effects of Information Technology on Financial Services*
     Systems. Washington, DC: Congress of the United States.

Personick, Valerie A.
  1983 The Job Outlook Through 1995: Industry Output and Employ-
     ment Projections. *Monthly Labor Review* (November): 24-36.

Podgursky, Michael
  1984 Sources of Secular Increases in the Unemployment Rate, 1969-82. *Monthly Labor Review* (July): 19-25.

Priebe, John A., Joan Heinkel and Stanley Greene
  1972 1970 Occupation and Industry Classification Systems in Terms of Their 1960 Occupation and Industry Elements. Technical Paper No. 26. Washington, DC: U.S. Department of Commerce, Bureau of the Census.

Richie, Richard W., Daniel E. Hecker and John U. Burgan
  1983 High Technology Today and Tomorrow: A Small Slice of the Employment Pie. *Monthly Labor Review* (November): 50-58.

Roessner, J. David
  1984 Impact of Office Automation on Office Workers, 4 Vols. Final report prepared for the Employment and Training Administration, U.S. Department of Labor.

Romero, Carol J.
  1985 Training for Work in the Computer Age. Washington, DC: National Commission for Employment Policy.

Rosenthal, Neal
  1985 The Shrinking Middle Class: Myth or Reality? *Monthly Labor Review* (March): 3-10.

Salerno, Lynn M.
  1985 What Happened to the Computer Revolution? *Harvard Business Review* (November-December): 129-138.

Schlefer, Jonathan, ed.
  1983 Office Automation and Bureaucracy. *Technology Review* (July): 32-40.

Schloss, Nathan
  1984 Use of Employment Data to Estimate Office Space Demand. *Monthly Labor Review* (December): 40-44.

Seskin, Eugene P. and David P. Sullivan
  1985 Revised Estimates of New Plant and Equipment Expenditures in the United States, 1947-1983. *Survey of Current Business* (February): 16-27.

Silvestri, George T., John M. Lukasiewicz and Marcus E. Einstein
  1983 Occupational Employment Projections Through 1995. *Monthly Labor Review* (November): 37-49.

296

Standing, Guy
1984 The Notion of Technological Unemployment *International Labour Review* (March-April): 127-147.

Stanford Research Institute
1984 Drop in Business Demand for Personal Computers. *The SRI Journal* (May): 4-5.

Strassman, Paul A.
1985 *Information Payoff: The Transformation of Work in the Electronic Age.* New York, NY: Free Press.

Strassman, Paul A.
1983 Managing the Costs of Information. Pp. 294-306 in Lynn M. Salerno, ed., *Catching Up With the Computer Revolution.* New York: John Wiley and Sons, Inc.

Sutherland, Roy A.
1982 Home Banking, Electronic Money Invades the Living Room. *The Futurist* (April): 13-17.

Tschetter, John
1984 An Evaluation of BLS' Projections of 1980 Industry Employment. *Monthly Labor Review* (August): 12-22.

Wang Laboratories
1985 *Issues in Information Processing: Cost Justification.* Lowell, MA: Wang Laboratories, Inc.

Werneke, Diane
1984 *Microelectronics and Working Women.* Washington, DC: National Academy Press.

Winston, Patrick H.
1985 The AI Business: A Perspective. *Manufacturing Engineering* (March): 75-78.

Young, Allan H. and Helen Stone Tice
1985 An Introduction to National Economic Accounting. *Survey of Current Business* (March): 59-74.

Zisman, Michael D.
1978 Office Automation: Revolution or Evolution? *Sloan Management Review* (Spring): 1-16.